The Canoer's Bible

The Canoer's Bible

REVISED EDITION

Robert Douglas Mead

Revised by J. Wayne Fears

⚓ **Doubleday**

New York • London • Toronto • Sydney • Auckland

PUBLISHED BY DOUBLEDAY
a division of Bantam Doubleday Dell Publishing Group, Inc.,
1540 Broadway, New York, New York 10036

DOUBLEDAY and the portrayal of an anchor with a dolphin are trademarks of Doubleday, a division of Bantam Doubleday Dell Publishing Group, Inc.

Library of Congress Cataloging-in-Publication Data
Mead, Robert Douglas.
    The canoer's bible / Robert Douglas Mead.—Rev. ed. / revised by J. Wayne Fears.
    p.   cm—(Doubleday outdoor bibles)
    1. Canoes and canoeing. 2. Canoes and canoeing—United States.
I. Fears, J. Wayne, 1938–   II. Title. III. Series.
GV783.M4 1989
797.1'22—dc19   88-27527
                                                                                      CIP

ISBN 0-385-24578-5

To James E. Mead,

my father,
who, so far as I am concerned,
began it all.

Acknowledgments for the Revised Edition

There are many who deserve credit for the updating of this book. Most noteworthy is the cowriter and chief researcher, my wife, Sherry K. Fears. She made the voluminous job of researching facts and current information look easy and helped pull the new manuscript together. Rachel Klayman of Doubleday exercised patience and understanding during the months the project was under way. A special thanks is due the canoe and canoe equipment manufacturers whose names appear in this book. We asked them for their assistance during their busiest time of the year, yet they came through with up-to-date information and photographs.

Many government agencies and canoe associations took time out of their busy schedules to answer questions and give advice on the content of this book. Since a list of these would require several pages, I wish to thank all of them collectively for their help.

To everyone who had a hand in the rewriting of this book, I offer my heartfelt thanks.

—J. WAYNE FEARS

Acknowledgments for the First Edition

This is the place for saying thanks, and I do so. My father, to whom this book is dedicated, heads the list; his ways as a canoer and camper became mine, duly modified by the difference in our temperaments. My wife and, later, our sons have been tolerant companions on canoe trips that go back to the early months of our marriage. My wife also took many of the pictures in this book not otherwise credited, my son Jim others; both my wife and my son Matthew have surrendered countless weekends to helping me illustrate this book, particularly in Chapter 3. Jim Hansen produced the prints from which many of these pictures are reproduced. Nancy Ulrich survived the typing of the manuscript. Among the several people who have shared their expert knowledge in several fields connected with canoeing, I particularly thank Ralph Frese—canoeist and canoe builder, proprietor of the Chicagoland Canoe Base. And finally, I express my thanks to the editors at Doubleday, Sandy Richardson and Bill Thompson, who in the first place suggested that I undertake this book and who have provided the encouragement needed in its writing and publication.

—R. D. M.

Contents

Appendices 147

INTRODUCTION

Why Canoe?

Something like two million Americans, individuals and families, own canoes today. Another six million rent canoes from time to time. Both figures are on the rise. What is it about canoeing that attracts people in such numbers?

The reasons why people take to the water with canoe and paddle are probably as various as the people themselves. Speaking as one among the millions, I would put at the top of my own list a delight in the waterside country itself, as experienced from the seat of a canoe. That delight connects country as different as the desert canyons of the Rio Grande and the lush pine and hardwood forests of northern Minnesota, the remote, almost unpeopled wilderness of the Canadian North and the populous environment of the Delaware River. Linked with that pleasure, fed by all the senses, is another, which you can cultivate equally in the half-forgotten stream on the edge of town or the mightiest river system of the continent: self-reliance. For the time that you are on the water in your canoe, you depend on no one but yourself, your own combination of strength, skill, experience. The canoe itself, slipping in silken silence through the water, is the intimate source of that feeling of independence. Of all the vehicles human inventiveness has evolved, none is more perfectly adapted to its physical medium.

One immediate consequence of that adaptation is that canoeing—viewed simply as a sport, a form of exercise—is remarkably democratic. You needn't, that is, be endowed with great physical strength to do it, nor do you need to develop a high degree of skill before you can engage in it with pleasure and satisfaction. Canoe and paddle respond equally to the very young and to those past middle age, to heavily muscled men and delicately constructed women. A husband-and-wife team is among the recent U.S. national canoeing champions; at other times, middle-aged fathers and their teenaged sons (or mothers and daughters) have been winners. In practice, that means that canoeing is one of the small number of things a family can do together on pretty much even terms and with appropriate satisfaction for all concerned—husband and wife, boys and girls, young and half-grown or adult-size children. To be a parent is also necessarily to be, consciously and unconsciously, one's children's first teacher—a role that the society we live in, with its reverence for professionalism and its superstitious bias toward technical arrangements in place of personal relationships, has made immeasurably more difficult than it once was. In the context of a canoe trip, however, whatever competence and wisdom one has communicate themselves immediately to one's children, without having to be asserted—and vice versa; and what you learn from each other and value is a good deal broader than simply how to take a canoe safely through rough water or build a fire that lights when all the wood is wet.

There's another thing about canoeing that recommends it to families and to anyone else who lives on a budget (and who doesn't?): simply, it doesn't cost very much. My own canoeing experience goes back to the Depression years of the early 1930s. As a family—father, mother, my two brothers, and myself—more than part of our reason for getting started was that a canoe trip was a vacation we could afford to take together.

These reasons for canoeing, which, with varying emphasis, most canoeists share, are also the reasons for the content of this book. You'll find a heavily illustrated outline of paddling technique and of canoe handling generally (Chapter 3), starting from the beginning, but useful (I hope) even to those who already know more than a little about these matters. Obviously, no physical skill can be learned solely from pictures and a written description. With this information, however, and with lots of practice graduated through increasingly demanding conditions—plus the kind of in-person tips you can pick up from other, more experienced canoers—you should be ready when the time and opportunity come for you to shove off on a canoe trip of your own. And that is the goal of this book: to assemble between two covers the knowledge and information essential to safe and enjoyable canoe travel on your own, whether that means a long weekend on the nearest river or a summer-long odyssey through the farthest wilderness.

Given that goal, three chapters of this book (2, 4, and 5) are concerned with kinds of equipment and supplies suited to canoe travel and camping in varied conditions and climates, beginning with the canoes and paddles. These chapters can serve as a buying guide as you assemble your own canoeing gear, but in many areas canoes and other basic equipment can be rented—an inexpensive way for first-time canoe travelers to check my suggestions against their own preferences. U.S. and Canadian sources for purchase and rental of all equipment and supplies discussed are listed in the Appendices, along with much other useful information.

And when you've mastered your canoe and collected your equipment? You shove off and travel, of course—as far as time and energy will carry you. The book's final chapters, then, have to do with planning and organizing a canoe trip, whether for one canoeload or a group, on your own or with the help that's available from canoe outfitters and guides—and with how to conduct the trip itself for everyone's safety and enjoyment. The book closes with an introduction, region by region, to the major canoeing areas throughout the continent, with sources for further information about each, which, again, are summarized in the Appendices. All of these are areas where extended canoe trips are possible, from a week or so to, in some cases, an entire season. Wherever you happen to live, there's no limit to the possibilities.

In all of this, I've tried to share with you the things I've learned in forty years of canoeing, first with my parents and brothers, later with friends, and now with my wife and our four sons. I've tried, that is, to set forth as plainly as possible how *I* do things, and why. This is not to say that I consider my way of canoeing the only one possible. You'll meet other experienced canoeists who do things a little differently or with different emphases. You'll have, in time, your own ideas. Indeed, I've never made a trip without learning something about canoeing or camping that, often, has seemed fundamental in retrospect. Nor do I consider myself the kind of superskilled canoeman who seeks out steep-pitched rapids for the fun of it or who will ever bring home a blue ribbon for flat-water or downriver racing. What I do know, however, is that my particular combination of experience and skill has carried me and the people I've canoed with through most of the kinds of conditions that canoers can meet with on this continent—and we've met them with enjoyment and assurance and without serious hazard even when, at the time, the going seemed toughest. That, I think, is the essential requirement any time you set out by canoe: to enjoy the trip; and to surmount whatever difficulties present themselves along the way, so that you, your party, your canoe and equipment come back again in safety. The two go together.

1 The Canoer's World

A few years ago, two of my sons and I headed our canoe down the 8 miles of river that connects two lakes called Darky and Minn, in the Quetico country, north of the Minnesota-Ontario border. It was a bright morning in early June, and on the river, sheltered from the wind by big pines thick on either bank, the weather was almost sultry, as on a meandering tidal stream of the far South. At times, the river elbowed out in a little lake, with dense growths of wild rice and white and yellow flowering lilies surrounding the channel, and squads of young ducks and loons feeding among them. Again, the river narrowed, cutting its way through indestructible rock, and there were the half a dozen rapids marked on the map for the boys to watch for and skim through, exercising skills they'd been practicing in the two weeks of our trip—though at this season the rapids turned out to be no more than momentary riffles in the smooth flow of the water. But, miles as we were from any other people, any town, we treated them with respect all the same.

Toward noon, with a final rush around a last bend, the river current broke against the deeper waters of a new lake, made choppy by a freshening breeze. We worked our way down it, pushing against the wind and waves, portaged into the next lake, and camped for the night on a tiny island a mile from shore, with just room for our tent, a fireplace, a dozen stunted pines and birches, and the two big rocks—one to fish from, the other for swimming—around which the island itself had grown, like a pearl. Another day and we were cross-ing an arm of a lake that still carries its *voyageur* name, Lac La Croix, the biggest in this border country, with water vistas of 5 miles or more in any direction. From our vantage point, hugging the water, feeling every pressure of wind and wave in the movement of the canoe and the muscles of our bodies, it was like putting out on an ocean. Our route that afternoon took us on portages around two waterfalls (where we paused to gather tiny wild strawberries growing cool in the spray, and ripe blueberries from a sunny outcropping above). We camped that night on an island dividing a third, much bigger fall and slept to its roaring lullaby: a ceaseless tumbling of waters like an image of irresistible force, pounding against smooth granite cubes of living rock that are its immovable object and its channel.

The next day—and next-to-last of our trip—was 20 miles of a long, narrow lake, with the wind building behind us until the following waves were breaking over the stern of the canoe. After the effort of keeping headed, we faced another river, sheltered now, but this time upstream, with the current against us and a series of rapids to push up and falls to portage around. Another day, and we were back at our starting point, the village of Winton, 90 miles north of Duluth—where roads end and the hundred or so people are mostly Finns whose parents or grandparents came there as loggers; their speech still sings with the music of that other northland of lakes and pines and rocky streams thousands of miles to the east.

Canoeing is an inexpensive family sport that almost anyone can enjoy. (Montana Travel Promotion)

CANOE HISTORY

Canoeing is one of the oldest outdoor activities in North America. The word canoe comes from *kanu*, a Carib Indian term referring to their sea-going dugouts. It is believed that the Carib Indians of the Caribbean Islands made the first canoes.

Indians in the southeastern part of the United States made similar canoes by burning and chopping out large logs until a long wooden shell was all that remained. Farther north, Indians made canoes by fastening bark to a frame contructed of branches. These canoes stayed basically the same for several hundred years and were used by trappers, missionaries, explorers, and other wilderness travelers until the late 1800s. It was then that canoes began to be made of such materials as cedar strips or canvas over a wood frame. These canoes were used mostly by sportsmen for hunting and fishing, with some people canoeing just for the fun of it.

By the late 1950s, canoes had advanced in design and materials to the point that the craft was relatively lightweight, not so tippy, and more manageable in the water. The environmental movement arrived with the 1960s, and canoeing emerged as "the thing to do." White-water canoeing became popular as a daring sport, canoe races were enjoyed by spectators and competitors alike, and canoe manufacturers set up shop everywhere.

This strong interest in canoeing has not lessened. Stronger and lighter materials have found their way into the canoe industry, making canoeing more fun than ever. Canoe camping is now being enjoyed by families, both at streams near home and at famous canoeing areas across the continent. Canoe racing has been added to the Summer Olympics, and more sportsmen are using canoes than ever before.

CANOE TRAVEL

Whether you call it tripping, expedition canoeing, cruising, or flat-water canoeing (the white-water enthusiasts' term, to set it apart from what *they* do), the elements of canoe travel are the same. Whether for a day or two at a time or for months, you are *traveling*: you have a sequence of places to get to and an objective at the end, even if it is only to complete the circuit and return to your starting point. Whatever help you may have in setting out or after you get back, while you are on your route you are *on your own: you* supply the power that drives you along. And whatever you require to sustain you on the way—food and cooking gear, tent and sleeping bags, clothes—you carry with you in your canoe and pack on your back over the portage trails between waters, which may be anywhere from a few feet to a mile or more. Traveling by canoe, you can, if you like, reach parts of this continent that are not in fact accessible by any other means. On the other hand, even when you are not traveling to or through actual wilderness—and there are literally thousands of fine, canoeable lakes and rivers within a few miles of major cities from Boston to Los Angeles—the effect will be

Thousands of canoeable lakes and rivers are found close to most American cities.
(Old Town Canoe Co.)

much the same. The nameless stream that you flash past on the turnpike with hardly a glance looks entirely different when seen from a canoe. By returning to this older mode of travel—as old as the Indians who preceded us on this continent—you return to an earlier viewpoint, a simpler and more basic way of doing things, and that is part of the lure of canoeing and one of its rewards. In either case, whether you are canoeing through deepest wilderness or within sight and sound of a million people, the effect is the same: you travel with the freedom that comes of being self-sustaining, dependent on no one but yourself.

That canoe trip of ours was typical in another way of what a new-time canoer can look forward to: it took us through most of the kinds of waters one is likely to encounter in traveling by canoe. There were lakes ranging in size from beaver ponds, no more than dots on our maps and too small to be named, to big lakes 5 or 6 miles across and 30 miles long, where the waves can build up almost like ocean combers to test the canoer's heart and nerves and skill. There were rivers connecting some of these lakes, to glide down or battle up with hard paddling, rivers that might spread lakelike, a mile at a stretch, half marshy at the edges, and then narrow around the next bend, running deep and swift, punctuated by rapids. And there was, finally, that succession of waterfalls to negotiate, from both directions—paddling through the turbulent eddies at the bottom to reach the carrying place, approaching from above with a different but equal caution.

The variety of water and weather that I led my boys through was no accident, of course. I had been canoeing that country with my father, brothers, mother, friends since I was a child smaller than my sons, and for their first sampling I picked from all those memories a route that would show them a little of every kind of thing that country has to offer. It's varied country—and big: the Boundary Waters Canoe Area, created in 1965 after decades of evolution and growth, runs for 200 miles along the top of Minnesota—more than a million acres, thousands of lakes, thousands of miles of canoe routes; and Quetico Park, across the border, is on the same scale. You could spend a lifetime canoeing that country and never know all of it.

The BWCA-Quetico long ago implanted my own notions of what canoeing might be, like a boy's first experience of the possibilities of love. But any canoe travel you're likely to do will partake of that variousness. Indeed, the possible combinations of the canoer's pair of elements, water and weather, must be infinite, and they can vary in one place from year to year, season to season, so that, even following the same route, no canoe trip is likely ever to be twice the same. Hence, if canoers had a motto, it might well be the Coast Guard's *Semper Paratus*—"ready for anything." Taking you the first steps toward being ready for anything when you step into your canoe is what this book is about.

Any canoe trip you make will involve you in a variety of waters, calling on several different specific canoeing skills, but, depending on where you live, one or another kind is going to predominate. We'll look at the possibilities in greater detail in a later chapter. Here, we'll be thinking ahead, since the kind of country you'll be canoeing determines not only the skills you need to master but a whole series of choices in equipment and clothing and in the canoe itself.

There is notable canoe travel to be had in every state of the Union, every Canadian province. East and west of the great central basin walled off by the Appalachians and the Rockies, river canoeing predominates. The range is from such big and comparatively gentle streams as the Hudson, the Delaware, and Oregon's Willamette, where you can make rewarding canoe trips of a week or two, to hair-raising roller coasters like Maine's Dead River and parts of the Connecticut in New Hampshire that reach or surpass the limits of what's possible in a canoe. In the East particularly, the horizons of the canoer's world tend to be seasonal. In the Northeast, rivers that fill in spring with melting snow and rain may be too shallow and rocky to afford much fun in summer; from Pennsylvania south, the season is earlier, and winter and early-spring canoeing has much to recommend it. Dams on these rivers present a hazard in the shape of unpredictable rise and fall in the water level—or, if you like a welcome change of pace in the form of portages.

Many of these waters that form the canoe traveler's world are what is known as "flat." This is not to say millpond-smooth, but with a current slow enough—under 4 miles an hour—that the canoer can usually travel at will in any direction, up, down, or across. Water flows because it follows a natural slope; the steeper the grade, the swifter the current. The difference between flat-water and white-

Streams with smooth water are known as "flat." (Michigan Travel Commission)

Water with lots of rapids and a steep gradient is referred to as "white water." (Wyoming Travel Commission)

water canoeing is very much like the difference between cross-country and downhill skiing. For the canoe traveler, white water is a part of the whole, an aspect of his sport. He knows how to handle it—and knows what is beyond the limits of himself and his canoe. Relying on himself even when in a party with several other canoes, he reads the water ahead and scouts the banks of rapids he has not tried. Knowing that he must depend on the gear in his canoe for days or weeks to come, he does not risk depositing it at the bottom of an impassable stream; he portages around the hazards he's not sure of or uses poles or a rope from the bank to let his canoe down the descent, under control. Any river he can go down he can also come up again, though the going against the current may be slow and wearying.

The white-water canoer, in contrast, seeks out the swiftest rapids, the steepest gradients, for a few hours or a day of split-second action—and plans his runs around cars or buses to carry him back by road to his starting point. Since his gear need be no more than a rucksack of lunch (and perhaps a change of clothes against the chance of a dunking), his canoe or kayak will be built light, fast, and nimble. In the past twenty years, the demands of white water have stimulated radical experiments in the design of canoes and paddles and in the materials they're made from, and the white-water canoers have developed the techniques to match them. Today, with the right equipment and careful training, it is possible to canoe—in control and with reasonable safety—streams that would have been suicidal for canoers of the past or their Indian predecessors. Many of these innovations in design and technique have become part of the flat-water canoer's arsenal—like the technical advances that from time to time come out of Watkins Glen or the Indianapolis 500—and we'll be looking at them in later chapters. Nevertheless, for the canoe traveler, white water—exhilarating, scary, or both together—remains only a part of the whole. His world is larger and more varied.

WHO CANOES

On canoe trips over the years I've seen just about the entire spectrum of human age and physical prowess. We've come across parties of boys in their middle or early teens . . . lissome girls who raced us over the portages . . . a young man and woman on their wedding trip . . . a pair of elderly ladies canoeing together, who looked like your favorite high school English teachers . . . whole families, mother at the bow, father at the stern, a crowd of children and a dog in between, among the packs. I was six or seven when my father let me take my turn at helping paddle our canoe (not *much* help, probably—my arms got tired). He was seventy when we made our last canoe trip together, with my four- and five-year-old eldest sons as passengers. The point is that you don't have to be an eighteen-year-old football player to canoe well and pleasurably. In a world of 7-foot basketball stars and 300-pound tackles, canoeing is one of the equalizers. One of my boys, who's 5½ feet tall and has the weight of a wombat dripping wet, handles a canoe as effectively in the water and on the portage trail as his brother, who's 6 feet plus and growing.

The reason for this is that, in whatever modern-design variants, canoe and paddle are among man's great adaptations to his physical environment: knowing how to use them effectively in getting through the waters makes it possible for one who is not so young or strong or big to keep up with those who are. That explains, I think, another fact of the canoer's world. Of all the forms of more or less strenuous exercise, canoeing is among the most gradual. *You* set the pace, adapting your body to paddle and canoe. You may feel tired on the first day or two, but you won't wake up stiff in the morning, with muscles that feel as if they'd been soaked overnight in epoxy. Hence, canoeing is not a sport that requires special conditioning. If you're snowbound in a city apartment and like busywork, do sit-ups for the sake of your back and stomach muscles; flex your arms and shoulders with dumbbells in your hands. But, above all, study and practice the basic skills in calm waters before you venture into the wilderness. The best conditioning for canoeing is *canoeing*, and the mere strength will come. On the first day out, plowing against the wind and waves, you may regret every cigarette you ever smoked—and you can count them off against your paddle strokes. By the end of the trip, you'll wonder why the first day seemed so tough. Such is the steady and unfailing process by which canoeing rebuilds your muscles and your mind.

CANOE CAMPING

Whether for a weekend or a spell of weeks, any canoe travel you do is going to include camping along the way. In its camping aspect, canoeing falls somewhere between backpacking and trailering. The differences are in what you can carry and the distances you can expect to cover.

For hiking any distance, the usual recommendation is a load of not more than 40 pounds. Whatever your personal limit, you're going to select what goes in your pack with extreme care and an eye to the bulk and the ounces. The hiker's tent, if he uses one at all, must be light and compact. Weight will also be an important factor in his choice of sleeping bag, and an air mattress or a foam-rubber pad to go under it may well be a luxury that won't fit in his pack. Cooking gear will have to be on the same small scale; food will be exclusively freeze-dried, weighing only a few ounces for a serving for two or four people, and the variety and speed of preparation offered by heavier and bulkier canned goods will be out of bounds.

For the canoe camper, the limits are a good deal less stringent. It still takes planning. Unlike his station-wagon-and-trailer counterpart, he can't

Unlike the backpacker, the canoe camper can take 200 to 300 pounds of gear, if desired.
(Coleman Company)

pack up the contents of his house (as it often looks) and move it to the nearest lake or mountain, but there's no necessity or minor camping comfort that he has to exclude, either. Depending on its length and design, his canoe will have a load capacity of anywhere from 600 to 1,000 pounds or more. With two people in the canoe, that translates into room for at least 300 pounds of gear—more than you'll ever need or want; even with a passenger, you still have, with a little care, adequate capacity without serious overloading. That means, for instance, that you can carry a tent big enough to avoid the claustrophobic sensation of trying to change your clothes lying flat on your back, as in the old-time Pullman upper berth. It means you can carry a full range of cooking equipment and eat your meals from a plate rather than a bowl or the common pot. It means you can use the bulkier—and less expensive—sleeping bags and stretch out at night on an air mattress or foam-rubber pad (unless you're accustomed to sleeping on mattresses as firm as Mother Earth and can't nod off any other way). And it means, finally, that you can allow yourself a few of those heavy little luxuries that come in cans.

To put this a little more concretely: on the canoe trip described at the beginning of this chapter, we carried food for the three of us, sleeping bags, and spare clothes in two large packs that weighed 50 or 60 pounds each at the start—the more you eat, the lighter they get, and of course we supplemented our diet with fresh-caught fish. Our cooking gear was in a small, separate pack, and our old balloon-cloth tent, weighing about 25 pounds, portaged handily on top of one of the big packs. The weights were not enough to be tiring over the fifteen or twenty minutes of a typical portage (in the old days, before the dried foods came along, we thought nothing of a pack weighing a hundred pounds or more). Actually, weight alone is less important than bulk. When it comes to portaging, it's very much worth some care in preplanning so as to fit your outfit into as few packs as possible. Trying to thread your way along a portage trail with a lot of small, loose articles dangling from your hands and arms and neck is a refined form of torture, and it's just such encumbrances that tend to get left behind when you shove off at the other end. How to avoid such nuisances and the lost time that goes with them will be taken up in a later chapter.

COMPETITION

As I mentioned earlier, canoe racing has become a popular sport, be it a local race sponsored by the Jaycees or the Olympic Games. While some races are limited to only "Pro-Class" competitors, many have "Open" or "Citizens" classes which are open to all paddlers. There are many kinds of races, both for flat-water and white-water enthusiasts, including marathon, slalom, poling, downriver, sailing, flat-water sprints, and ocean.

Marathon racing is the oldest form of canoe competition, as it was enjoyed by North American Indians hundreds of years ago. Today, marathon races vary but are generally long-distance—over 5 miles—endurance runs with the winner being the canoe with the shortest elapsed time from start to finish. Most marathon races are broken down into divisions for women, men, youngsters, mixed, and seniors (over forty).

Some marathon courses require portages around dams, shallow water, etc. Marathon races governed by the U.S. Canoe Association have rules concerning specific hull configurations for major marathon classifications with limits on waterline widths, bow and stern height, overall hull lengths, and decking lengths.

Perhaps the most popular, and certainly the most fun to watch, is white-water racing. This takes place in swift water with lots of rapids and rocks. White-water racing can be either of two styles: open canoe or closed canoe.

In open-canoe races, the paddlers battle Class II and Class III waters. Two major events are usually held: downriver racing and slalom racing. The downriver event may be 8 to 25 miles long, with the fastest canoe being the winner. The slalom event is shorter, only a quarter mile, but the paddler must pass between 20 to 30 sets of poles, called gates, without hitting them. The winner is determined by the speed of the run, less penalties for missed gates and touched gates.

Closed-canoe white-water racing is similar, but it takes place in Class III and Class IV waters, requiring closed canoes or kayaks. The downriver events are usually 3.6 to 7.2 miles long, and the slalom has 25 gates over a distance of 800 meters.

Americans have participated in Olympic flat-

Canoe racing has become a popular sport and is now a part of the Summer Olympic Games. (North Carolina Travel)

water competition since 1924. Today, Olympic canoeing is governed by the American Canoe Association through its National Paddling Committee for U.S. events and the International Canoe Federation for international events. The Olympic events are comprised of 5,000- and 10,000-meter events. Only ranked paddlers are considered for Olympic competition.

Poling and sailing are perhaps the least known of the canoe-race categories. The sailing event is based on the means by which many earlier western explorers got their canoes upstream in favorable winds—rigging them with sails. In the poling race,

the contestant must use a pole to propel and maneuver his canoe up and down a stream and around floating buoys.

Those interested in canoe competition should contact the American Canoe Association for information on canoe clubs and races in their local area.

HUNTING AND FISHING

Sportsmen have rediscovered the advantages a canoe offers for getting into remote corners of the backcountry. A canoe can reach fishing waters iso-

Fishing is a fun part of most canoe trips. (Jim Henry)

Hunters traveling by canoe reach some of the least-disturbed game habitat in North America. (J. Wayne Fears)

lated from ski boats and high-powered bass boats. It can be used on a small lake or to reach parts of rivers often overlooked by other anglers. Many canoers become fishermen after they have taken up canoeing. Fishing is a fun way to spend the last couple of hours of the day, and a delicious meal of fresh fish is a great way to end a day of canoeing.

Hunters have also found the canoe to be an ideal way to reach some of the best game habitat in North America. The canoe is quiet, and now that high-tech canoes in a camouflage pattern are available, they are almost impossible to see against brush. The canoe can take a pair of hunters and enough gear to stay in prime hunting country for a week, and across waters no other craft could negotiate. After all, the canoe was the craft of choice of American hunters several hundred years ago.

CANOE REWARDS

The canoer's distances, like his equipment and supplies, are on the generous side compared with hiking. In country like the Boundary Waters Canoe Area-Quetico, you'll travel 15 or 20 miles a day, with portages, without feeling pushed—and have time to explore, take pictures, perhaps do a little lunchtime fishing, and still stop early enough in the afternoon to make camp, have a swim, eat dinner in daylight, and take your canoe out afterward, unloaded, to match wits with the local fish in the magical twilight calm of their feeding time. On that trip with my sons, our loosely planned itinerary took us through a generous 120-mile loop of the Quetico, and even at that we spent four or five days of our two weeks in stopovers, loafing, fishing, exploring. Going downstream, you may well cover two or three times these average distances with no greater effort; the speed of the current is a bonus adding onto the 4 miles an hour you earn by paddling.

Canoe travel is, in a word, a life of leisure, provided you've mastered the basic skills. Getting those skills is what we'll be doing in this book, beginning with the gentle art of paddling.

Provided you've mastered the basic skills, canoeing can be a leisurely pastime for one day or one month. (Coleman Co.)

2 Canoes and Paddles

On our family canoe trips back in the 1930s and early '40s, we never used anything but wood-and-canvas canoes built in Maine, where canoeing as a white man's sport began. After World War II, when some genius in the Grumman Aircraft Company had the idea of switching a surplus plant to canoe building, using techniques developed for planes, we began using the aluminum canoes that resulted. Quite recently, I've been converted to fiberglass canoes.

My personal experience with the various types of canoes is, in effect, a capsule history of canoe building over the past forty years. Yet I believe that, in all that time, I never gave more than two minutes' thought to the many variables in the design of canoes and the materials they're made of or to the differences these might make in handling or durability. If that sounds a bit stupid, I can only say that to me a canoe was a canoe and that was all there was to it.

It wasn't until one year when I had to decide on the ideal canoe for a long and potentially hazardous trip to the Arctic, that I began seriously to investigate and think about the real differences in canoe design and materials. Then—with the realization that in the remote reaches of the Canadian Northwest I would be betting my life on the choice I made—I discovered that the range of possibilities was so huge as to make a really confident decision seem nearly impossible. There are at least eighty canoe builders in the United States, each offering from two or three to a dozen or more different canoe designs in several different sizes—say a thousand different canoes to choose from. I can't pretend to have studied or tested more than a tenth of these. In what follows, therefore, we'll be looking at a few makes that represent the main possibilities and the practical factors you'll want to consider in any canoe you choose for your own use. Your reasons for deciding on any particular canoe may be entirely different from mine, but the principles involved will be the same, and in that sense the solution to my quandary should make yours a little easier.

Before entering into this decision-making process, I would suggest that you become familiar with the parts of both the canoe and paddle. When you are talking with a canoe renter or salesperson, chances are they will use these terms in your conversation, and it will help you to know what they are talking about.

BUY OR RENT?

You don't have to own a canoe, and if you're a first-time canoer, renting is probably your best way of finding out if you really like the sport—and what to look for when and if you do decide to buy your own canoe. Then, too, renting means you don't have to haul the canoe around with you on top of your car—or store, repair, and maintain it when you're not canoeing. Outfitters in towns around the major canoe areas all rent canoes. With the prolif-

Parts of a canoe

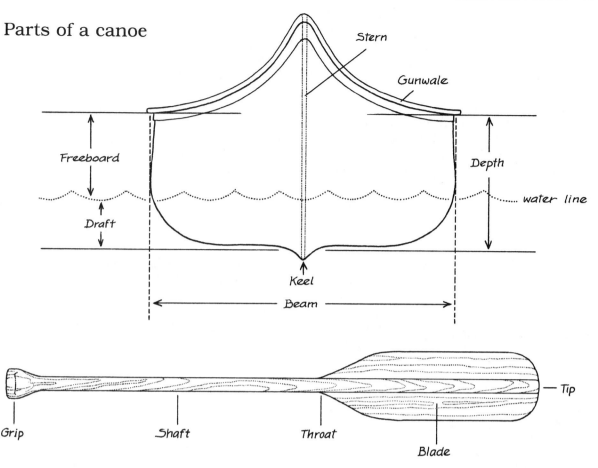

Parts of a paddle

Jackie Aher

eration of general rental services, by calling around in your area you'll probably be able to find an agency that will rent you a canoe to try out for a day or two on a local lake or river.

CHOOSING YOUR OWN CANOE

The Indians, who invented the canoe, evolved dozens of distinct designs, from the shallow-draft dugouts of the southeastern United States to the oceangoing giants of the Pacific Northwest and the kayak-form canoes of the Arctic and sub-Arctic. Even the birch-bark craft of the central forest lands had almost as many variants as there were tribes, some heavily built, with keels, others light and keel-less, sometimes covered with bark other than

birch. As canoeing, in the nineteenth century, changed from a means of commerce to a sport, canoe designs multiplied, and modern materials and manufacturing methods have still further complicated the picture. Faced with this bewildering variety and the contradictory claims that go with it, I've sometimes thought that a skilled pair of paddlers would manage equally well in a tin bathtub—that subtle differences in design matter less than who's using them. But that's a very partial truth, at best. The real point is that some canoe designs are better suited to some conditions than to others; and, since all will be used in a variety of conditions, each is to some degree a compromise among competing possibilities. From your standpoint as a canoe user and potential canoe buyer, the essential factors, in order of importance, are size and capacity, weight, cost, materials, general stability, and that half-tangible, design, which I'll try to illustrate. Just how you balance these factors will depend on the uses you expect to make of your canoe.

Size and Capacity. Traditionally, canoes have been built in lengths ranging, in 1-foot increments, from 13 to 18 feet. A few models are built as short as 11 or 12 feet, and a few makers offer canoes as long as 20 feet or more. Recently, racing standards established by the canoe associations have encouraged the makers to produce an 18½-foot canoe, comparatively long and narrow across the beam (*beam:* the distance between the sides at the center of the canoe, usually around 3 feet). Not all sizes, of course, are available in all designs or from all makers. From the standpoint of handling, the 17-foot version of the traditional design was supposed to provide the best ratio of beam to length. In general, the longer the canoe, the easier it will paddle and the more it will carry. Conversely, the short canoes will be broad in relation to their length, comparatively harder to paddle but a little more maneuverable—and they'll carry appreciably less.

Many makers specify the capacity of their canoes in pounds. By that standard, the theoretical load you can expect to carry will range from around 400 pounds for a 12-footer to about 800 pounds in a typical 17-foot canoe and as much as one thousand pounds in a few 18- or 18½-foot canoes. These capacities represent a limit of safety which in some places is a matter of law. All allow for 4 to 6 inches of freeboard (*freeboard:* the distance between the water and the gunwales at the lowest point). The differences in what different canoes of the same length will carry—and the differences are considerable—are due to a combination of several factors: beam, the center depth of the canoe, the natural buoyancy of the materials it's made from, and the size of its flotation tanks.

Wood is the oldest material from which canoes have been made. This modern canoe is made from wood strips. (Old Town Canoe Co.)

These theoretical load capacities are, of course, no more than that—theory. What counts is your own ability and experience, the kind of waters you'll be traveling, and whether you're aiming for canoe trips of a couple of weeks or more or only a few days at a time. So, to translate theory into practical terms, you can figure that any canoe shorter than 15 feet is essentially for one person and his gear—or two not very big people and their lunch and tackle, out for a day's fishing. A 15- or 16-footer should be adequate in most conditions for two people with reasonable baggage. (On our family canoe trips when I was a kid, we sometimes traveled safely with a canoe as short as 15 feet, which with a passenger—myself—and a fair amount of baggage meant only an inch or two of freeboard; but I *don't* recommend it to you.) In New England, where a big canoe is unhandy to maneuver on rivers that are typically narrow, fast, sharp-turning, and shallow, and a canoe trip as long as a week is unusual, the smaller sizes seem to be preferred for general use. Elsewhere, if you want to make your canoeing a family affair, you'll choose one of the bigger canoes, with room for a couple of children as passengers and as much in the way of food and camping gear as you're likely to need. The more traveling you do—and hence, the more varied conditions you'll meet and the bigger your loads—the longer the canoe you'll want; it will give you a little extra freeboard, which at times you'll be mightly glad to have. But there's a limit: weight.

Weight. Not being a big guy myself, I rank weight high on my list of what's important about a canoe, and, other things being more or less equal, I'll usually prefer the lightest canoe I can get. The difference is not so much in paddling as in portaging. If you're under 6 feet, an extra 15 or 20 pounds may not mean much on a flat, broad portage, but you'll find it a lot more tiring to lift and put down again, more awkward to maneuver through narrow spots or over fallen trees. When the going gets tough—steep, rocky, muddy—the added weight might sometime mean a fall and a damaged canoe or a twisted ankle. (If you're stuck with a canoe that's a bit heavier than you feel you can manage, you can use one of the two- or three-man carries described in the following chapter, but they'll make your portaging a little more time-consuming.) Before you buy your canoe, by all means get your

dealer to put a yoke on it and let you try it out for weight. That's the best way to decide, if you have any doubts.

Leaving aside the small canoes, most 15-footers will weigh in at something like 50 pounds, and each foot will add another 10 pounds or so, give or take 5 pounds either way, depending on the design. Particularly in fiberglass hulls, additional weight doesn't necessarily mean greater strength; it may simply mean the maker is not very smart in his use of materials and his manufacturing techniques. One fiberglass canoe that I've used a lot and consider well designed and sturdily built is an 18½-foot Sawyer that comes in at just 70 pounds on the family scale. We'll look more specifically at weight and other differences when we consider the various representative makes, and you'll have your own ideas about which is going to be best for you. But keep the weight factor in mind; it can be important.

Materials.   Today there are many choices of canoe materials, and it is a good idea for anyone thinking about purchasing a canoe to study the various materials to see which best suits his needs.

During the first half of this century, canoes made from canvas stretched over a wooden skeleton were the most popular type made. (Old Town Canoe Co.)

Wood—The first canoes were made of wood, and today the canoer can still purchase wood canoes. While these crafts are both beautiful and sturdy, they do have some drawbacks. Due to the amount of hand labor involved in making them, they are relatively expensive. Regular maintenance is required, including washing and occasionally varnishing. When repairs are called for, the skills of a craftsman are likely to be needed.

Most wood canoes are handmade from northern white cedar or western red cedar planking. The white cedar ribs are hand-bent, and all hardware is made of brass. The exterior is given a protective coating of clear fiberglass. A 17-foot model will usually weigh from 70 to 85 pounds. Wooden canoes are available from Great Canadian and Old Town Canoe Company, as well as several custom canoe shops.

Wood-and-Canvas—Wood-and-canvas was for nearly fifty years virtually the only type of canoe made. Cedar is the most usual wood for ribs and planking; various hardwoods are used for gunwales, decks, and seats. The hull is built up around a wooden form that determines its basic shape, then covered with a tightly stretched heavy grade of canvas. The canvas is finished with a marine paint topped by varnish, and all exposed woodwork is varnished.

Contrary to what you might suppose, I don't believe that a wood-and-canvas canoe is any more likely than aluminum or synthetic to smash if you drive against a rock; nor is it significantly easier, in my experience, to cause a leak in (by gashing through the canvas). If you do get a leak, you can use tape for a quick repair, as with other canoes, and patch in a square of canvas when you get home. However, if you were using a wood-and-canvas canoe much in rapids, the chances are that you'd scratch up the canvas enough, even without cutting it, to require repainting and revarnishing after every trip. Maintenance in general is a problem. Using the canoe a lot, you might have to put on a new coat of varnish as often as once a year, and you wouldn't want to store it outdoors, as you can aluminum and most synthetic canoes.

There are other disadvantages to wood-and-canvas canoes. Although it's possible to build them very light (and hence a bit fragile under hard use), most are rather heavier than typical aluminum or fiberglass canoes of the same size. In addition, if you have the misfortune to capsize one, the interior wood will soak up the water, takes days to dry out again, and weigh like lead until it does.

A 17-foot wood-and-canvas canoe weighs from about 75 to 85 pounds. They are available from Old Town Canoe Company.

Aluminum—When aluminum canoes appeared after World War II, they opened up fast-water rivers that in the past had been out of reach to all but the most skilled and venturesome canoeists. Aluminum canoes are generally less expensive than synthetic models, and with normal use, they are virtually maintenance-free. The metal will take a lot of scratching without showing or requiring the kind of protective repairs that canvas would need. Dents can be pounded out with a rubber hammer. On the down side, they can be cold or hot and can be noisy in rocks. A 17-foot aluminum canoe may weigh anywhere from 65 to 85 pounds. Canoes made from aluminum are available from Alumacraft Boat Company, Grumman Boats, Sportspal, and Meyers Industries.

Fiberglass—The first synthetic material used to make canoes was fiberglass. It was the fiberglass-canoe makers who first started experimenting with canoe styles, resulting in a multiplication of new designs.

The reason for this wealth and diversity of fiberglass designs is that in its fabricating techniques the material stands somewhere between wood-and-canvas and aluminum. There's considerably less hand work in making a fiberlgass canoe than in one of wood-and-canvas, but changes in design aren't limited to the costly metal forms that permit relative mass production in aluminum. The fiberglass canoe is formed within a rigid shell, starting with a layer of colored resin or paint, followed by several layers of glass fabric (held together and made rigid by resin that's sprayed or painted on, then usually hand-rolled to remove air bubbles and excess liquid) and ending (the inside of the finished canoe) with a final layer of colored resin and/or paint. When all is dry, the canoe is taken out of the form, and thwarts, gunwales, seats, and decks (or end caps, another term) are riveted into place. The glass fabric supplies the canoe's strength. Beyond a point, the resin, which bonds the layers of fabric

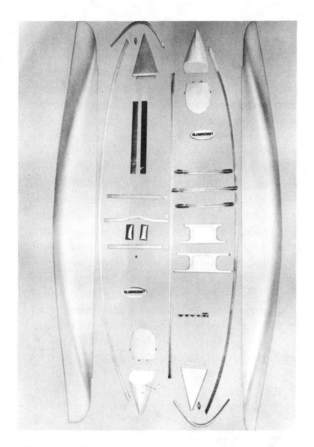

together, simply adds weight. Hence, when the process is skillfully done, it's possible to produce a fiberglass canoe that's appreciably lighter and probably stronger than the same size in wood-and-canvas or standard-weight aluminum—and often a touch lighter than light-weight aluminum as well. As a matter of physics, fiberglass and resin formed by the process described test at twice the strength of tempered aluminum of the same weight. Hence, in theory, a fiberglass canoe should be twice as strong as an aluminum one of the same size and weight (theory again—in fact, the differences in

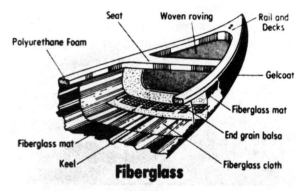

The parts of an aluminum canoe, ready for assembling: the two halves of the stretch-formed hull, with gunwales, stems, decks, and foam flotation; seats and ribs (above, center); thwarts and carrying pads (below, center); with the keel in the middle. (Alumacraft Boat Co.)

Fiberglass canoe construction: layers of gelcoat, fiberglass cloth and fiberglass mat, and woven roving. (Old Town Canoe Co.)

Aluminum canoes are durable and require little maintenance. (Sportspal Canoes)

weight and strength are less). Never having smashed a canoe of either kind, I can't tell you exactly what that difference in strength means in practice—how much more abuse one will stand than the other before it gives up. I *can* tell you that in fast rivers fiberglass will flex and rebound against blows from rocks that would dent an aluminum canoe and impede its performance.

As my description implies, unitary construction is the desirable norm for a fiberglass canoe—that is, it's made in one piece, built up within a single, undivided form. Some makers, however, mold fiberglass canoes in two symmetrical halves, either divided down the middle from bow to stern, as in aluminum construction, or occasionally from side to side amidships, and then hold them together with fiberglass-and-resin laminations, inner or outer keels, or the equivalent. Such two-part con-

struction isn't necessarily a sign of poor quality—some hull shapes couldn't be made any other way without destroying the mold each time—but I'd be wary of it; in selecting a canoe, look for seams that indicate two-part assembly and ask the dealer or manufacturer about this specific point.

In fiberglass canoes, excessive weight—a difference of as much as 10 to 20 pounds for the same size—may indicate a cheaper and less effective manufacturing technique: resin sprayed on rather than brushed (the better makers also squeeze out the excess by hand with rollers to make the finished product lighter). Another shortcut is the use of "chopped" fiberglass, which can be sprayed on (and will need more resin to hold it together), rather than single, all-over fiberglass mats. Inspect the floor of the canoe. You should be able to see and feel the weave of the glass fabric. If not, beware!

Fiberglass offers the canoe maker much flexibility in design. (Sun River Canoe)

21

The most obvious drawback to fiberglass is that it scratches. Not only rocks but waterlogged tree branches jammed below the surface and even sand will leave their marks on the canoe's smooth, shiny skin. (Aluminum also scratches, but the marks aren't nearly as visible.) Since these abrasions are on the underside, you don't have to look at them when you're paddling, but they're ugly and in time will cut through to the glass fabric underneath. At that point, although the canoe won't leak, a repair is in order, using either the old standby, waterproof tape, or epoxy or resin, sanded smooth. Even fairly small irregularities in the surface may impede handling. Since a keel-less fiberglass canoe is most vulnerable to damage at bow and stern just below the waterline, some makers offer protective aluminum or stainless-steel bang strips at those points, an extra I strongly recommend.

Apart from the scratches, fiberglass in itself takes even less maintenance than plain aluminum, which in time will corrode. A few high-priced fiberglass canoes have wood trim, which will have to be varnished from time to time; most use anodized aluminum instead.

A 17-foot fiberglass canoe usually weighs in the 70- to 85-pound range. These canoes are made by such makers as Chicagoland Canoe Base, Sawyer, Great Canadian Canoe Company, We-no-nah Canoe Company, Old Town, Mad River, White Canoe Company, and Sun River Canoe Company.

Several makers have improved fiberglass by adding other fabrics. Sawyer adds Du Pont Kevlar as a reinforcement and calls the hull material Goldenglass. We-no-nah adds Compet polyester and calls it Tuf-weave. Old Town uses Coremat as a special stiffening layer.

Polyethylene—One of the most common materials used for building high-quality, inexpensive canoes is a plastic called polyethylene. This is a tough, yet flexible material that conforms to various shapes. Coleman is one of the major canoe manufacturers using polyethylene; the version they use is called RAM-X.

Coleman extrudes RAM-X into sheets, which are then heated and vacuum-formed over a mold into 13-, 15-, and 17-foot canoes. When it comes off the mold, the material has a memory which it will retain indefinitely.

If a RAM-X canoe is dented in use, it will return to its original shape. The material is flexible, with superb impact resistance even at low temperatures. It also resists surface abrasion and will show only minimal surface marring after repeated use.

RAM-X never needs to be repainted because its color permeates the material. It also has ultraviolet inhibitors, which means you can leave it sitting in the sun for extended periods of time without fear of it softening, cracking, fading, or becoming brittle.

In the water, RAM-X becomes very resilient or slippery. Its flexibility allows Coleman canoes to slide over rocks or obstructions. It's also quiet, so there's no banging or clanging when running over gravel bars or if you bump the canoe with your paddle.

Another property of this material is that it won't conduct cold or heat. It's always comfortable to kneel in, even on the hottest days. The smooth interior finish won't scrape or cut either.

After repeated use, some marring or scratching of the RAM-X will occur, and this is natural. However, the canoe is molded so that the bottom is thicker than the sides. If the material should ever puncture or wear after a long period of service, Coleman offers a repair kit.

Because RAM-X is buoyant, it reduces the amount of additional flotation that is required to support the canoe if it's swamped or overturned.

Old Town Canoe Company has a polyethylene hull material they call Crosslink. By rotationally molding polyethylene into three layers, Old Town has made a breakthrough in manufacturing an extremely strong, abrasion-resistant hull. The outer layer is made from cross-linked polyethylene, giving the canoe its attractive and abrasion-resistant hull. The interior layer is also constructed from cross-linked polyethylene and gives the canoe a cool, durable finish.

The key to the exceptional strength of the canoe lies in its central foam core layer. This polyethylene foam core provides stiffness and eliminates the need for the framework which is required in other polyethylene canoes. This method of construction, combined with durable cross-linked polyethylene, produces a canoe that can take great abuse and be popped back to its original shape with minimum distortion.

A 17-foot polyethylene canoe will weigh around 78 pounds.

Polyethylene canoes are strong, lightweight, and relatively inexpensive. (Coleman Co.)

Royalex—Another space-age plastic being used in canoe hulls is Royalex, a sandwich material made of vinyl on either side of an ABS plastic core. It is most often used on white-water canoes, as it is very durable, bending when it strikes rocks and logs, then returning to its proper shape. A Royalex canoe is quiet, easy to paddle, and virtually maintenance free. It is also a good insulator against heat and cold.

A 17-foot canoe from this material will weigh between 70 and 80 pounds. It is used as a hull material by Blue Hole Canoe Company, Mad River, Old Town, and White Canoe Company.

Kevlar 49—This Du Pont cloth weave is one of the strongest but lightest-weight materials used in canoe-hull construction. Mad River introduced Kevlar to the canoe industry in 1974. Pound for pound, it is stronger than steel, and its low density makes it about 20 percent lighter than fiberglass. About the only drawback to Kevlar is that it is expensive. It is often used with other materials such as foam core to make efficient, ultralightweight canoes.

A 17-foot Kevlar canoe will weigh in the 45- to 55-pound range. Canoes with Kevlar hull material are made by Mad River Canoe Company, We-no-nah Canoe, Blue Hole Canoe Company, and Old Town Canoe Company.

Synthetic materials for canoe hulls are changing rapidly, and I'm sure that by the time you read this, there will be new space-age materials in canoes that weren't in use at this writing.

Design.   Every canoe hull design is a combination of three sets of curves. Just how they're combined and the degree of curve in each dimension determines how the canoe will handle, both in general and under various conditions. The differences in handling that you'll actually feel are as subtle as the curves involved, as infinite as the possible combinations, but the more experienced you are as a canoeist, the more you'll feel—and appreciate—the differences. Each emphasis in design offers a particular advantage—and a corresponding disadvantage—depending on the circumstances. It's in that sense that there's no "perfect" canoe for all conditions: every design is to some extent a compromise.

You can study a canoe hull *from below, from head on,* or *from the side.* In each of these positions, you'll see a different set of curves, each of which has its own importance. For the purpose of this discussion, we'll consider only the double-ended canoe, nearly always identical in its lines at bow and stern; a square-stern canoe won't be first choice if travel under your own power is your primary aim.

Looking at the canoe *from below* (or turned on its side), what you see is the bow line. If it's relatively sharp and long ("fine" is the designers' term), curving gently back to a comparatively narrow beam, the canoe will cut through the water better, be easier (and faster) to paddle. Conversely, a blunter, fuller, more steeply curving bow line, broader in the beam, will be a little heavier to paddle but also more buoyant, with a greater carrying capacity—because of the greater volume enclosed by the hull. Other things being equal, the full bow line is probably more apt to ride *over* waves than *through* them, hence will be drier in rough water.

When you look at the canoe *head on,* what you're seeing is the bottom curve, in effect a cross section. Here again, a continuous curve from gunwale to gunwale means speed and maneuverability—but a reduced load capacity. A flat-bottom canoe, on the other hand, will carry more (and not ride quite so deep with the same load) but feel a little heavier in the water. There's a difference in stability, too. In flat water, from calm to lightly wavy, a curved-bottom canoe is going to feel tippier than one with a flat bottom: it will sway a little from side to side with each paddle stroke (though with experience you compensate for that movement). In bigger waves, on the other hand—violent rapids or a storm—it's possible for a wave to grab the broad plane of a flat-bottom canoe and shove the canoe on over, where one with a curving bottom, affording less leverage, will recover and pop upright again like a cork. If you're a first-time canoer, you'll probably do best under most conditions with a flat-bottom canoe, and if you're renting, as I've suggested, that's exactly what you'll get: the aluminum-canoe builders don't make them any other way.

Viewed *from the side,* in profile, a canoe presents its third set of curves (and also an important difference in depth between bow and center, which

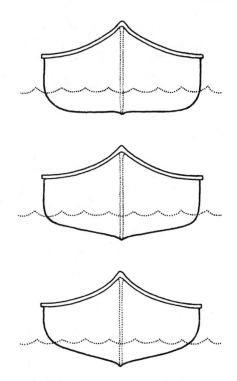

Top: canoe hull design—comparatively flat-bottomed, shallower draft for the same capacity than a rounded bottom, but slower; will feel more stable.
Center: shallow "V" canoe hull design—comparatively rounded cross section; fast, but somewhat deep draft; will feel somewhat unstable to the inexperienced canoer.
Bottom: Rounded design which will feel very unstable to the inexperienced canoer. (Jackie Aher)

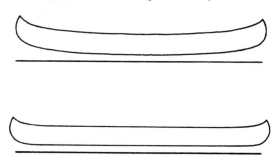

Top: canoe hull design—a rocker-bottom canoe (continuously rounded from bow to stern), somewhat reducing load capacity and increasing draft but appreciably more maneuverable than a flat-bottom canoe.
Bottom: canoe hull design—a flat-bottomed canoe, providing great load capacity with comparatively shallow draft, probably easier than a rocker-bottom to hold on course. (Jackie Aher)

Kevlar canoes are among the strongest and lightest available. (J. Wayne Fears)

we'll come back to in a moment). Here, too, the choice is between a flat bottom and a continuous curve from bow to bottom and up again at the stern (called a "rocker bottom"). The curving profile will turn a little faster, important in rapids, but, other things being equal, sit deeper in the water and carry less. There's not, in my experience, any difference in stability.

Three dimensions are important variables in canoe design: bow and stern depth (usually the same), center depth, and beam. Bow/stern and center depths are generally in rough proportion to over-all length: the longer canoes will be a little deeper at both ends. In the 17-foot canoe, the range in bow depths (measured, with the canoe flat on the ground, from its lowest point to the peak of the bow) is from about 16 to 26 inches; 20 or 22 inches is typical. The higher the bow, the less likely you are to take on water as you slice through waves or the swirling turbulence of a rapid—but you'll also be more vulnerable to the cross winds you'll meet in lake canoeing, which can make it tough work trying to hold a course. After a day of that, you may feel too tired for dinner before crawling into your sleeping bag for the night! A canoe cut low in the bow to minimize this cross-wind effect will have to compensate in some other direction—with a rocker bottom that helps the canoe ride over the waves, perhaps with longer decks, or end caps, which of course reduce somewhat the usable space inside the canoe.

Again in the matter of center depth, canoe design has two opposite desirables to reconcile. You want it low enough so that the canoe won't be excessively affected by wind, high enough for adequate carrying capacity and safe freeboard with a load. In a 17-foot canoe, a 13-inch center depth is typical, with a range from 11 to 15 inches. The 4-inch difference may not sound like much, but it can mean a lot if you find yourself in the middle of a lake with a storm coming up and the waves beginning to build. A rocker bottom will compensate to some extent for a low center depth. Another answer is to stretch the canoe out by a foot or more, increasing its capacity and general buoyancy.

The final dimension that matters is the canoe's beam, measured at the center from outside to outside at the gunwale level. A beam of 36 or 37 inches is usual for a 17-footer, though in the Canadian Far North, where canoes are still the workhorses of a frontier society, they're built up to 45 inches and will carry a correspondingly huge load, 1,600 pounds! A narrower beam, down to 33 or 34 inches, makes for easier paddling, but with some sacrifice in capacity.

Before we leave the general question of canoe design, let's run through the practical effects of the basic options. For speed (which is also to say easy paddling even when you're not in a hurry), look for a fine entry line at the bow, a continuous curve in the cross section, a narrow beam, and a low profile at bow and stern and amidships; other things being equal, a long hull is always faster than a short one. These are the characteristics found in canoes designed for racing, with exact dimensions and proportions controlled by a complex formula devised by the American Canoe Association. The disadvantages of such a canoe in ordinary use are that it tends to plow through waves rather than ride over them, so that it will take water in conditions where a blunter, deeper canoe would stay dry; it's also less maneuverable and will feel less stable to an inexperienced canoer—the two paddlers need to be quite sensitive to subtle changes in balance; and, finally, it will carry less. The opposite extreme, is a canoe that's comparatively blunt in the bow line, broad-beamed, flat-bottomed both in cross section and in bow-to-stern profile, and high at bow and stern and amidships. It will ride the waves better, ride higher in the water with the same load (providing extra margin in shallows), and seem more stable; it will also be slower, take more effort to paddle, and be more vulnerable to cross winds. Some of the classic canoe designs of the past combined features of these two extremes: a fine entry line flaring to a full cross section behind the bow, rockered at bow and stern for maneuverability, comparatively flat-bottomed amidships for stability and capacity. A few modern builders make a hull with similar characteristics, and it probably comes the closest of any to being the best design for all purposes, but the prices are high.

There's one other matter of canoe design, much debated among canoers and canoe builders: the keel. As we noted earlier, a keel of some kind is a structural necessity in an aluminum canoe, but in wood-and-canvas or synthetic there's a choice—and room for argument about how a keel or the lack of one affects handling. A narrow bar centered on the bottom of the canoe and running its length below

When a motor is needed to get across big stretches of water, a motor mount attachment is a useful accessory for the canoe. (Coleman Co.)

the water line, a keel improves "tracking"—makes it easier to hold your course when you've wind to contend with—and also protects the bottom from rock damage. From that standpoint, the deeper the better, and five eighths or one inch is standard, depending on the maker. In shallow water, though, a keel means just that much greater draft, and the extra inch can make the difference between sliding over a rock and getting stuck—or dumped. What's more, just because it does tend to hold its own straight line, a keel of any kind impedes the kind of fast turns and sideways maneuvers that are essential for getting through rapids. The aluminum-canoe builders' answer to that problem is what's called a *shoe keel*, flattened down to three eighths inch to reduce the drag in turning. Conversely, the keel-less synthetic canoes favored for white-water use get their tracking characteristics from the complex combinations of curves discussed earlier. If most of your canoeing is likely to be on the lake systems of southern Canada and the upper Midwest, with those big stretches of windy water to get across, a keel's your best bet. And if fast rivers or a mixture of flat water and fast water is what you have in mind, you'll find the going a little better with a keel-less model.

One final point about keels: if you're buying (or renting) an aluminum canoe, turn it over and sight along the keel—it should be absolutely straight and without dents or bends. Any irregularities in the

keel can add a lot to the difficulty of holding a course.

Adaptations of canoe design for motor use are outside the purview of this book, but if you want to combine paddling with a small kicker for getting across big stretches of water, avoid the usual square-stern canoe—the extra drag makes it a real brute to paddle.

Instead, take a motor mount with you. This is an attachment that mounts to the gunwales just behind the stern seat and has a wooden block to clamp a small outboard motor onto. Once you are through using the motor, you can take the attachment off and you are back enjoying the paddling efficiency of your canoe. Most canoe manufacturers have motor mounts that fit their canoes, or adjustable motor mounts that will fit most canoes are available.

CHOOSING THE RIGHT PADDLE

There was a time when a paddle, like a canoe, was pretty much standard in its design and the only real question was getting the right length. That, too, has changed, and again it's the specialized demands of the racers and white-water enthusiasts that have led to new designs and the use of new materials—from which the rest of us can benefit. Today, besides the traditional, one-piece, solid-wood paddle in spruce or a hardwood such as ash or maple, you can choose among laminated wood, fiberglass, composite, or plastic, with shafts of aluminum, PVC, or wood, and several different styles of grip. Before we turn to the various materials—which make possible rather wide variations in design and hence in paddling techniques—let's think about the real basics: over-all length and blade width.

The old rule of thumb for length is that with the tip of the blade resting on the ground, the top of the grip should come about to your nose when you're standing up straight. Another way of accomplishing the same measurement is to take the grip in your right hand as if for paddling and reach your arm straight out from the shoulder; then, with your left arm fully extended in the opposite direction, you should be able to wrap your fingers around the tip of the blade. Either way, you won't go far wrong. The result, if you're 5 feet 8 inches (as I happen to be) will be a paddle of 63–65 inches. In practice, I like it a couple of inches shorter than that in the bow, a little longer in the stern, where steering strokes are longer and deeper.

The object here is to get a paddle long enough to give you maximum leverage for your reach when you're actually paddling. Since modern paddle blades vary quite a bit in length—from 17 to 27 inches or more—what we're really concerned with, then, is the length of the shaft (including 1 to 3 inches of grip) plus the blade, whatever its length. To go at the question from that angle, try a paddle out sitting down in a chair, as if paddling. Toward the end of a stroke, with the upper hand wrapped over the grip and your lower hand around or just above the throat of the paddle, both arms should be fully extended with a paddle of the right length—the upper arm straight out in front of the opposite shoulder and raised at an angle of about 45 degrees, the lower pointing down and back, a little behind your body. The distance between your two hands in that position plus the length of the blade yields the right paddle length for you. (With my arms and height, that comes out to about 42 inches for grip and shaft, which with a blade of, say, 22 inches gives a total of about 64 inches—about right for me at the stern; with a longer blade, the whole paddle would naturally be longer too; for use in the bow, I'd shave off 2 or 3 inches.) As you see, it comes out about the same as the old rule of thumb.

By whatever route you reach it, this standard for length is about right for general travel in a canoe of conventional design—lakes, rivers, some fast water. Up to a point, the longer the paddle, the more leverage you'll have (if your arms are long enough), hence the stronger your strokes—particularly the pries and draws (defined in Chapter 3) you need for quick maneuvering in rapids. For this reason, the white-water people tend to use paddles that are longer by 5–6 inches than is normal in general canoeing. The limiting factor is that the long paddle gets in the way in shallows and is more likely to be cut up on rocks or broken off at the shaft—especially if what you're prying against is a submerged boulder. Conversely, in some of the the synthetic canoes designed for flat-water racing, which have a low profile and seats set comparatively far down, you can do with a shorter paddle—say 60 inches or less (you don't have as far to reach to

the water). Even here, though, my own preference is still for a longer paddle—but perhaps that's no more than early training and habit.

One of the best developments in the field of canoe paddles is the bend paddle. The bending of the shaft forward near the top of the blade permits the paddle to force the canoe forward through more of the stroke. Bent shaft blades are vertical at the stroke's end, so no water is lifted and there is no loss of momentum; thus, greater paddling efficiency. The downside of the bend paddle is that it gives high performance in forward movement but can result in some loss of control in tight maneuvers. These popular paddles are available in several bend angles, but the most common are the 5-, 10-, and 14-degree bends. The 5-degree bend is so nearly straight that it is about the same as a straight paddle. The 10-degree bend is good for general canoeing where the J stroke and tight maneuvers are common. The 14-degree bend gives the canoe maximum straight-ahead power. Almost every canoe paddle manufacturer offers bent paddles.

How wide should your paddle blade be? If you make the dealers' rounds or study the manufacturers' catalogs, you'll find some as narrow as 6 inches, others, designed for racing, up to 12 inches (they look like wooden snow shovels). These are maximum widths—the blade is always tapered at the top, often at the bottom as well. The length of the blade is equally important: what matters is not width (though that's what the makers advertise) but area—the greater the area, the stronger your thrust through the water. Or, to put it the other way around, with a big paddle you'll paddle somewhat slower for the same forward speed than with a narrower one. (The voyageurs used paddles only 3–4 inches wide and paddled correspondingly fast—a stroke a second, which is the tempo of paddling songs like "Alouette.") A one-piece, solid-wood paddle in the traditional teardrop, or beavertail, shape—the blade long and tapered at both ends for strength—will be from about 6 inches wide to a maximum of 7½–8 inches. A typical blade in this design is 6½ × 27 inches, with the widest point (and hence the center of power) about a third of the way up from the tip. That gives you a total effective blade area of just over 100 square inches, provided you get the whole blade in the water at each stroke. That's standard for cruising and makes for a steady 30 or 35 strokes a minute, which you should be

Canoe paddles come in a variety of designs and are made from materials ranging from wood to Kevlar. Note the differences in blade and handle designs of these paddles. (Jackie Aher)

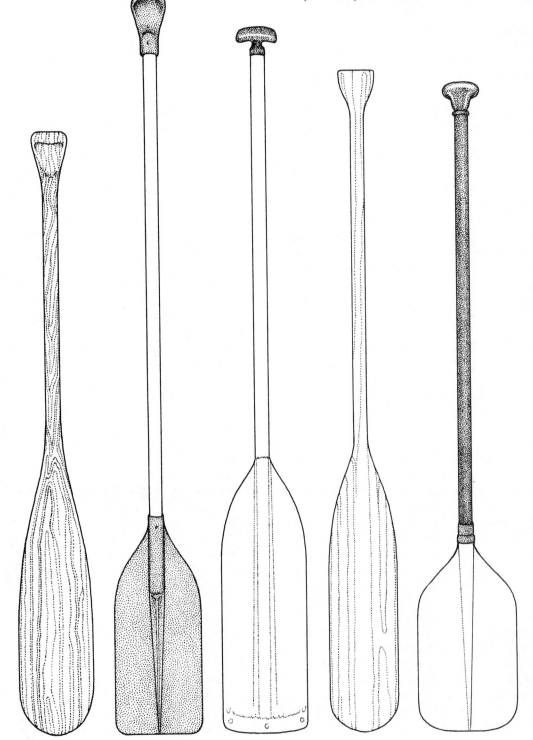

able to keep up all day without tiring.

Laminated-wood or synthetic paddles don't have to be tapered at the tip for strength, and the blades can therefore be built quite a lot broader and shorter than the traditional style. A typical design suitable for general canoeing will have a blade 8¾ × 22 inches, squared off at the tip, with sides that run straight half or two thirds of the length before tapering in to the shaft: an area of around 150 square inches. Bigger paddles (9 × 25 inches, say, with an area of about 175 square inches) are used for racing and for white water. The boiling turbulence of deep, difficult rapids produces an effect rather like a partial vacuum, and it takes a big paddle to get enough purchase on such water to pull through it and control one's course. The big blades, indeed, make for fast, precise steering in all conditions—the zigzag course, for instance, that you'll follow to get through the chop of a gathering storm without swamping.

Apart from the advantage in steering, a big blade doesn't seem to provide a proportionate saving in

Examples of high-quality wooden paddles.
(McCann Paddles)

Many high-quality white-water paddles are made from fiberglass, such as these Sawyer paddles.
(J. Wayne Fears)

When selecting a paddle, be sure to get one long enough for maximum leverage for your reach. (Gerald S. Ratliff)

effort in normal cruising. With a 140-square-inch blade, a paddling rate of 30 strokes per minute feels about right to me, but using a smaller, 100-square-inch paddle I have to up the tempo only to about 32–33 to maintain the same speed. I'll leave it to the engineers to explain why!

Whatever length and design of paddle you choose, you should have the same size blade at bow and stern. A difference at either end will make accurate steering a lot harder.

The traditional paddle grip is pear-shaped, 2–3 inches long and flaring out from the shaft (about 1¼ inches in diameter) to a width of 3–4 inches. That's the style I'm used to, but the T-shaped grips available on laminated or fiberglass paddles—

either straight or curved at both ends—give you something to wrap your fingers and thumb around and hence a little more control. The T grip is favored for white water, but it's a little more fragile, I think, when it comes to poling in rocky shallows (remember, to save the blade, always turn the paddle upside down when faced with that kind of situation).

Paddle weight is worth thinking about. The range is from just under a pound to nearly 3 pounds; 2 pounds is typical. Spruce and some plastic or synthetic paddles tend to be rather light, ash or maple a little heavier. A lighter paddle will probably seem less tiring if you're paddling long distances—a statistician has calculated that an extra

One of the most efficient paddle designs is the bent paddle, as it moves the canoe forward through more of the stroke than a conventional paddle. (Jackie Aher)

pound means lifting seven additional *tons* in the course of a day's canoeing—but the practical effect isn't as great as the difference in weight may suggest.

All paddle materials have their good and bad points. A good solid-wood paddle is cut from the heart of the tree, and its elegant, traditional lines make it remarkably strong. The blade itself will abrade, perhaps split, as it slides over rocks in shallow rapids. The shaft tends to rub against the gunwale as you paddle and will in time wear to weakness—that's the point, just above the throat, where a wooden paddle's likely to break, though it's never happened to me. With a lot of use, the varnish on the grip will wear through, the wood

get rough enough to cause a blister if it's not sanded and revarnished. Any wooden paddle, solid or laminated, will have to be revarnished periodically, perhaps once a year if you're doing much canoeing.

A laminated paddle is made from many strips of wood glued together. Many companies coat the wood strips with fiberglass to give them strength and to get a better seal, as a gouge in the wrong place can let water in and cause the strips to come apart. Most laminated paddles are stronger than solid wood paddles. Another advantage of a laminated paddle is that the blade can be made much wider than solid wood. Paddles of wood and laminated wood are available from Sawyer Canoe Company, Grey Owl Paddle Company, Mad River

Canoe Company, Mitchell Paddles, Inc., Bending Branches, McCann Paddles, White Canoe Company, and Great Canadian Canoe Company.

There are many choices of canoe paddles made from strong, lightweight synthetics. As an example, one top-of-the-line paddle is We-no-nah's Max-craft. It has a featherweight, rigid foam core wrapped in a woven skin of graphite, fiberglass, and Kevlar. Impact-resistant epoxy protects the blade rim. The shaft grip is heat-shrunk PVC, and the top grip is plastic. This 49-inch-long paddle weighs a mere 15 ounces. Barton Paddle Company makes an ultralight paddle from a foam core carbon fiber. Sawyer Canoe Company makes high-quality canoe paddles from fiberglass, as well as Kevlar. The Coleman Company uses polyethylene to build strong paddles. Iliad combines a blade of fiberglass/epoxy with an aluminum shaft to produce quality paddles. The Norse Paddle Company has a similar paddle with a fiberglass blade and an aluminum shaft, and the Mohawk Paddle Company makes a less expensive paddle with an aluminum shaft but with a plastic blade. The Carlisle Paddle Company has an aluminum paddle that has been coated with polyethylene to eliminate oxidation and to keep fingers warm. It is also quieter to use.

These are but a few examples of the various synthetic materials that are now available in paddles. By the time you read this there will probably be many more, as the quest for stronger, lighter, and quieter paddles continues.

If I'm doing much canoeing in rocky conditions I've found it's prudent to protect the tip of my paddle blades with tape. The better makers of paddles of all types will furnish their paddles with the tips reinforced with metal—copper or brass was the old standby, aluminum or stainless steel today. Fiberglass and resin are also used to reinforce the tips of wooden paddle blades, an improvement you can easily make yourself.

There's one other type of paddle you may sometime be glad to know of: the double blade. It's primarily for getting around in a kayak, but if you want to travel any distance by yourself in a 16- or 17-foot canoe, you'll find the going a lot easier with a double blade than with a single paddle. Normal lengths are 8–9 feet, prices roughly double those for a comparable single-bladed paddle in laminated wood or fiberglass. Those who use them usually prefer to have the two blades set at right angles to each other, and most are jointed in the middle so they can be taken apart for carrying, portaging, or storage. Designs and materials vary even more than in single-blade canoe paddles, but I'd stick with those of the canoe builders in preference to the more extreme (and expensive) makes that are really meant solely for kayak use.

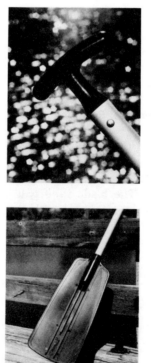

Coleman Marine has a line of T grip paddles featuring blade and handle material of Covel. Covel is more impact resistant and withstands exposure to the elements much better as well. The shafts are annodized aluminum, and the blades, which are 8 inches wide, are reinforced to prevent blade chatter. They are available in lengths of 52, 58, and 62 inches. (Coleman Co.)

3 Handling Your Canoe

Back in the days when I was learning to ski, the *Schilehrer*, in his Germanic English, was constantly barking at his charges, "Ski in control!" Signs dotted around the warming hut underscored the point. Much the same idea applies to canoeing, too: *Canoe in control*. Learn to handle your canoe in all the conditions you're likely to encounter, so that it does what *you* want it to do, with ease and safety—not the other way around. That's the goal that will engage us in this chapter.

The chances are that sometime or other, perhaps at a summer camp, you learned something about paddling a canoe, if only to pass one of those water-safety tests. Perhaps you made a canoe trip or two, back then or since, or you've tried levering a rented hulk around a pond in a city park. If so, you can skim any of the following basics that you already know. Remember, though, that the technique of canoeing does keep evolving and, we hope, improving, along with the canoes and paddles it's done with. Personally, I like hearing and reading others on matters I think I know, on the chance of picking up something new or seeing a familiar aspect from a fresh viewpoint. I hope you will, too.

We'll start at the beginning: getting your canoe into the water and yourself into it—and out again.

GETTING IN AND OUT

Both the canoe and the paddle are made up of parts, which have names. So that we can talk about handling them, we need to be clear about what these terms mean (see diagram).

Like any other boat, a canoe has a *bow* (front) and a *stern* (back). Bow and stern are each usually covered by a short *deck*, which may be extended in canoes designed for white-water use; some recent designs are fully decked (see Chapter 2), with small cockpits for the two paddlers. *Gunwales* ("gunnels") run from bow to stern along the tops of the sides and are braced by one to three *thwarts* placed laterally between the gunwales—the longer the canoe, the more thwarts it will have. If you have to portage the canoe, you'll use a *yoke*, either mounted on the center thwart or positioned just in front of it and attached to the gunwales. Wood-and-canvas and aluminum canoes are built up symmetrically from a shallow *keel*, running along the bottom from just behind the bow to just in front of the stern; while the function of the keel is primarily structural, it has some effect on handling and stability, though just how much is a much debated matter among the various builders (see Chapter 2). Such keeled canoes are usually strengthened with internal *ribs* running from the keel up the sides to the thwarts. Nearly all canoes have *seats* of some kind mounted between the thwarts at bow and stern, though some purists prefer to paddle from a kneeling position and most canoers will take to their knees in difficult white water—not necessarily to say their prayers but to lower the center of gravity.

The paddle has a *handle*, or *grip*, at the top, and a wide, thin *blade* at the business end. Between the two is the *shaft*. The reinforced place where the blade narrows into the shaft is called the *throat*.

The easiest way to get a canoe into the water is for two persons to take it between them. With the canoe right side up and pointing toward the water, you stand on opposite sides at the center, facing each other, and lift the canoe by the gunwales, with your hands on either side of the center thwart or yoke so that it balances. Then walk toward the water, lower the bow into the water so that it floats, and work your way hand over hand along the gunwales toward the stern until almost the whole length of the canoe is in or over the water. One person then places one hand under the stern for support and with the other takes hold of a thwart or the near gunwale and swings the bow in until the canoe is parallel to the bank, when he sets the stern in the water. One person can do this, too. Standing at the middle of the canoe, lift it by the near gunwale and center thwart so that the bottom of the canoe rests on your knees and you're balanced in a half-sitting position, leaning back. Then sidestep toward the water, lower the bow into the water, and work your way back toward the stern, as before. Either way, have your paddles where you can reach them as you hold onto the canoe, so that you won't have to run back to get them while your canoe drifts gently into the sunset.

The canoe can be launched sideways, saving a little time, if there are no shrubs, trees, or big rocks in the way—on a beach, for instance. Two people align the canoe with the shore, then lift at bow and stern. One person will balance the canoe on his knees the same as for an end launch, walk it to the water's edge, then lower the far side till it floats, while gently easing the near side off his knees, holding it by the near gunwale.

Ideally, for loading the canoe and getting in you'll have a soft bank with enough water to float the canoe and no rocks or logs to put scratches or worse on the bottom of the canoe. Then, while one paddler squats in the middle to hold and steady the canoe, the other loads. Being symmetrical, the canoe will float exactly level, when it's empty, and that's about how you want it when loaded; distribute your gear or passengers from bow to stern and side to side so they'll balance. The bow seat is a little farther from the bow than the stern seat is from the stern, with the result that if both paddlers are the same weight the canoe will be a little higher in the bow. That's fine for flat water if there are no waves or wind to contend with. If you're going to

One-man end launch: lift the canoe onto the knees and sidestep toward the water.

Lower one end of the canoe into the water so it floats.

Then pass the canoe along by the near gunwale until it's fully afloat.

One-man side launch: lift the canoe onto the knees parallel with the bank, walk it to the water's edge, and slide it down broadside into the water.

Two-man end launch: lift the canoe on either side from the middle, lower one end till it floats, then pass the canoe, along the gunwales, into the water.

Two-man side launch: holding the canoe at either end, lower it gently into the water—quicker and more convenient for loading if the bank is clear enough to permit this method.

Loading: one partner holds and steadies the canoe while the other loads, lifting pack by the top flap and sliding it gently down the gunwale; the load should be distributed so the canoe is trim at bow and stern.

Boarding: the bowman usually boards first, holding his paddle, keeping low and grasping the gunwales for balance while his partner holds and steadies the canoe.

be mostly in fast or white water, the canoe will handle more easily if it's exactly balanced—compensate by moving some of your load forward or back.

With the canoe loaded, you're ready to get in—bowman first while his partner steadies the canoe. Paddle in hand, step to the far side of the canoe, keeping low, with your other foot on the bank and grip the outside gunwale to help your balance; or steady yourself and the canoe by bracing the paddle blade on the lake or river bottom, on the far side of the canoe. Then take hold of the near gunwale with your other hand, lift your other foot into the canoe, and take your seat. You can then use your

Shoving off: with the bowman in place, his paddle at the ready, the sternman shoves the bow out from the shore, then steps in, holding his paddle, and pushes off with the other foot.

Changing position in the canoe: keep low, with hands on both gunwales for balance.

paddle to hold the canoe in place while your partner gets in, moving in the same style, and shoving off as he lifts his foot into the canoe.

Not all landings are open and easy, of course. With obstructions in the form of rocks or fallen trees, you may have to stick the canoe out into the water at an angle from the shore and load from the stern. In that case, rest the tip of the stern on the bank while the sternman braces it between his knees. Have your packs within reach. Then the bowman steps in, lays his paddle in the bow, and the sternman passes him the packs. The man in the canoe keeps low, feet wide. To minimize movement, I generally set one pack at a time on the stern seat, where the bowman can reach it; he then shifts it forward into position, resting it on the thwarts along the way. By the time all the packs are in and he's in his seat, the stern should lift free of the bank. Then, if you're the sternman, you can lift it gently forward, stepping over the stern and shoving off as you do so. Don't forget your paddle!

In getting into or out of a canoe or moving around in it once you're out on the water, you're making use of a couple of basic physical facts: the canoe's symmetry and your own—which is what balance is all about. When you move, balance a foot on one side against a foot on the other, a hand steadying you on one gunwale against a hand on the other; that way, you'll keep your head and torso in balance and where they belong, low and directly over the keel. Once in and on your way, avoid sudden, excitable movement. Perhaps a sudden gust wafts

Landing: the bowman stops paddling and upends his paddle to pole with the grip while the sternman steers the canoe in to the bank.

your hat or drinking cup into the water—don't lunge for it! Your partner in the stern can pick it up as it floats past or circle gently back to retrieve it before it sinks. While caution and control are in order, you needn't be afraid of the canoe. It will probably feel, if you're not used to it, tippier than it really is: it moves with your movement, like a living creature, leans with you as you lean over the side to get a drink or study a water flower—and then pops upright again. In a lifetime of canoeing, I've never managed to upset a canoe—except once, on purpose, at a summer camp, and then it proved to be surprisingly difficult.

Landing the canoe and getting out are, as you'd expect, pretty much the reverse of getting in and shoving off. To avoid the scrapes of a fast and hard landing, the bowman stops paddling ten or fifteen feet from the shore and holds his paddle ready to fend off rocks or logs and bring the canoe to a gentle stop. Generally, the paddle should be inverted when used in this way, since a rock concealed beneath a rippling surface might break the blade: for this final landing maneuver, use the grip end, *not* the blade. From the stern, I like to take the canoe in on a smooth arc so that it comes up broadside to the landing place. Steadying himself on his paddle, the bowman can then get out and hold the canoe for his partner. Unless you're landing on a soft, gently sloping bank or a sandy beach, you'll do best to load and unload while the canoe is fully afloat, to avoid possible damage. Don't walk in the canoe when it's drawn up on land. It's not that it isn't tough, but you may add some needless dents that will mean weak spots and trouble later on.

SEATS AND STABILITY

Seated in the canoe, brace your feet and legs so that your knees won't stick up in the way of your paddle strokes and you won't slide around on the seat as you paddle, wasting energy. In a canoe of normal dimensions, I mostly tuck my feet under the seat, crossed at the ankles, toes firm against the bottom of the canoe. If you tire of that position, you can extend one leg (the one opposite the side you're paddling on), bracing with your foot against a pack or the side of the canoe. Beginners tend to slide over to the side they're paddling on, lean out with each stroke. Don't. The movement makes it

Leg and foot positions for paddling: both feet tucked under seat, knees down and out of the way.

Leg and foot positions for paddling: a change, one foot under the seat, the other forward, braced against the bottom of the canoe.

harder for your partner to paddle and sets up a side-to-side tipping of the canoe that could be dangerous. With a little practice, you become astonishingly sensitive to the canoe's lateral balance. If your partner leans to one side, you lean a little to the other to compensate. As you reach forward to stow a paddle or get out a camera for a picture, you grip the gunwale with your other hand, maintaining equilibrium. All these little movements soon become automatic, very much as in the complex balancing act that a child masters as it learns to walk. Indeed, the two processes are much alike, with the difference that a canoe is a simpler, more elegantly symmetrical body than the human one—its shape is naturally in balance and will stay that way if you let it.

In a modern canoe, the seated position is the norm for both comfort and stability, and that's the assumption behind most of what I have to say about paddling later in this chapter. In rough water, though, you can reduce the chances of spilling by shifting to a kneeling position, lowering your center of gravity slightly. Given the purpose, a low kneeling position is best: leaning back on your heels, back and buttocks braced against the seat.

On a canoe trip, most of your travel will be in a loaded canoe—another assumption underlying my views on canoeing technique. An empty or lightly loaded canoe—as it will be if you take off for a day's fishing and exploration or a weekend of downriver paddling—is a different proposition, appreciably less stable. In that case, one or another kneeling position is very much in order. The low kneeling position is the most comfortable, but your strokes will be stronger from an upright kneeling position. Even better is the one-knee position favored by canoe racers: you kneel on the side you're paddling on, the other knee up and braced well forward, the torso erect; your whole body should be rotated slightly toward the paddle side, and the two paddlers will be balanced toward opposite gunwales. The purpose of kneeling in a lightly loaded canoe is not only to lower the center of gravity but to shift the two paddlers forward or back to suit various wind and water conditions. Generally, and particularly in rough water, the canoe will handle best if both paddlers kneel within a foot or two of the center thwart. If you canoe much by yourself, the one-knee position near the center thwart will be best for balance and efficiency.

Low kneeling position, which may be advisable in rough water but is not the norm in modern canoes designed for seated paddling.

One-knee position: best for balance and a strong stroke in an empty canoe; both paddlers are positioned near the middle and pivoted slightly toward their paddle sides.

If you paddle any distance on your knees, you'll want to pad them—with a small pack, a spare life jacket. For more permanent kneeling pads, see the suggestions in Chapter 4.

BASIC PADDLING STROKES

When it's moving forward, a canoe turns from the back as if on a pivot directly under the sternman. This fact defines the quite different roles of the two paddlers. The bowman has comparatively little control over the direction in which the canoe moves. His job in essence is to supply motor power—and serve as lookout. From where the sternman sits, he often can't see obstructions directly ahead, especially on a bright day, with the sun glittering on the water. The bowman needs to keep his eyes open and call out any dangers he sees coming up—or shove off with his paddle from the big rock that suddenly looms just below the surface, before the canoe comes to a grinding straddle on top of it. The sternman, in contrast, picks the course and has, or should have, full control over the direction of movement. These differences mean that the two canoers use a different repertory of strokes. If you're new to canoeing, you'll study these strokes and master them—in smooth water—separately, but in practice they're not so distinct: as you travel by canoe, you see every movement with your eyes, feel it with your body. Your progress through water is a matter of constant subtle adjustment to the motion of your canoe, and as you make those adjustments one stroke shades into another.

Paddling Bow. If you're paddling on the left side, place your right hand over the end of the grip—*not* around the shaft below the grip—and take the shaft in your left hand just above the throat so that your left arm is about at a right angle to the blade. Paddling on the right, you reverse the grip—left hand on the grip, right hand on the shaft. From either side, you reach and lean forward as you take the stroke so that the paddle blade enters the water at or in front of the bow and at a right angle to the surface of the water and the keel of the canoe. Then pull back with both arms in a strong, smooth movement—the resistance you feel is the canoe pulling forward through the water. As you make the stroke, the paddle will naturally pivot on your lower hand until the blade is pointing back and down, a little behind you. Then bring the blade out in a sharp swing forward for the next stroke. As you do this, rotate the paddle forward with your upper hand so that the blade travels parallel to the water. This is called *feathering* and saves resistance when you're traveling against the wind—enough to be worth making it a habit even on calm days.

Which side you paddle best doesn't seem to be affected by whether you're right- or left-handed, but you do need to practice this basic stroke until you can do it equally well, with equal strength, on either side. There will be water situations in which you *have* to be able to paddle on one side or the other, and if your upper arm and shoulder tire over a long stretch of paddling, a switch to the other side comes as a welcome relief. When you change sides, you'll also be changing the position of your hands: as you bring the paddle out at the end of the stroke, swing the blade up and forward with the lower hand so as to clear the bow; at the same time, grasp the paddle throat with the other hand and slide what was the lower hand up the shaft to the grip. You should be able to change sides gracefully, without missing a stroke.

After much thought and experiment, I find that the strongest, least tiring stroke is made with both arms straight, or nearly so, throughout the stroke (the upper elbow may bend slightly). It helps, too, to keep the shoulders straight, not hunched, the torso erect, so that your lungs fill freely with every breath. The grasp of the upper hand should be firm, fingers over the grip, thumb around the shaft, to control the angle of the paddle blade through the water; the lower hand should be loose and relaxed, since the angle of the paddle at that pivotal point above the throat changes constantly throughout the stroke. "Long and strong" is a good bowman's motto: with the hands as far apart as possible for maximum leverage, reach as far forward as you can, pull hard against the water, and bring the blade back as far as you can reach while keeping the arms straight.

As bowman, you set the pace—you can't see what your partner's doing, but he can see you and will try to match his rhythm to yours. How fast? It depends somewhat on the size of the paddle blade and the kind of water you're in. For normal flat-water canoeing, I favor a long, steady, strong pull, about one stroke every two seconds (which probably sounds faster than it is). Against wind or strong current—sometimes it seems that, like Alice, you need all the paddling you can do to stay in one place—you'll tend to paddle slower, adjusting to the greater resistance you feel, but *don't*: that's the time to raise the beat. Conversely, riding a down-river current, you can often slow down and let the water do your work for you.

To slow the canoe or back off from a danger spot or out from an awkward landing place, you need to be able to *back-paddle*, which is simply the reverse of the basic stroke. Reach the paddle backward and put it into the water about in line with your seat, then push it forward and bring it out. This back stroke will also tend to turn the bow of the canoe toward the side on which you're paddling, and you can use it, therefore, to help your sternman make a turn a little faster, if need be.

While the bowman really needs only his two basic strokes, forward and back, there are a couple of others the canoe traveler can borrow from the technique of white water. They're called the *draw* and the *pry*, and are essentially bow turning strokes, used in fast currents when you need to get out of the way of trouble *fast* and the sternman can't see what's coming as well as you can from the bow. In such waters, in fact, you reverse the normal

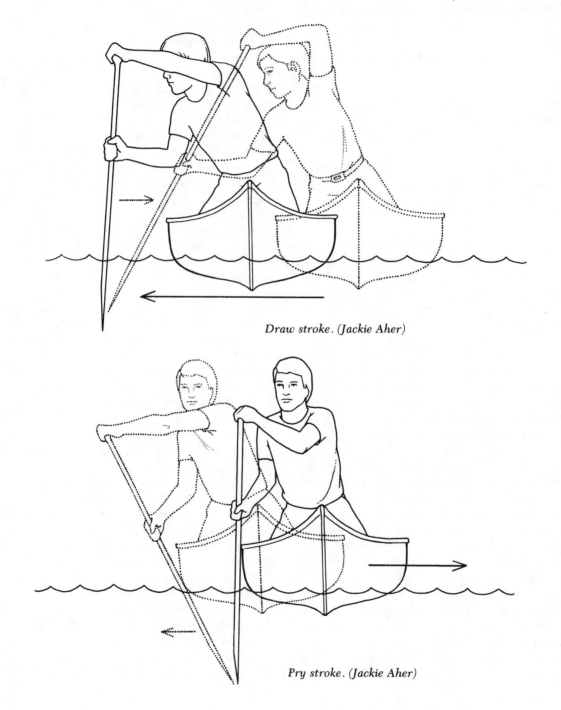

Draw stroke. (Jackie Aher)

Pry stroke. (Jackie Aher)

flat-water situation: the bowman may not set the basic course, but he does make the small quick adjustments, and when he swings the bow in one direction or the other, his partner must follow his lead.

To make the *draw*, reach the paddle out away from the canoe, keeping the blade parallel to the keel and, as you set it into the water, pull it toward you. This will swing the bow *toward* the side on which you're paddling.

You can think of the *pry* as the reverse of the draw—putting the blade into the water next to the canoe and pushing it away, keeping the paddle nearly vertical; or (as the name implies) as a levering movement, where the lower hand holds a nearly fixed position near the side of the canoe (or on the gunwale) and serves as a fulcrum while the upper hand moves toward you. The stroke is done both ways and serves to swing the bow *away from* the side you're paddling on.

As with your other basic strokes, you need to be able to do both the pry and the draw equally well on either side. Moreover, since the times you need them will be in fast-moving water where quick reactions can save you a ducking—or worse—it's worth learning to do them both with your hands reversed from the normal (right hand above, left hand below, when you're paddling on the *right* side—and vice versa). That way, in a pinch, you can switch sides without changing the position of your hands—saving a fraction of a second that might just be vital.

Paddling Stern.   If you were paddling by yourself at the stern, using the basic bow stroke, each stroke would swing the bow ten or fifteen degrees away from the side you're paddling on. This is the effect of the leverage mentioned earlier. You compensate for this by paddling on the opposite side from your bowman and timing your strokes to his, but that's usually not enough. Unless you correct for your extra leverage, the canoe will travel in circles, going nowhere. The solution is to combine the strong, forward-moving pull of the bow stroke with a subtle angling of the blade that compensates for the offside thrust: the *J stroke*, the basic steering stroke at the stern.

To make the J stroke, reach and lean forward and set the blade in the water vertically, at a right angle to both the water surface and the keel of the canoe. As you pull the paddle back, keep the shaft close to the gunwale, and at about the midpoint of the stroke rotate the near edge of the paddle blade toward the rear with your upper hand so that as you finish the stroke, with the blade reaching back behind the stern, the blade is turned inward at an angle of about 45 degrees to the keel line, which is also the natural direction for the canoe's forward movement. The first half of the stroke supplies the power to move the canoe forward; the second half, with its rotation of the blade (which, on the left side, if carried far enough, would make a figure like the hook of a J), balances the swing that follows from that power and holds the canoe on a straight course. In general, when the weather's reasonably calm, you want to hold as straight a course as possible—the shortest distance between two points, meaning a saving of time, effort, and paddle strokes. To do that, pick a distant landmark—a tree, a big rock at the water's edge, a point of land—and keep your eye on it and the bow of the canoe pointed toward it. Adjust each part of the J stroke so that you hold that course—extra power at the start, a little more angle at the finish, as needed. Make it a habit to feather the blade as you bring it out for the next stroke.

Like other paddle strokes, you should practice the J stroke until you can do it equally well—and automatically—on either side. In normal conditions, you'll change sides only as often as necessary to give yourself or your bowman a rest, and when you do change, learn to do it quickly, without breaking the rhythm. When I'm paddling stern, I like to bring the paddle straight up, *over* my head, so as not to wet a passenger or scatter drops of water on the packs in front of me in the canoe.

The double movement of the J stroke—the power pull at the start, the rotation of the blade during the second half—is not easy for a beginner. The foundation is mastery of the basic bow stroke, then hours of practice with the steering hook of the J stroke so that you can do the whole thing in rhythm with your bowman, with maximum forward thrust and, at the same time, holding an efficient straight-line course. An alternative, which I think makes an inherently stronger stroke and which you may find easier to learn, is one I call the *V stroke*. You begin with the outside edge of the paddle blade angled back at about 45 degrees and hold that angle all through. Toward the end, check the blade mo-

Forward movement with bowman using J stroke. (Jackie Aher)

mentarily and at the same time rotate the outside edge forward to slice up and out of the water for the recovery, making the second arm of the V.

Unless you're traveling in a dead calm, you may not need to steer on every stroke in order to hold your course. A head wind striking the bow at an angle opposite your paddle side, for example, will balance the turning effect of your strokes at the stern with little or no steering effort on your part. Indeed, it's likely to overcompensate, a problem we'll take up later in this chapter.

Turning Strokes.   A more extreme version of the J stroke or V stroke will turn the canoe in a gradual arc toward the side you're paddling on. For a faster turn toward the paddle side, hold the blade at the end of the stroke at a right angle to the direction of travel and move it out, away from the canoe. For a gradual turn in the opposite direction—away from the side you're paddling on—use the *C stroke*, or *sweep*. Start it at the same point as the J or V,

Turning stroke. (Jackie Aher)

but as you bring the paddle back, move it out from the canoe and back again toward the stern so that the paddle travels in a half-circle course through the water. For a quick swing toward the paddle side, use the paddle as a rudder, dragging it behind you with the blade at a right angle to the keel line— or bring the blade forward through the water in a *backstroke* like the one described earlier at the bow; if you have to turn fast in the opposite direction, switch sides and rudder or back stroke on the other side, a maneuver you should be able to make

in emergencies without changing the position of your hands (in which case it would be called a *reverse rudder* or *reverse backstroke*).

For fast turns with less loss of forward movement, you can use the two bow turning strokes, the draw and the pry—but remember that they have the opposite effects at the stern. The draw will pull the stern *toward* the paddle—and hence swing the bow *away from* the paddle side. The pry will push the stern *away from* the paddle—and turn the canoe *toward* the side you're paddling on.

LIFTING AND CARRYING

The basic strokes we've been reviewing are all you need to get from point to point as you travel by canoe. How about those points along the way where you're *not* paddling but carrying, or *portaging*—the old voyageurs' term—your canoe and packs, between two lakes or around rapids? Once the canoe's up on your shoulders, its natural balance makes it surprisingly easy to carry over distances of up to a mile—as long as you're likely to encounter. The effort—and the risk of dropping the canoe or falling—comes in getting it up there and setting it down again. There are several ways of minimizing that effort.

For a start, since the paddles are a nuisance to carry separately, wedge them into the front half of the canoe. How you do this will depend on the layout of the canoe, but in a typical 17-footer with a thwart right behind the front seat, the paddle

Correct portaging technique minimizes the effort involved in getting around rough water.
(Old Town Canoe Co.)

blades fit neatly between seat and thwart, pressed together at the tips, with the grips angled back toward the gunwales, pressing against the carrying yoke from above. With other canoes you may have to reverse this, facing the blades toward the stern, or tie them in with quick-release elastic straps. However you arrange it, the object is to keep the paddles with the canoe so they'll be handy when needed and not have to be carried separately.

Since a yoke is almost indispensable for convenient one-man carrying, I wouldn't rent or buy a canoe without one. In a pinch, you can usually wedge the paddles to do the job—blades pointing toward the stern and positioned to rest on your shoulders—but it's an uncomfortable makeshift for anything more than a short distance.

For the lifting process, let's assume that you're right-handed, hence approach the canoe from the left side (lefties can reverse the following description). Facing the canoe just in front of the yoke, lean over and grip the near gunwale with your right hand and reach across with your left to take the opposite gunwale a little farther forward (or the front thwart, if there is one and you can't reach the gunwale). Then, if you're big enough—6 feet or more, say, with arms that are correspondingly long and strong—you'll swing the canoe up in one smooth motion and set the yoke pads down on your shoulders. If you're smaller, you'll do what I do: swing the canoe partway up and over, with the stern down so that it's resting on the ground, then step backward, sliding your hands along the gunwales until you can lower the yoke onto your shoulders. Either way, once up, the canoe should balance with the stern a little down, the bow a little up, so you can see where you're going. If you have it balanced right, the canoe should stay put without your having to hold on, but it's well to reach forward to the gunwales or paddles with one or both hands to steady your load. If you haven't got the balance quite right, hunch your shoulders, lifting a little on the thwarts, to jump the canoe forward or back a fraction of an inch. Usually, once the canoe is unloaded, you and your partner will carry it between you up from the water to a reasonably level place where you can pick it up. If you're big and wearing waterproof boots, take the canoe halfway out of the water, step into the shallows, and lift as described—you'll save a little time and shorten the portage.

Getting ready to portage the canoe: wedge the paddles into the canoe so they'll be out of the way and won't have to be carried separately.

One-man canoe lift: grip the gunwales.

Then swing the canoe up and over with the stern resting on the ground, and lower the yoke onto the shoulders.

With the yoke properly positioned, the canoe should balance on the shoulders, bow slightly up, hands used only to steady it, with a minimum of effort.

Setting the canoe down: lower the stern to the ground.

Then slide it gently down to the ground or sidestep it into the water.

If you tire before you get to the end of the portage trail, avoid setting the canoe down—the effort of doing that and getting the canoe up again pretty much nullifies the rest. Instead, look for a natural canoe rest—a smooth branch growing horizontally 7 or 8 feet off the ground, or a pair of trees growing close together so as to form a V a little narrower than the canoe. You can then let the stern down to the ground and slide the bow of the canoe a foot or two over the branch or into the crotch and take your rest without the work of setting the canoe down and lifting it up again.

When you reach the other end of the portage, look for a good loading place and step to within a foot or two of the water. Let the stern down to the ground, take a firm grip on the gunwales, and swing the canoe over your head to your right (if you're right-handed), lowering it gently onto your knees. You can then rock the canoe over your knees until the bow floats, and slide it on in from the stern; leave it half out till you're ready to load.

If you're using a car carrier to transport your canoe to your starting point, you can get it on and off the usual passenger car by yourself. To take it off the carrier, angle the canoe and slide it so that the stern half is sticking out to one side while the bow is still supported by the carrier—you can then get your shoulders under the yoke, lower the stern, and lift the bow clear. Reloading works in reverse: rest the inside stern gunwale on the carrier and slide the bow on, stepping out from under the yoke so that you can take hold of the outside gunwale and ease the canoe onto the rack. A van or camper, being higher than a passenger car, will have to be loaded over one end, resting the bow of the canoe on the roof rack, then sliding and lifting it into place, a job best done by two people.

Even a little guy like my third son can portage a canoe by himself, but, at least for a beginner, there's a certain knack to it that takes practice. Your partner can help you lift the canoe by standing a foot or two in front of you, facing you so as to see what you're doing, and reversing the movements already described (where you take the far gunwale with your left hand, he uses his right, and so on— or vice versa if you're left-handed): grasping the gunwales, he lifts when you do, steadies the bow while you lower the stern to the ground for support, then holds the bow up till you're in position and ready to let the yoke down onto your shoulders.

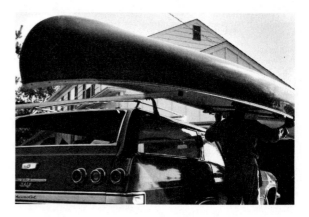

Loading the canoe onto a cartop carrier: lift the stern slightly and slide one gunwale onto the rear rack.

Then lift the bow onto the forward rack, grip the outer gunwale, step out from under the yoke, and slide the canoe onto the carrier.

Setting the canoe down again at the other end can be managed the same way. (This two-man lift also works with the helper facing forward and duplicating your movements.)

Two or three persons can carry the canoe between them. Two people can take the canoe at either end, where the gunwales come together at bow and stern. You then lift the canoe and let it down so that the gunwales rest on your hands with your elbows braced against your ribs. Or, standing at bow and stern on opposite sides of the canoe, you can carry the canoe *upright* on your shoulders, as the voyageurs often portaged their big 30- or 35-foot freight canoes. With three people, one can take

Two-man canoe lift: the portager and his helper grip the gunwales with opposite hands and swing the canoe up . . .

. . . and over, with the stern resting on the ground; the helper then supports the canoe while the portager steps backward so that the yoke can be lowered onto his shoulders.

the yoke on his shoulders while the other two provide support and balance at either end. All these methods are tiring over any distance, compared with the normal one-man carry, but they may be preferable for children or small adults. On a very steep portage or one that's cluttered with big rocks and fallen trees, you may be glad of one of these forms of help no matter what your size.

The pads on your carrying yoke will be made of leather or vinyl and filled with foam rubber (soft) or horsehair (firm and durable but getting scarce). I find both kinds comfortable, but if your shoulders get tender you can use a sweater to provide extra padding. My father protected his knobby gymnast's shoulders with a cushion contrived from a pillow and an old pair of my football shoulder pads. Now that federal law requires life preservers in a canoe, you can use one in the same way.

SPECIAL CONDITIONS AND TECHNIQUES

The canoeing techniques we've discussed so far all assume that you're traveling flat water, with little in the way of wind, waves, or current to contend with. How do you handle these conditions? And what about rapids? Basically, you'll be adapting your standard techniques, but there are several little tricks that will help you do that. Let's consider.

Waves. On a good-sized lake—which in canoeing terms means 2 or 3 miles across and up—strong winds and big waves can build up in a hurry. (Big rivers can produce the same conditions.) Because of that, it's a good rule to stay within half a mile of shore so that you can get in fast if a storm blows up. In rough water, you'll generally find the going easier close to shore, where the water's shallower, the waves smaller (and the river current slower)—but keep your eyes peeled for big rocks that may be just below the surface and can overturn or smash your canoe. You can spot them by the circular ripples they make as the water rises and falls, perhaps flecked with foam. Weather as it affects canoeing is so complex and variable that it can be judged only from much experience, but a few pointers can be given. For one, beware of the black clouds and rising wind that portend a storm. If you're on the water, work in close to shore so that you can get out fast when the storm breaks; if you're on shore, better stay there till you can see what's coming—maybe it's time for making camp early and getting inside the tent, where you can stay dry. In general, on a windy day, don't judge a good-sized lake by what you can see from water level near shore: it may not look rough, but scattered whitecaps in the shallows probably mean that there are a lot, farther out where you can't see them—waves big enough so that it may be impossible to turn and head for shore once you're out there among them. If in doubt, look for a hill near shore that you can climb for a better view.

Most canoes will be safe, manageable, and dry in waves of a foot or two even when a full load leaves only six inches or so of freeboard amidships, twice that (or more, depending on the design—see Chapter 2) at bow and stern; some canoes built especially for rough water will stand waves twice that size. When properly loaded, a canoe headed into the waves lifts to ride up and over them and down the other side as if on a miniature toboggan run. On the other hand, if the waves are closely spaced from crest to crest, the canoe will slap down between them with a splash that, if they're big enough, will put water in amidships. *Any* water in the canoe is a nuisance, wetting you and your packs, but at a cupful a time it will accumulate until it can be dangerous—making the canoe heavy and hard to steer, altering balance and stability as it sloshes back and forth. It's well, therefore, when you're planning a trip, to find out in advance how much your canoe will stand. Take the canoe out near home with a load on a windy day and experiment. When you know what the canoe is capable of, you can adopt the right tactics in the rough weather you're almost certain to meet in the course of an extended trip.

With its sharp bow, a canoe tends to plow through waves that it meets head on; it gets its lift from the flaring out of the hull a foot or two back from the bow. In moderate to big waves, you can increase that natural buoyancy (and lessen the slope the canoe has to climb) by setting your course at an angle of 20 or 30 degrees to the waves. By doing that, you lessen your chances of taking on a dangerous amount of water even in very choppy weather, keeping the canoe nimble and responsive.

When your intended course is down a lake against wind-blown waves (wind blowing against a strong river current can produce much the same effect), you'll have to tack, as in a sailboat, to keep your general course and avoid getting too far out: travel at an angle across the waves and away from the shore, then swing toward the shore so that you keep the same angle to the waves but on the other side of the canoe. The turn needs to be made quickly and with care; the waves will try to swing you on around, lengthwise in the trough, where you'll take on water, perhaps tip over. In rough water, the sternman must be doubly watchful—one eye on a landmark ahead for the general course, the other on the waves in front of the bow to gauge the right moment to zigzag. (Call out as you start the turn so your bowman can assist with a pry or draw.)

Heavy waves taken at an angle to the bow make it difficult to hold a course (hard work, too); the normal steering stroke may simply not be strong enough to compensate. It will help if you both paddle on the same side, opposite the one that's meeting the waves. Then, with you both using a straight bow stroke (or perhaps even the turning C stroke at the stern), you should be able to balance the wave pressure. Watch, too, for any point of land sticking out into the lake—there will be a lee, or patch of calmer water, on your side of it, and you can get into it for a rest—or put ashore to wait out the heavy weather.

Paddling with the waves behind you will be easier—and faster—but requires the same angling and tacking course as paddling into the waves. A big wave from straight behind can as easily come over the stern as one from the front over the bow.

It will sometimes happen that you'll hit a spell of weather rough enough to keep you ashore for several days. If you *have* to travel—because the vacation's near the end or you're running out of food—you can do so in early morning and again in late afternoon and early evening, and camp and rest in between. Even in the worst of weather, the wind will usually drop, the waters calm, at the beginning and end of the day. The sun, warming and stirring the air, is the factor, of course. To take advantage of the calm, you'll have to start well before dawn, when there's barely light enough to see, and by midmorning in the aftermath of a storm the wind may be blowing hard again and keep up till nearly sunset.

Wind and Current. In lake travel, you may face strong winds that don't necessarily build up into heavy waves. A following wind is a delight, carrying you along effortlessly—the bowman can raise his paddle like a sail and the sternman has little to do but rudder. Paddling into the wind, of course, is another matter. Course permitting, paddle as straight into the wind as you can—a crosswind tends to swing the canoe around and requires that much more effort at the stern to hold the course. If the wind's from the bow quarter and you're loaded a little heavy in the stern, the bow will tend to swing with the wind—and conversely if the wind's off the stern quarter and you're light back there. I've found also that with the canoe stern-heavy in a wind coming squarely from either side, it's the stern that tends to swing around, again making it tough to hold the course. The sternman will be most conscious of this and can help somewhat by sitting well forward on the seat (or by sitting as far back as possible if it's the bow that seems to be swinging); if he has a pack within reach that he can easily shift, that will do some good, too. However, since the wind keeps on changing direction, you're generally better off with the canoe as nearly balanced as you can manage. From the vantage point of a canoe, the whimsical changeableness and general orneriness of wind is the subject of an ancient joke in my canoeing family. To us, the wind is a very sensitive being who'll play tricks on you if he hears you talking about him. So we never refer to "the wind" when we're canoeing, we talk about a certain "Mr. Smith": "Mr. Smith is nice today" or "Mr. Smith seems a little touchy." After a day of paddling against the wind, you'll wish you could invent a charm of your own.

If you have "Mr. Smith" against you and are carrying a passenger, it will sometimes help to hand the passenger your spare paddle, which he can use sitting or kneeling in the middle of the canoe. It's awkward and tiring paddling from that position—the widest part of the canoe—for any length of time, but for a short spell it can make the difference between forward progress and standing still, like a squirrel on a treadmill. The same resort will also work if you're trying to get upstream against a strong current.

In paddling downriver, the general rule is to keep the canoe in line with the current. The shape of the bank and the bottom may well generate crosscurrents that feel very much like crosswinds and are handled about the same way—it may help you hold your course, for example, to have a little more weight in the bow than in the stern. In general, you won't need to paddle hard, but make enough effort to keep moving a little faster than the current so that you, and not the river, control your direction. As with waves, the current will be easier in the shallows near the riverbank than out in the middle; and it will be slower on the inside of a bend than on the outside. Both these facts are worth remembering when you're paddling upstream—and sometimes down as well.

Rapids. Any time you're canoeing, but above all in wilderness travel, rapids are to be approached with caution and respect. A few writers have made shooting rapids sound like a lark, but you won't find that attitude among serious white-water canoers or racers. In going down rapids, a ducking, lost gear, or a damaged canoe is the least of your risks; if you're spilled into the turbulence that swirls around submerged rocks and ledges, you may come out badly skinned or with a head injury that's a prelude to drowning in the deep pools below. It happens.

Hence, when you're traveling a river, caution begins with an accurate, large-scale map that marks the rapids ahead. Study it. Have it handy in a pocket or spread open on the bottom between your feet. And keep your eyes peeled. If the wind's behind you, you may not hear the rapids till you've come too close for comfort. Remember, too, that rapids exist because there's a drop in the river bed at that point—you may see only the smooth, dark lip of the water, not the white water and spray. As you get close, keep to one bank or the other. Usually, rapids are fast not only because there's a drop but because the river narrows. As a result, the current will be slower near the bank just above the rapids, perhaps gently eddying, and you can land there with little risk.

Rapids have been given a difficulty rating by the American Whitewater Affiliation so that maps, charts, etc., can indicate rapid class. This rating system is also valuable to use when describing a set of rapids or river to someone. Here are the various classes and their descriptions:

Class I—Moving water with a few riffles and small waves. Few or no obstructions.

Rapids are classed based on their difficulty. This is a Class II rapid. (Blue Hole Canoe Co.)

Class II—Easy rapids with waves up to three feet and wide, clear channels that are obvious without scouting. Some maneuvering is required.

Class III—Rapids with high, irregular waves often capable of swamping an open canoe. Narrow passages that often require complex maneuvering. May require scouting from shore.

Class IV—Long, difficult rapids with constricted passages that often require precise maneuvering in very turbulent waters. Scouting from shore is often necessary, and conditions make rescue difficult. Generally not possible for open canoes. Boaters in covered canoes and kayaks should be able to Eskimo roll, which is a righting maneuver used as a self-rescue method for overturned decked boats.

Class V—Extremely difficult, long, and very violent rapids with highly congested routes that nearly always must be scouted from shore. Rescue conditions are difficult, and there is a significant hazard to life in the event of a mishap. Ability to Eskimo roll is essential for kayaks and canoes.

Class VI—Difficulties of Class V carried to the extreme of navigability. Nearly impossible and very dangerous. For teams of experts only after close study and with all precautions taken.

If rapids on a river generally fit into one of these classifications, but the water temperature is below 50 degrees Fahrenheit, or if the trip is an extended one in a wilderness area, the river should be considered one class more difficult than normal.

Always study rapids from the bank before running them. Rapids that look easy from the river may be impassable when viewed from the bank. (Blue Hole Canoe Co.)

If there's one invariable rule for canoeing rapids, it's this: never try to run them without landing first and walking along the bank to see what's ahead. Rapids that look easy from above may be impassable 50 yards down. Nor is past experience always a guide. A rapid that was easy in spring high water may be too choked in summer with deadwood and boulders to be taken. So *look it over first* and figure your route as you would at the top of a difficult ski run.

By the time I've done that advance scouting and planning, I'd just as soon portage—which is one reason white-water canoeing as such is beyond the scope of this book. Nevertheless, there is a certain excitement in going down rapids, and there will be times when the riverbanks are so high and steep that you have no alternative. In that case, in planning your course you need to "read" the water, and you'll be looking for the deeper channels where the current won't land you on a submerged rock an inch below the surface. Look for a V in the current with the base pointing downstream—it's made by a pair of upstream rocks, and if the space between them is wide enough, it's probably deep enough for you to get through. If the V points upstream, it indicates a single obstruction, and you'll need to steer to one side or the other. "Standing waves"— waves that seem confined to one patch of water— are another indication of a channel that's probably deep enough to be safe: the waves are made by the water piling up as it drops between obstructions. If the waves are not too high for your canoe to ride over without taking excessive water, that's the spot to head for: the choppiness may bounce the canoe like a car on a potholed road, but you'll soon be past it. Unlike standing waves, a smooth, dark hummock of water indicates a single big boulder just below the surface, and hitting it could be disastrous. White-water canoeists call such formations "pillows," but as someone has remarked, these pillows are stuffed with rocks—they're to be avoided.

If, in your advance inspection of a rapids, you see the turbulence of many small rocks below the surface so that there's no clear, deep channel, you may be able to let your canoe down in safety, half empty, from the bank by means of a rope, or line (the technique is known as *lining*). One person can maneuver the canoe with 40 or 50 feet of rope tied at bow and stern and his partner in the canoe for more delicate guidance with a paddle; or the two of you can manage it with separate ropes 20 or 25 feet long. (For river travel, it's advisable to have bow and stern lines—painters—permanently attached.) But as I've already suggested, you may well decide that portaging is less trouble.

With caution as the watchword, the foregoing

This canoer is using the technique known as "lining" to get his canoe through a set of rapids. (J. Wayne Fears)

The one-man lining technique. (Jackie Aher)

The two-man lining technique. (J. Wayne Fears)

advice will get you safely down the kind of occasional fast water, riffles, or small rapids you're likely to meet in the course of normal distance canoeing. Don't, however, try anything more serious or prolonged without study, instruction, and careful practice with your partner in easy waters. In the Appendices, I've listed some books that describe white-water technique in detail. Such reading needs to be filled out by the kind of guidance you can get from experts by joining a local canoe club. And there's no substitute for practice. Under any conditions, bow and stern need to work as a team, but in rapids their coordination becomes doubly important, and as I suggested a few pages back, their respective roles are rather different. The sternman sets the general course, but he can't see what's immediately in front of the canoe: he must rely on his partner at the bow for the minor course corrections needed to avoid obstacles he can't see from his position at the stern. Hence, the bowman must watch the water ahead—for the circle of ripples that signifies a rock just below the surface—and react fast with a draw or pry stroke, a quick shove with the paddle. The sternman must watch both his partner, assisting the changes of course, and the water farther ahead. Paddle just hard enough to keep ahead of the current, hence keep the canoe properly aligned. The keynote is concentration and the teamwork that can only be developed by careful practice *before* you need it.

It will happen from time to time that you'll have to get yourself *up* a rapids, an entirely different proposition from descending—for instance, a brief stretch at an approach to a portage. If the distance is short, the current not too strong, the water at least a foot or two deep, you'll probably manage with a spell of fierce paddling. Or invert your paddles and *pole* your way through the fast spot, pushing with the paddle grip against the stream bed. As I suggested earlier, you turn the paddle upside down to avoid cracking or breaking the blade, a point important enough to bear repeating: Whether pushing against fast water or holding the canoe steady at a landing, always use the grip, not the blade. You can use the same paddle-poling technique to get yourself through a shallow reedy stretch more effectively than by ordinary paddling, and again it's well to turn the paddle up in case there are rocks among the muck. Such half-swampy areas are part of the cycle by which nature, often

assisted by beavers and their dams, endeavors to convert a lake back into solid land, and since they're likely to occur at one end of a lake, you will sometimes have to get through them to reach a portage.

For getting *up* or *down* a short stretch of fast, shallow water, the best method will often be for you and your partner to step out into the stream. The canoe, riding lighter and higher, is less likely to be damaged on the bottom, and you can make sure with a little judicious lifting over the shallowest spots. You can get out and wade a few steps with equanimity if you're wearing the kind of boots recommended in Chapter 5—high enough and reasonably waterproof. Remember to stow your paddles with care so as not to knock them out as you ease the canoe over the rocks. The only thing more disheartening than watching your paddle sail off down the current is losing the canoe itself. Hang on to both!

Poling, properly speaking, was a method the voyageurs often used to get up a lengthy stretch of rapids, perhaps to avoid a long or difficult portage. The technique is also used in the shallow, gentle, meandering streams of southern New Jersey and in swampy rivers on south to Florida. To do it, you'll need a straight, slender hardwood pole (such as ash) 10 or 12 feet long, which in wild country you can cut on the bank. It should be carefully trimmed to save your hands; for permanent use, the lower end is tipped with a metal ferrule.

Poling is done from a standing position, your feet braced wide for balance, one ahead of the other so that your whole body is angled slightly toward the side on which you're poling. Two canoers may pole in unison, on opposite sides; more commonly, it's done from near the stern while the bowman keeps his paddle ready to change course or fend off snags. Poling is a stop-and-go movement. You lever the canoe forward until the pole's leaning at an angle, "walking" your hands up to the top; then lift, swing the pole forward, and let it slide straight down, brace against the river bottom, and lever forward again. Against a very strong current in a deep river, you may have to tow, or *track*, the canoe from the bank—the same general idea as the one described a few paragraphs back for letting a canoe down a rapids. (A pole can also be used for getting a canoe down a rapids that's fast, shallow, and not too heavy, digging the lower end in among the rocks and then slowly letting the canoe down to the next

*Poling may be used to move a canoe upstream or through shallow, slow-moving water.
(The Coleman Co.)*

stopping point while you drag the pole along the bottom to keep the canoe from going too fast; old-timers call this *setting*.)

SOME OPTIONS

All the canoeing techniques we've discussed so far assume two paddlers who supply all their own power. There are alternatives.

Solo Canoes. Solo canoeing has grown in popularity, and several canoe manufacturers now make one-man models. These canoes are 12 to 15 feet in length and weigh from 30 to 50 pounds. Solo racing canoes may weigh as little as 25 pounds. Among those manufacturers making solo canoes are Mad River, Old Town, We-no-nah, Sawyer, and Blue Hole.

In the quiet of early evening, you may feel like paddling out by yourself for a little fishing or simply to be alone. In a canoe of normal length (15 feet and up), the bow will be too high to steer easily from the stern. It will balance better if you sit in the bow seat *facing* the stern and paddle in that direction. Smaller canoes (12 or 13 feet) are designed primarily for one person (they'll carry two and a minimal amount of gear) and are usually pad-

Solo canoeing has grown in popularity both in competition and in backcountry tripping. (Grumman Boats)

Solo paddling—low kneeling position.

Solo paddling—one-knee position. Less comfortable for long distances but more efficient; in either case, the solo paddler should be near the middle of the canoe for balance.

dled from near the middle. Although easy to handle because small and light, they're still slow for real travel: with a single paddle, half your effort goes into steering. One solution for one-man travel is a double-bladed, kayak-style paddle. Another, favored by some Maine canoeists seventy-five years ago, is light oars and a rowing seat, as in a single scull, and a few canoe makers still build such a rig (see Chapter 4).

If you have to paddle any distance by yourself, using a single-bladed paddle, and the water's not dead calm, you'll balance better and be more efficient in one of the kneeling positions described earlier in this chapter. The one-knee position is the strongest and least uncomfortable. In a two-man canoe, your position should be a little back of amidships (farther forward for paddling into the wind), your body angled toward the paddle side so that you can reach the stroke easily while counterbalancing with feet and legs toward the opposite side of the canoe. The J stroke is made a little differently in solo paddling: begin by reaching out with the inside edge of the blade angled forward, then bring the paddle diagonally back toward the gunwale and slide into the regular J stroke. The beginning of the stroke is a modified draw stroke, which swings the bow slightly toward the paddle side, helping, with the hook of the J, to balance your off-center paddling.

Sailing. Sails? Historically, the fur traders carried sails and mounted them on masts cut on shore for

The use of a sail on the canoe dates back to the fur trade era of the early 1800s. (Sportspal Canoes)

an occasional run up rivers and across such big lakes as Superior and Winnipeg. You can do the same with a poncho tied to a pair of paddles, using the spare as a rudder. The mast has to be positioned about where the front seat is, thus excluding paddling from that position and travel with both a passenger and a sizable amount of gear. Several canoe builders, such as Old Town, Grumman, and Sawyer, sell sailing rigs adapted to their own designs.

Motorized Canoeing. Many hunters, fishermen, and guides like to use a small motor on their canoes. It can get you fairly quickly through familiar waters to more remote areas and can be easily mounted on a bracket between the gunwales of a double-ended canoe. With that arrangement, a 1–2-horsepower motor is *plenty* from the standpoint of safety and speed (a little faster than paddling)—especially if you have to portage it; and the small motor uses a minimum of gasoline, another problem in wilderness logistics. If you're going to use a motor much, a square-ended canoe, with a mount at the stern, may be the solution; it will carry a 3-horsepower motor safely. These canoes are available from Coleman, Mad River, Great Canadian, Sawyer, Old Town, Grumman, and Sportspal. Such a canoe will paddle fairly well, though appreciably slower than the usual double-ended canoe, and, in addition, the square-end canoes I know of are rather heavily built, slow-moving without their motors and burdensome on portages. My father went through a motor-canoeing phase. Eventually, we decided that we preferred the silence, broken only by the plunk of our paddles, the water whispering against the sides of our canoe, and the sounds of our own voices and the loons', raised in conversation or song.

Many sportsmen and guides like to use a small motor on their canoes in order to move quickly from one location to another. (Coleman Co.)

4 Equipping Your Canoe

Once you've settled on your canoe and acquired a set of paddles, you've got the essentials for successful canoeing. There are, however, several kinds of equipment that you'll find in the manufacturers' catalogues (or in some cases you can make for yourself without too much trouble) and may want to give some thought to. Some of these accessories are more or less necessary if you're going to be traveling much by canoe. Other items represent special adaptations of the canoe that in all likelihood you'll never try, and still others come under the heading of luxuries more encumbering than useful—like a transistor radio clipped to the handlebars of a bicycle.

CANOE PROTECTION

Unlike most canoes, a few are not decked at bow and stern. Short thwarts provide structural support at those points and give you a handle to grab when taking the canoe in and out of the water, as well as a convenient tie point for cartop carrying. The catch is that if you're canoeing in water the least bit choppy, with anything approaching a maximum load, you'll take water over the bow (and probably at the stern if the waves are behind you). It may be only a few drops at a time, but if you're crossing a mile or so of open water, that can add up to an inch or two sloshing around in the bottom of the canoe—not dangerous, probably, but it will gradually soak whatever's in your packs. The solution

is to order the canoe with *end caps*—molded fiberglass decks about 3 feet long, riveted to the gunwales at bow and stern, with a raised lip on the inside to deflect water. They'll cut down slightly on usable space but will make the difference between canoeing dry and having to head for shore when the water's even a little rough.

With end caps on a fiberglass canoe, you'll have to have some means of tying the canoe to front and rear bumpers when you're carrying it on top of your car. The handiest thing is a rope *loop* or a metal *painter ring* anchored in the bow and stern about six inches above the water line—specify it when you place your order. On aluminum canoes, such as Grumman, such a ring or loop is standard; other makers use a *painter strap* bolted to the bow and stern decks or have a hole drilled through the decks to hold a knotted rope for the same purpose. If you don't find one of these items in the maker's specifications, inquire and have it installed at both ends. If you're canoeing much in white water, you'll find other uses. Twenty or 30 feet of rope securely tied at both ends makes it fairly easy to let a canoe down through shallow rapids ("lining")—you and your partner can maneuver the half-loaded canoe from the bank—or to haul it up again ("tracking"). The same geology that creates rapids may also mean a shoreline too steep to haul a canoe up when you want to take a rest, reconnoiter, or stop for lunch. In such conditions, those long bow and stern lines can be used to secure the canoe to a tree or a rock. White-water canoers and kayakers make it a point

White-water end cap: a long deck of molded fiberglass to keep waves from washing in at bow and stern.

never to hit the rapids without such lines, not only for the functions indicated but for rescuing a boat that the force of water has jammed against a rock—a situation in which I hope you'll never find yourself.

If you use long lines at bow and stern, you can hold them coiled and firmly inside the canoe with rubber *tie-downs*—short lengths of rubber cord with hooks at either end. The same thing, wrapped around a thwart, will also serve to hold the spare paddle in the canoe and out of the way (or use heavy twine tied with a hitch that can be undone with one hand); a longer piece can be used to tie a pack into the canoe, if you find yourself unavoidably in the kind of rough water where capsizing (and losing your baggage) is a real possibility.

As I indicated earlier, I don't tie my packs into the canoe, primarily because I don't believe that, with reasonable canoe sense, one need ever get into a situation in which there's a serious risk of capsizing. Beyond that, I'm not sure that the obvious method, lashing the packs to the thwarts, would be effective; it's quite possible for the weight of the packs to tear the thwarts loose if the canoe does indeed turn over. Nevertheless, I know some very competent canoers who do tie their packs in, and if you're so minded, you might attach a couple of pairs of cleats or small eyebolts to the gunwales for the purpose, keeping them well away from interfering with paddling at bow and stern. With

rubber rope of the right size (or ordinary rope), they should protect your gear in any emergency that could possibly arise.

To keep yourself and your cargo dry when canoeing rough waters, you might want to consider an all-over spray cover, a waterproof fabric fitted over the gunwales from bow to stern, with elasticized openings over the two seats. At this writing, only Mad River and Old Town offer spray covers for their canoes. Unless you own one of these canoes, you'll have to rely on your own ingenuity with some help from your local canvas shop.

Another bit of canoe protection worth knowing about is what's called a *stem band*. The stem is the rounded structure, above the water line at bow and stern, joining the two sides of the canoe: on an aluminum canoe, a narrow exterior strip of metal sealing the two halves; on others, generally internal (though some wood-and-canvas canoes are made or can be ordered with external stems). Since the bow stem takes the greatest impact in any encounter with a rock, a metal covering at that point will help avoid the need for serious repairs and generally lengthen the canoe's life—traditionally a brass plate attached with screws, though aluminum is now normal. A stem band may or may not be standard on a wood-and-canvas canoe; check, and specify if it's not (minor cost). Most synthetic builders do *not* offer a stem band (the "bang strip" mentioned in Chapter 2), but I'd ask about it and get it if it can be supplied. The wood-and-canvas builders (and Sawyer in fiberglass) will also supply, as an optional extra, a similar protective strip running the length of the keel line—useful for the same reason as a stem band but less necessary. One advantage of an aluminum canoe is that it has no need for either of these extras: the metal keel and stems provide all the protection needed.

Unless you have a boathouse or a spare slot in your garage, you'll presumably store your canoe outdoors. Since I prefer to keep my canoe off the ground to avoid scratches and general banging around, I set it, bottom up, on a pair of saw horses made of two-by-fours. You can make a sturdier, and more permanent *canoe rack* from a pair of four-by-four posts, set about 3 feet out of the ground and 8 or 9 feet apart, with two-by-four crosspieces about 3½ feet long (and braced against the posts to prevent warping). Either way, you'll have to tie the canoe down, using ropes or the straps from

Spray covers do an excellent job of keeping you and your cargo dry in rough waters.
(Wyoming Travel Commission)

your cartop carrier—unless you enjoy watching it being lifted by every passing wind and dropped with a clunk. There's no need to cover an aluminum or synthetic canoe. With wood-and-canvas stored outdoors for any length of time (or one of the deluxe synthetic canoes trimmed with wood), use a large sheet of heavy plastic, carefully tied or taped around the canoe.

Paddles are best stored indoors. So that they won't be stepped on and broken if left standing in a corner (and wooden paddles have a tendency to warp), I'd suggest a rack that can be attached to a wall in the basement or the garage; make it with a two-by-four-inch board, for example, with pairs of pegs cut from half-inch dowels to support the paddles by their grips.

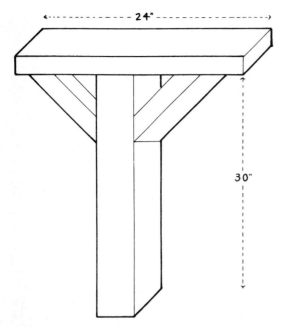

Canoe storage rack, using two-by-fours for crosspiece and braces and a 4 × 4-inch post set in the ground; the 30-inch height is the minimum for conveniently setting the canoe down or picking it up by yourself. Two such racks are needed for stability, positioned 8 to 9 feet apart for a canoe of average length; the canoe should be tied or strapped down. For two canoes side by side, use crosspieces 7 feet long, with a post at either end, and omit the braces.

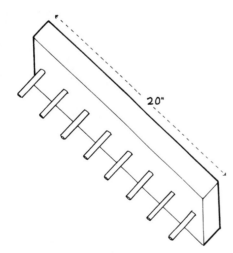

Paddle storage rack, made with a 2 × 4-inch board and ½-inch dowels spaced 2½ inches apart on centers. The rack shown is the minimum size to hold four paddles hung by their grips, with some overlapping of the blades.

For canoe repairs, as I've suggested in earlier chapters, cloth adhesive tape, inside and out, will do temporarily for cuts or small holes in any canoe material. For greater permanence, I use epoxy, molded in place with tape, which doesn't require clamps, warmth, or exposure to air in order to set. A small hole in aluminum can be fixed with aluminum paste applied like plastic wood and held in place with tape or fabric till it's hard, when it can be filed or sanded smooth; a big gash should be smoothed and flattened at the edges, then covered on the inside with an overlapping aluminum patch sealed with liquid rubber and riveted in place (*not* welded; the heat softens the metal). Small cuts in canvas (which will let water into the wood planking underneath) can be sealed with a waterproof cement; a hole is patched with a piece of muslin or light canvas slipped between the fabric and the planking and cemented.

The canoe manufacturers and their dealers sell cleaners and waxes suitable for aluminum and synthetic. Unless your canoe has been exposed to one or another form of industrial discharge, hosing down with a sponge is enough to get rid of the inevitable mud and sand. Apart from looks, a coat of wax (as in the old Simoniz treatment for cars) may be slightly functional in helping a canoe slide off rocks and provide some protection against minor scratches. Nicks in wood trim (or paddles) should be touched up at the end of the season with marine varnish, preferably the same kind used by the manufacturer if you can get it. With hard use the wood may, after several years, have to be sanded down and revarnished. A major repair to a synthetic canoe is probably best done by the manufacturer, but you can buy a repair kit and do the job yourself.

PERSONAL FLOTATION DEVICES

So far we've been thinking only about protecting the canoe. But what about the passengers? National law has now answered that question by requiring a life jacket, or personal flotation device (PFD) as they are now most often called, for everyone in the canoe. The PFD must be a Coast Guard-approved model that is in serviceable condition, readily accessible, and of an appropriate size for the person using it.

Most experienced canoers prefer the Type III

A PFD must be of an appropriate size for the person using it. (Coleman Co.)

Be sure the PFD you rent or own is in good shape before embarking on a canoe trip. (J. Wayne Fears)

Every person in the canoe must have a Coast Guard-approved PFD. (Old Town Canoe Co.)

PFD. It is designed so that the wearer is in a vertical and slightly backward position in the water, keeping the wearer from turning facedown in the water. A Type III PFD can be comfortable to wear and comes in a variety of styles that can be matched to use.

Be sure that the PFD you rent, purchase, or borrow is in good shape and try it on for fit. Do not alter it in any way and don't use it as a canoe fender or kneeling pad. Inspect your PFD periodically to ensure that it is free of tears, rips, or holes. Avoid PFDs that are filled with kapok. Kapok fibers may become waterlogged and lose their buoyancy if the vinyl inserts are cut or punctured.

Not only are PFDs good for flotation, but in cold water they can also increase the wearer's survival time from the effects of hypothermia.

The law doesn't require you to wear your PFD, but it should be kept within easy reach and be worn, at the very least, in rough water or if bad weather threatens. Nonswimmers and children should be required to wear a PFD at all times when they are on or near water.

Most canoe dealers and sporting goods stores can help you select the best PFD for canoeing. Get the best you can afford and use it. Your life may suddenly depend upon it.

Old Town carrying yoke: hardwood with foam padding, clamps that screw down to gunwales so it can be adjusted or removed when not needed.

CANOE FLOTATION

Most canoes are either naturally buoyant or are made so with built-in flotation devices, but those that aren't buoyant need something equivalent to a life jacket—flotation bags, which are made of plastic and are inflated, sealed, and inserted inside the craft. Styrofoam blocks and inner tubes from tires are also used. The greater the volume of flotation, the greater the displacement of water when the canoe is capsized and the easier the rescue. Be sure flotation devices are attached securely to the canoe. Flotation bags for canoes are available from Old Town, Mad River, and Blue Hole.

Sawyer carrying yoke: aluminum with foam padding, bolted to center thwart.

TRANSPORTATION

Moving your canoe from place to place begins on your shoulders. There's more than one way of doing this (see Chapter 3), but with a little practice, a satisfactory *yoke*, and perhaps an assist from your partner in lifting the canoe, you'll find it easiest on your own. Hence, even if the only portaging I did was from the car to the nearest stream bank, I wouldn't buy a canoe without a yoke. (You can, as I suggested in Chapter 3, portage a canoe by wedging the paddles between the front seat and the thwarts so that the blades point toward the stern and rest on your shoulders, but it's not comfortable for more than a short distance.) Most canoe builders have their own design of yoke in aluminum or wood, bolted or riveted to the gunwales or attached

with wing nuts (hence movable); some supply a yoke in place of the center thwart, others in addition to it. Either way, it should be positioned a couple of inches ahead of the canoe's midpoint, so that the bow will balance up and you can see where you're going. The modern, foam-rubber shoulder pads are softer but less durable than the older horsehair, which has pretty well gone the way of the horses themselves. (The Canadians still seem to like an elegantly carved, unpadded yoke, which, though I've never tried one, looks more suitable to oxen than to humans.) Even so, if you have knobby shoulders you may want some extra padding—a sweater or jacket wrapped around your neck, perhaps a life jacket, which otherwise would have to be carried separately.

Cartop Carriers. A cartop carrier will do the job better and be easier on your nerves at highway speeds. The most popular rack, especially for cars without rain gutters, is the inexpensive foam block carrier kit. It is simply four foam blocks that snap onto the canoe's gunwale. The kit includes rope and hardware necessary to secure a canoe to the cartop. Many canoers whose cars have rain gutters prefer the Quick-n-Easy or Yakima clamp-on rack, which has a hardwood bar upon which one or two canoes can rest. The bar is 60 inches wide for one canoe or 76 inches wide for two canoes. Yakima has an entire system of racks that can fit nearly every car on the road. A variety of canoe cartop carriers is available from most canoe retail stores.

Whatever the design, strapping or clamping the canoe to the rack isn't enough for highway speeds; it should also be tied at bow and stern to the car's bumpers. Since most modern car bumpers don't have a place to tie to, get a set of Voyageur's Limited nylon bumper hooks, which snap onto the bumper. The hooks have an eye to which you can secure a rope. The hooks are strong, resist water, and won't scratch the car's finish.

Regardless of what type cartop carrier you use, be sure to check your canoe and carrier often when traveling.

If you want to lock your canoe to the car, Mad River has a locking system that secures canoe to rack and rack to car.

For peace of mind: a sturdy bar-type canoe rack such as the Yakima two-canoe rack. (Yakima)

Inexpensive foam block carrying kits are easy to use when attaching the canoe to the vehicle top and require very little storage room. (Coleman Co.)

Canoe Trailer. There's one other solution to the problem of transporting your canoe from waterway to waterway, and that's a *trailer*. That's not as extravagant as it may sound. Great World is one source for a canoe trailer that will carry several canoes, with or without a compartment for baggage. Or, with a little ingenuity, you can build your own and save some money. You can start with a small, stock trailer, though you may have to replace the hitch to get adequate clearance for a canoe; then build up from the trailer's four corner a well-braced framework to support a conventional canoe rack. The trailer itself will carry as much gear as you're likely to need. If you do much canoeing with a lot of camping equipment, the trailer will carry everything and still leave plenty of space for comfort inside the car, and that's why some canoers use it.

5 Gear

CLOTHING

There's really no article of clothing that I'd call essential to canoeing. If you've done other kinds of camping, you'll use what you have; or make do with the tired old garments you wear for working around the yard or house. If you stick with canoe camping, you'll evolve your own preferences in clothes, depending on where and when you travel. There are, however, a few general principles to bear in mind.

Bulk, in the first place, is important. In buying clothes or packing for a two-person canoe trip, don't take more than you can fit in a single pack, and preferably less than that. Avoid nonessentials that you may never wear: you don't need two sweaters unless you know it's going to be cold enough so that you'll have to wear both a fair amount of time (and that's *cold!*). Don't take a windbreaker when a rain suit will do the same job, probably more effectively.

In line with that advice, my canoe clothing list works out as follows for a two-week trip: boots, trousers, shirt, hat, a rain suit, and a light sweater for the cool nights and mornings that are likely in most canoe country even in mid-summer; and a somewhat Spartan maximum of four sets of socks, underwear, and handkerchiefs or bandannas. For a shorter trip, you can cut down on the latter; for a longer one, soap the dirty socks and underwear occasionally, then tie them behind the canoe to rinse while they drag through the water (they'll dry stretched across your packs or the bottom of your

A rain suit on a canoe trip can double as a windbreaker, eliminating the need for another garment. (J. Wayne Fears)

upturned canoe when you stop for lunch). I also take a spare shirt and pair of trousers to have something dry to change into after a rainy day; and a pair of cotton work gloves—not for paddling but for handling hot pots over the cook fire.

That basic list, well chosen, will do for all seasons except the depth of winter, when you're probably not going to be canoeing anyway. In really cold weather, I add a second, heavier sweater and a suit of long underwear. I've never used the sort of down-quilted jackets or parkas that are currently popular among skiers (I don't use them for skiing either, for that matter); the bulk and restrictiveness would rule them out even if the high prices didn't. In cold weather, from the freezing point on down, several thin layers, topped by a light, windproof jacket or parka, will always be more effective than one thick one. As you warm up with exercise, you can shed a layer or two and stay comfortable—and safe; overdressed, you'll sweat, even in extreme cold, and your own sweat will have a dangerously chilling effect.

There's one other factor to bear in mind any time between the first of May and the end of September: the billions of insects who share this planet and its waterways with us. In some parts of the continent, there are flies—deer flies, horseflies, little bulldog flies, other local names and types—that will bite ferociously if they get the chance, but mosquitoes,

in my view, are worse for sheer numbers. There's nothing quite so unnerving as walking in to an apparently peaceful meadow and being greeted by swarms of the little devils streaming up from the ground, covering your body black while they strain to make a meal of you. Hence, any time you're canoeing in the mosquito season, wear long trousers and a long-sleeved shirt, both of material tough and thick enough to ward off insects—*not* shorts and a T-shirt; and they'll also protect you against sunburn, which on a bright day on the water can sear even the toughest human hide.

Detailed lists of canoe-oriented clothing and camping equipment are included in Chapter 8, with sources for all of these items in the Appendices. Although we're concerned here with the principles behind these recommendations, a few items are important enough to bear special comment.

Both for loading and unloading the canoe and for support on a rough portage trail, you'll need a pair of boots high enough and waterproof enough to protect your feet and ankles. A 9- or 10-inch boot (midcalf) is about right; a smooth sole (not lugged) won't track dirt into the tent. Several makers produce silicone-tanned leather boots of this type that are guaranteed waterproof, if periodically treated with silicone in liquid or paste form. Or, for less money, you can start with an ordinary work or

North American waterways are often populated with biting insects. Insect repellent should always be packed during the warm seasons. (J. Wayne Fears)

Long sleeves are a good idea for canoers, not only for warmth, but for protection from the sun and biting insects. (Old Town Canoe Co.)

hunting boot of the right height and make it adequately waterproof with one of the waterproofing grease or wax compounds available from most outfitters. (Rubber boots are waterproof, of course, but provide less support than leather, and I find them sweaty.) In all seasons, I like thick wool socks inside my boots (such as the Norwegian Ragg type)—they're comfortable, and, unlike cotton, continue to insulate even when wet.

During cool or cold weather, a thick, soft wool shirt (what's known in the trade as a jacket-weight material, a 20-ounce fabric) has the recommendation of being bugproof, and it will take a good deal of wetting without the chilling effect of cotton. A good wool shirt shouldn't *feel* scratchy, though if you can't stand wool you might try one of the thick cotton flannels (chamois cloth)—mosquitoproof and fairly warm on a cool day but not so good as wool when wet.

Whatever trousers you settle on should be loose-cut for easy movement: most blue jeans are too tight for comfort. I like a tighly woven cotton twill (it dries quickly), with long underwear underneath in cold weather. In choosing shirts and trousers,

look for ample pockets, with button flaps that will hold whatever odds and ends of survival equipment you carry on you.

A good sheath or folding knife with a 4- or 5-inch blade is useful in so many ways on a canoe trip that I think of it as an article of clothing.

Since much of the canoe country is also rainy country, you'll travel often enough in wet weather to need adequate rainwear.

A high-quality rain suit made by companies such as Peter Storm or Kool Dri can be a good investment. There is also a wide variety of outerwear featuring Gore-Tex that can serve as rainwear, yet lets perspiration pass to the outside, keeping the wearer dry regardless of how hard it rains or how hard he paddles.

Any form of poncho, open at the sides, is just about worthless. A crushable waterproof hat with a 2- or 3-inch brim keeps sun as well as rain out of your eyes and is handy for anything from carrying water to fanning a reluctant fire.

TENTS

As with canoes, you can rent tents and sleeping bags from outfitters in the vicinity of the leading canoeing areas. If you're trying the sport for the first time, it's a good way of postponing an investment till you're sure you want to make it, and it's a means, too, of finding out for yourself the desirable properties before you make the commitment of purchase. Except for outfitters for whom the rental business is a front-line sales technique, the rental equipment will probably be on the heavy and bulky side, chosen for harder and more careless use than you'd give your own gear.

If you're buying a tent primarily for canoeing, the right choice will make a big difference both in the ease with which you travel and your comfort in camp. You're looking for something between the backpacker's nylon upper berth and the car camper's Taj Mahal.

The best size for canoe camping is what most tentmakers call a four-man tent, meaning a floor area of at least 65 or 70 square feet. It's still small enough to fit into a compact space—level tent sites aren't always easy to find—and will be luxuriously unconfining for two people, with plenty of room for bringing your packs in at night and storing a

Since many canoe campsites do not provide a sure footing for tent pegs, freestanding tents should be considered. (Coleman Co.)

The best-size tent for canoe camping is the four-man tent, such as this Diamond Brand tent, which gives ample room for two canoers and their gear. (J. Wayne Fears)

little dry kindling for the morning fire in case it rains. A tent that size allows you to snuggle a couple of children in with you, in comfort, and is feasible for four adults provided they don't walk in their sleep; a bigger party will need a second tent. For myself, I likewise prefer a tent high enough for dressing and undressing, making life a little easier at the start and end of the day; but, as I said, I'm careful to stake it tight against overnight storms, particularly if I have to pitch it in an exposed spot.

Regardless of size, several features are virtually indispensable. One, certainly, is a sewn-in floor, heavy and waterproof enough so that in a downpour water can flow under it, if need be, without coming through. Another is attached mosquito netting at the door and any windows and a waterproof storm door than can be zipped up or tied down when it rains.

Since many campsites, such as sandbars or the wooden platforms found in the Okefenokee Swamp, do not provide a secure footing for tent pegs, a freestanding tent should be considered. Investigate the streams or lakes on which most of your canoeing will take place and select a tent which will work best in those circumstances.

A few other features are desirable but not essential. A ventilation window, covered with mosquito netting and hooded against rain (or with a curtain that can be drawn down from the inside), will help keep down moisture from condensation in the tent. For mosquito netting and doors, the newer nylon zippers are less likely than metal to corrode and jam. And although it's not easy to find any more, I like a tent with an awning in front; it helps keep rain out, provides extra support when tied to a couple of trees, and gives you a dry spot for cooking on a rainy day.

Today's canoer can choose from a wide variety of tent shapes. There are small backpack tents, wedge styles, hoop tents, geodesic domes, wall tents, lean-tos, and A-frames. Of all these choices, one of the best is the four-person dome tent, such as is made by Coleman, Eureka, Diamond Brand, and North Face. They are freestanding, can withstand high winds, pack compactly, are lightweight, go up quickly and easily, and are insectproof. While these tents are not inexpensive, they are a good investment when you consider that with care, they will give years of service. They are spacious enough to sleep four adults or two people with a lot of gear. Also, they are high enough to dress in or to spend a day or two waiting out a storm without getting claustrophobic.

On the whole, your best bet when it comes to picking out a tent is a retailer with a good representation of types and makes, either a sporting goods store or one of the big mail-order camping equipment operations that produces its own catalog; *not* the manufacturer.

SLEEPING BAGS

As with a tent, you don't have to start by *buying* a sleeping bag; you can rent—from the same kinds of places that rent tents and other camping equipment. Or you can take a couple of blankets off your bed, double them over, and pin them together with

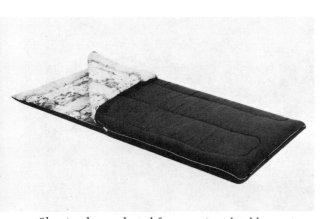

Sleeping bags selected for canoeing should contain an insulator that does not lose its insulating capabilities when damp, such as this PolarGuard bag.

blanket pins to form a double-walled, rectangular envelope that will be about as effective as a medium-grade sleeping bag. This old-fashioned alternative is more of a nuisance and rather less comfortable than a sleeping bag, but it's a lot less expensive.

Selecting a sleeping bag for canoeing should be done with great care. A sleeping bag is essential for sleeping comfort and may become a survival item. When you decide to buy a sleeping bag, your first consideration should be its capability to retain heat produced by your body. The holding of this heat is made possible by the insulation with which the bag has been filled.

Many types of insulation fillers have been tried

Keeping the sleeping bag clean and dry is very important on an extended canoe trip. (Coleman Co.)

A self-inflating foam pad combines the best qualities of both the foam pad and air mattress.

in sleeping bags, but there are six widely used fillers.

Duck or goose down has long been considered the best sleeping bag filler by most outdoorsmen. It compacts well for packing and springs back quickly to provide good insulation, but it has a drawback as far as canoeing is concerned. When it gets wet, down collapses and loses its insulating value; thus, it is not recommended for canoeing use.

PolarGuard is a man-made insulating filler that many canoers favor. It will keep the user warm even when wet, as its fibers absorb less than 1 percent moisture and it has 83 percent more loft than down when wet. Its drawbacks are that more PolarGuard is needed to equal the same amount of loft as down, which means a little more weight to carry, and it doesn't compress easily.

Hollofil 808 and Hollofil II are also popular synthetic insulating fillers used in many medium-priced sleeping bags. They absorb less than 1 percent moisture, so even in the worst dunking, they still retain their insulating qualities.

Quallofil is an insulating filler that is considered by many to be a high-tech substitute for down. It is almost as compactible as down, has outstanding insulating value, and retains its insulating qualities even when wet. Canoers who embark on Far North expeditions are choosing Quallofil as their sleeping bag insulation filler.

For summertime canoeing, Thermolite insulating filler is a good choice, as it is lightweight, inexpensive, and warm when wet. A sleeping bag filled with Thermolite will keep you warm in temperatures down to 60 degrees and compacts into a bag the size of a loaf of bread.

Since sleeping bag construction varies greatly among manufacturers and many of the cheap bags are rip-offs, the best rule to follow is to buy a sleeping bag from a reputable dealer who handles brand-name sleeping bags, such as Coleman, Moonstone, Red Head, Camel, North Face, and Marmot.

BETWEEN YOU AND THE GROUND

As a young sprout wrapped in my Hudson's Bay blanket stretched out on a quarter-inch layer of fallen pine needles that felt as soft as a bed at the Waldorf, I rather scorned anyone who needed a mattress to lull him to sleep. Now that my bones have grown middle-aged and creaky, though, I wouldn't venture forth on a camping trip without that luxury.

There are three basic alternatives: a plastic-foam pad, an air mattress, and the self-inflating foam pad. A plastic-foam pad is more an insulator than a mattress. If the weather's at all cool, you need one under you to retain heat. In summer, though, you may well find a pad sweatily overwarm (like a foam-rubber mattress) and generally uncomfortable to sleep on unless you're used to a board-firm mattress at home. In addition, if the pad's thick enough to be useful it makes a bulky roll that's awkward in any pack. For these reasons, I prefer an air mattress about half inflated (too much air and it's uncomfortably firm). Apart from comfort in sleeping, the air mattress, when empty, folds flat, is easy to stow, and in a Duluth pack makes an effective pad between your back and any hard lumps of equipment inside.

However, on a cool night an air mattress is definitely *not* warm: the air cells act like the coils of a refrigerator, drawing off your warmth. One answer to that problem, admittedly a nuisance, is a thin sheet of plastic foam (cheap, easy to pack, obtainable at most hardware stores) between you and the mattress.

There is a mattress that combines the best qualities of both the foam pad and the air mattress—the self-inflating foam pad. Made by Cascade Designs, Inc., the trade name is Therm-A-Rest. This type of mattress rolls up into a small roll when not in use. To inflate, all you have to do is open the valve. The foam core expands and draws air into the mattress, making it a comfortable ground insulator. This type mattress has been the choice of several Mount Everest expeditions.

SAFE DRINKING WATER

There once was a time when safe drinking water on a canoe trip was not a problem; you simply dipped a cup of water and drank all you wanted. That's no longer the case, as many streams are contaminated with products and waste from man. However, a lot of remote backcountry lakes and streams are unsafe from a cause other than man, the one-celled parasite called *Giardia lamblia*. This

The Katadyn Pocket Filter is one of the best defenses against Giardia. *(J. Wayne Fears)*

small parasite is little larger than a red blood cell and inhabits the small intestines of its host, which can be a beaver, muskrat, dog, or many other animals, including man. While in the host animal, a protective cover is formed around the parasite. Next, this parasite is passed from the host in fecal material, often finding its way into streams and lakes where it survives over three months in water of about 40 degrees. This parasite is killed when water is frozen or when it reaches temperatures over 176 degrees.

When a person drinks water in which *Giardia* are found, the results can include nausea, abdominal cramps, and almost always watery diarrhea, which may persist for several weeks. Cases of this condition, known as giardiasis, have occurred in wilderness areas throughout North America as far north as Alaska and the Yukon. Most of the cases were in areas where beavers are found, thus the nickname "beaver fever."

There are two recommended methods of making water safe to drink. The first is to boil the water ten minutes before drinking. The second treatment is to filter the water through a highly specialized filtration system. The one compact model that canoers should consider is the Pocket Filter made by Katadyn USA, Inc. These units weigh about 1 pound and pack easily. They consist of a replacement purification canister and a pump assembly to force water through a microfilter.

Since giardiasis is becoming an increasingly significant problem in North America, don't give in to the temptation to drink from the crystal-clear river.

CAMP COOKING

The canoe-country outfitters are generally prepared to rent basic cooking and eating equipment (pots, grill, plates and cups, cutlery, etc.) at reasonable rates. They'll also put together a food supply for a trip of a specified length at a flat rate per person—always, it seems, on the assumption that canoers are equipped with Paul Bunyan appetites; and they will, of course, fill specific food orders from whatever lines they carry, usually assisting the process with checklists you can go over well in advance. Even if you take one of these easy routes, though, you need a general idea of what's essential, and why. That's what we'll be considering in this chapter, in the broadest terms. Later we'll get down to the specifics you'll want to keep in mind when doing your own planning, with checklists that I hope you'll find helpful.

Open Fire vs. Stove. There are two different cooking techniques used in canoe camping. The first is the use of a small stove for cooking. This is required in many areas due to the shortage of fuel wood for an open fire, the danger of forest fires, or to reduce the damage to the landscape from open fires. Also, many campers don't want to take the time to cook over an open fire, don't have the pioneer skills needed, or prefer the compactness offered by a small stove, two-person cook kit, and freeze-dried food. Meals can be prepared much more quickly this way; as soon as you can boil water, you are eating.

The second technique is open-fire cooking. This is more often practiced in remote areas where fuel wood is readily available and in good supply and where there are either established fireplaces or there is no immediate danger of overuse of the area. Many campers utilizing this technique enjoy using the skills necessary to build a cooking fire and cooking over the fire. Perhaps they don't like freeze-dried food, or they may like to cook from scratch. Some like to cook freeze-dried food over an open fire. Whatever the case, we will take a look at both techniques so that you can decide for yourself which fits your plans.

Stoves—Although an open fire is generally the most interesting means of camp cookery, there are times and places in which it's not possible or practical. In some of the best canoe country, fires may be restricted or forbidden because of a midsummer dry spell. In heavily used areas, firewood can get too scarce to be relied on. In such circumstances, for a family-size canoeing party, you'll find it difficult to do without one of the two-eye stoves. The Paulin stove uses propane gas and is available with either two burners or three. I prefer the old reliable

For large groups, the two-burner gasoline stove minimizes cooking time. (Coleman Co.)

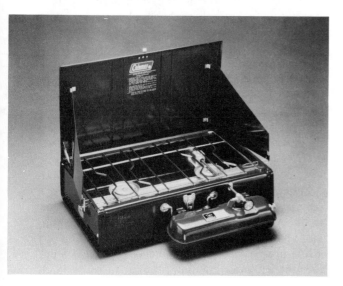

two-burner Coleman stove because the fuel, which is similar to white gasoline but more refined and less smoky, is easier to come by. Both are efficient for cooking but bulky, require substantial quantities of fuel in heavyweight containers, and are as awkward to fit into any pack as they are cumbersome to carry separately. Except by necessity, I wouldn't use either for canoeing.

The alternative is one of the small, single-burner stoves designed primarily for hiking, where every ounce must be seriously considered. Some of these burn alcohol (Optimus), while others use one or another compressed gas in a specially designed container (Bleuet, Olicamp Scorpion II, Paulin, Grasshopper). The Swedish Svea burns white gasoline, which you can buy at many gas stations, and ingeniously uses its own heat to pressurize the fuel, producing a blowtorchlike flame; I've found mine simple to use and reliable. The Primus, another European make and a name nearly synonymous with camp cooking, also uses white gasoline, but in a tank that has to be pumped up periodically, as with the Coleman Peak I or Sportsman stoves (Phoebus and another Optimus work on the same system). Cartridges are required for the various compressed gases, while for the two gasoline stoves you'll need one or two quart-size aluminum fuel bottles. With any liquid fuel, don't forget to take a small funnel to minimize spillage when you fill the stove. Carry extra fuel in small fuel bottles such as those made by SIGG and Nalgene. They are lightweight, don't leak, and are dent-resistant.

Of the three fuels (there are also stoves that burn

When freeze-dried foods are used, a compact one-eye stove is a good choice. (Coleman Co.)

Fuel for stoves and lanterns should be carried in compact, lightweight, and safe fuel bottles. (Nalge Trail Products)

kerosene, but except in backwoods areas it's becoming hard to get), white gasoline burns hottest, is most readily available, and is cheap for what it does. Compressed gas, besides being quite expensive and obtainable only in specialty stores, becomes less efficient as you climb above sea level. Such a stove as the Svea, which is primed by lighting a little of its fuel in the vicinity of the pipe connecting the tank with the burner, has the recommendation of simplicity (pumps, relying on airtight seals and valves, are not altogether reliable) and is safer than it sounds. It may, however, be hard to get going in cold weather or high, thin air.

In stormy weather, you'll have to take the stove and your cooking inside the tent, where caution is in order. In that confined space, it's well to provide a flat rock as a base, both to reduce the risk of knocking the stove over and to insulate the tent floor from heat, which can melt nylon and scorch canvas.

Although the small stoves are designed for one or two persons, it's possible, with a little holding of the breath, to cook enough stew, say, for five or six on one of them, the catch being that it will handle only one thing at a time and is rather slow with a big potful. As insurance against a wet day, though, or for a quick pot of lunchtime coffee, it's

worth having one in your cooking kit, even if you rely on a fire the rest of the time.

Fires and Fire Making—A number of writers on camping and wilderness survival describe methods of starting a fire with everything from the Indian fire bow and drill to a bit of plastic that can be used as a burning glass, but, for all practical purposes, cooking over a campfire begins with an adequate supply of dry matches. Indeed, the prospect of *not* being able to get the fire started when you need it is so depressing that several precautions are in order, a series of increasingly sure defenses against cold and hunger, if you like, to fall back on.

For ordinary use in camping, I rely on wooden safety matches, allowing about a box per day. Although you have to have the box to strike them on, I think that in damp weather they're less prone than the big, nonsafety wooden kitchen matches to soak up moisture and become useless. (Paper matches are no good at all.) The match supply should be kept in a plastic bag, tightly tied, well inside a pack, where rain's not likely to penetrate. For emergencies, most outfitters sell a small, waterproof metal match safe with a hinged screw top that holds ten or twenty kitchen matches; get one and carry it in a pocket. As a further precaution, you can waterproof a small supply of kitchen matches by dipping them in paraffin or lacquer. A few outfitters sell waterproof matches. Finally, I've taken to carrying a throwaway butane lighter in case all else fails. Although it's not much good in a wind, with careful shielding it's a sure source of fire, with a fuel supply that should last a month or two even with constant use; more to the point, if you're a smoker, the lighter will reserve your matches for more serious purposes. Acquire a supply of fire lighters (small, compressed blocks of sawdust, impregnated with resin and kerosene, that can be lighted with a match even in the rain) and resolve always to carry them with your cooking kit. A little dry newspaper, sealed in a plastic bag, is also useful in wet weather, though not so sure as a fire lighter.

For cutting the wood that goes into your fire and for a good many other campsire jobs, you'll need an ax. A full-size, single-blade head with a short handle (about twenty-four inches) is best, since it will fit in a pack, where the longer handle will stick out and leave an opening for rain to come in; a hatchet is too light for serious work. Whatever you use, be sure to get a stout leather case for the head to protect whatever's next to the ax in the pack. (Ax sheaths are not easy to come by in these decadent times, but can be made fairly easily from leather, heavy vinyl, or oilcloth.) Sharpen the ax well, before you set out on your trip, and it should see you through; though, with patience, you can touch up the edge with the same Carborundum you use for your knives (or carry a small file for the purpose).

From the safety standpoint—an ax, carelessly used, *is* dangerous—a few canoeists prefer a folding saw, of which there are several makes available. It will do to cut down a small tree or saw it into fireplace lengths (slow going, though), but it's no use for trimming branches, splitting wood, or sharpening tent stakes, and it won't pound your stakes into the ground, either. (When driving stakes with an ax, by the way, use the flat of the blade butt, not the butt itself.) As a compromise, you might use, with your ax, an inexpensive Varco pocket saw, an 18-inch strand of sawtooth wire with a ring at either end (holding the rings with your thumbs, you can cut down a fair-sized tree; strung over a lithe sapling, it makes a small bucksaw). In its protective plastic case, the pocket saw belongs in your pocket along with the waterproof match case, a tool for survival in the unlikely event you lose your entire outfit.

One of the first making-camp chores, along with setting up the tent, is collecting a firewood supply. Look for dead trees an inch or two in diameter that are still standing (wood that's been on the ground for a year or two is likely to be rotten, but it too will burn on a good fire, though smokily). The small trees can be broken off at the base and broken up by hand into fire lengths. On a river, you can count on plenty of well-dried driftwood along the high-water line, already, if you're selective, broken up to the right size; being impregnated with minerals from the water, though, it makes a smelly fire much inferior to the aromatic sweetness of seasoned pine. In beaver country, you can collect incomparable wood from the top of this industrious animal's lodges or dams. He and his family will already have eaten the bark from these discards, so you're not depriving him.

Whatever your wood source, it's handy to sort the supply into two piles, on either side of the fireplace: big pieces for burning, the trimmed branches and twigs for kindling. Avoid big logs, which are a lot of work to split with an ax; in general, use your ax no more than absolutely necessary. There are a few precautions you probably learned long ago in summer camp. One certainly is deliberation. Don't be in a hurry when you're using an ax. In cutting a tree down, take time to look around and make sure there's no undergrowth that will catch your back swing or stand in the way of a strong, accurate cut; clear anything that may interfere before you start chopping, and when you begin, stand with your legs braced wide apart and as far from the cut as you can get them. In trimming branches, stand on one side of the fallen tree and cut the branches along the other, letting your arm and the ax handle swing like a pendulum, working up from tree butt to top—the weight of the head will do the work. In cutting up the wood, use a good-sized fallen log as a chopping block, wedged with rocks if need be to hold it firm. Make sure there's no spectator looking over your shoulder before you take the first stroke, and, again, brace your legs solidly and keep them as far as possible from the cutting point. You're less likely to be hit by a flying piece of wood if you cut your tree from the middle, cutting each piece successively into halves until they're short enough for the fire.

Since prebreakfast woodcutting consumes some of the pleasantest moments of the day, avoid it by saving enough wood over from the night before. Cover the woodpile with a poncho or rain shirt weighted with rocks, in case it rains. Or take enough wood and kindling to start the morning fire under the tent awning or into the tent itself; or leave some under the upturned canoe. As a matter of woodsmen's courtesy, before breaking camp, collect some spare wood for the next guy, who may well arrive when it's dark, cold, or rainy—or all three at once.

A good many national, state, and provincial parks in the canoe country now require you to use established campsites along the water routes, where permanent fireplaces and grills are provided. Elsewhere, the chances are that any appealing site will have been used before by someone who will have bequeathed you a fireplace. If you do have to start from scratch, look for an open, level spot downwind from your tent site, preferably with a boulder to serve as a fireback. Clear twigs and pine needles,

In areas where an open fire is permitted, traditional cooking skills may be used. (J. Wayne Fears)

which might spread the fire, down to bare earth or rock. Build the fireplace sideways to the prevailing wind, using rocks, say a foot long by half a foot wide and high, overlapping them and wedging them with pebbles, rather as with a child's building blocks. A foot or a foot and a half high is adequate for containing the fire and sheltering it from wind, and is also enough to support whatever type of grill you're using.

In making a fire, I start with a few of the smallest, driest twigs I can find, broken into lengths of a couple of inches (if they don't break with a snap, they're green and no good). Pine is best for the purpose. Other woods, such as birch or willow, may seem dry but retain enough moisture to be hard to light. Arranged tepee-fashion, the twigs should light with a single match, and as the fire catches I feed it from all sides with successively larger twigs until it's going well and ready for the bigger pieces. I then put a pair of logs on either side of the fireplace and lay several across them to catch from the kindling; then a second layer of wood at right angles to the first, loose enough for a good draft. If wood is abundant, I put in as much as I can fit in this manner at the start; it makes a fast, roaring fire that will burn down to hot, steady coals by the time you're ready to cook. My father, however, whenever he made a fire, invariably repeated an old Indian saying: "White man build big fire, stand far away. Indian build little fire, stand close." For saving both wood and work, it's a good principle.

Contrary to what you may have heard, the bark of the white birch is not necessarily an ideal natural tinder. The flaky, paper-thin outer bark of a dead, standing birch, which you can remove with your fingers, does fairly well when torn into strips. The inner bark, dead or alive, standing or fallen, is more likely to smother the match (birch seems to rot from the inside out). *Don't* use your knife on a live birch; you'll go too deep, and the girdled tree will die.

If it's well sited in an adequate fireplace, the fire you cook dinner on will probably have burned down safely by bedtime; except in unusually dry weather, you really don't need to put it out with water. In breaking camp, however, pour a pail of dishwater all over the breakfast fire until it's really dead, no longer giving off smoke (the hot rocks may still steam a bit, but that's harmless). In our American mania for self-accusation, we've made it sound as if all forest fires are caused by careless campers. That's nonsense. In my observation, lightning is the more common offender, and it's probable that a periodic burning over is an essential stage in the natural cycle of a living forest. Nevertheless, fire, like other powerful natural forces, *is* dangerous and it can be immensely destructive, not least of the country where canoeing and camping are best. Treat it, always, with caution and respect. Too much dousing before you shove off is obviously better than not enough.

Cook Kits—All things considered, I prefer open-fire cooking to using any stove compact enough to be practical for a canoe trip. The fire provides enough cooking space for several pots at a time—a main dish, vegetable, dessert, coffee, even the after-dinner dishwater—and if the fire's properly made it will give a range of heats, from barely warm to blazing, depending on where you set your pots. Besides, it's cheery and warming at the end of the day, it smells good, and by the side of a wilderness lake its gray-blue column of smoke, rising to heaven like an offering of incense, is your signal to God and the world that another party of humans has taken up residence. At any rate, the equipment suggested here assumes you'll do most of your cooking over a fire, but it can be adapted to even the smallest of stoves, which you may want to carry in any case.

If you are canoeing with just one or two other people and using freeze-dried food, then you will not need a large cook kit. One of the small cook kits from Coleman, Olicamp, Primus, or Mirro will probably be all you need. Even with large groups, the cooking is often done in pairs using small stoves and cook kits. However, for open-fire cooking for a family or several canoers, a larger cook kit is called for.

For a start, you'll need a set of pots—a big one of, say, 8–10-quart capacity and two or three smaller ones that nest inside; a frying pan, preferably with a handle that folds out of the way for packing; and a set of plates, mugs, and bowls (for desserts or morning fruit or cereal) made to nest inside each other and fit in the pots. I use metal plates and mugs—they'll dent, where plastic will break—but they can be touchy to handle with hot food in them. I still carry a small coffeepot that fits inside the smallest cooking pot, but I've long since lazily abandoned real coffee—boiled, perked, dripped—in favor of instant. For all pots, I prefer *firmly attached*, semicircular (bucket style) handles that lie flat, out of the way, for packing; the removable kind tend to get lost or give way at the critical moment if carelessly put on. Tight-fitting lids are essential for keeping out ashes and whatnot. The big pot does fine for carrying water to your cooking area, and when you're traveling by canoe the water supply's always at hand; I don't, therefore, bother with a separate water container,

Cook kits come in a variety of sizes. Select the cook kit that is designed for your size group and for the type of menu you have planned. Left to right: one-person kit, six-person kit, two-person kit. (J. Wayne Fears)

A compact one-person cook kit takes up little room and works fine for freeze-dried foods. (Primus)

For larger parties or more elaborate menus, the four-person cook kit may be required. (Primus)

though there are inexpensive, collapsible plastic jugs (2½ or 5 gallons) that are light and fairly durable. On the other hand, if the water can't be trusted—an unfortunate possiblity even in some quite remote areas—a large container is essential, so that you can fill it from any safe springs along the way or, failing that, purify water in quantity.

When cooking on an open fire, the pots will collect soot and dirt on the outside, so a canvas carrying bag with a drawstring top is a must for packing. Particularly when cooking over a wood fire, I don't do much more than rinse the outsides of the pots—scouring them after every meal is a dirty and time-consuming job that can just as well be saved till you get back home, when you'll want to clean all your equipment anyway before putting it away. Instead, I pack each pot in a paper bag cut to fit, so that the soot on the outside of one isn't transferred to the inside of the one it's packed in.

As I suggested earlier, a pair of cotton work gloves belongs in the bag with the pots and plates, partly to keep soot off your hands but chiefly because the pots will be hot to handle in the course of cooking.

Inexpensive and nearly indestructible eating utensils, in chrome plate or stainless steel, are available at the nearest hardware store. You'll need a knife and fork and small and large spoons for each member of your family or party, with a couple of spares all around; and a spatula, long-handled fork, can opener, and at least one really sharp, all-purpose knife, with a small Carborundum or sharpening steel to touch up the blade (sharpen it well before the trip). Unless you make it yourself, a *caddy* to hold all this—a roll-up bag with slots for each kind of implement—is harder to come by.

The storage of beverages and foodstuffs can be made easy by using leakproof bottles made of "food-grade plastic" by Nalge Company. They are lightweight and virtually indestructible.

Store beverages and foodstuffs in leakproof plastic bottles for compact packing. (Nalge Trail Products)

For cooking over a fire, a grill of some kind is a great convenience. I prefer a light wire grill with legs that fold flat, such as those made by Mirro, and a canvas bag to pack it in.

There are a couple of less expensive, small backpackers' grills without legs—they have to be set up between two rocks, and it takes a certain amount of ingenuity to get them both level and stable, at the right height for cooking. In a pinch, you can do without a grill. For example, a pair of crotched saplings stuck in the ground on either side of the fire and braced with rocks will support a cross bar from which you can hang your pots. Any such arrangement takes time to set up, though, and risks spilling your dinner into the fire if someone stumbles against it in the twilight.

One of the natural laws of camp cookery is that dishwashing follows eating as night follows day. As we sit down to eat, I fill the biggest pot with fresh water and set it on the grill so that it will be hot when the meal's over. Then, while we sip the after-dinner cup of coffee, we toss coins or play cards for the privilege of washing the dishes (the dishwasher gets his hands *really* clean). The hot water is mixed with cold to a bearable temperature and

divided into two pots, one for washing, the other for rinsing. A bar of Ivory, which you can also use for washing yourself, does as well as any, assisted by a wash rag and a scouring pad.

You *can* leave the utensils to dry by the fire, but drying them is an important final step in the cleaning process, particularly for the knives, forks, and spoons. I carry a couple of cloth dish towels for the purpose—you don't mind losing or throwing out the pressed paper-cloth kind you can buy at the supermarket, but they're less absorbent.

After the evening meal, you can save time by stacking the dried plates and cups around the fireplace, bottoms up and weighted with rocks in case of an overnight wind. Make a point of tidying away all your food and equipment, ready for the night, as soon as the dishes are finished, so you won't

Cooking dinner: the fireplace, hastily made from rocks picked up on the beach, braces the grill, provides a shield against wind, and keeps the fire from spreading. (Jim Mead)

have to do it while stumbling around in the dark (suggestions later in this chapter for protecting food). Then you're ready for the evening, whether that means an hour or two of sunset fishing, reading, singing, playing cards, or simply sitting around the fire and talking. And so to bed!

Food. There once was a time when the bulk of a canoe's load was made up of food, but this no longer has to be, thanks to much-improved freeze-dried food. Some still like to carry along some fresh food as well as canned goods on their canoe camping trip. But with the wide selection of trail foods now available in canoe and backpack shops, as well as freeze-dried foods found in the supermarket, it is not necessary. With freeze-dried foods, almost anyone can prepare a gourmet meal using only boiled water, and it takes only a few minutes, leaving more

Almost anyone can prepare a gourmet meal with today's wide choices of freeze-dried foods.
(J. Wayne Fears)

time for canoeing, fishing, etc. Companies such as Mountain House, Backpacker's Pantry, and Smoky Canyon offer a wide variety of good-tasting foods that are quick and easy to prepare. Many similar but less expensive foods are available at the local supermarket. By combining foods from both sources, an interesting variety of meals can be built into the wilderness menu. If you are using lightweight foods from a supermarket, remove the foodstuffs from the cardboard boxes, being careful to save cooking instructions, and place them in Ziploc bags. It makes the load a little lighter and much easier to pack.

When planning the menu for a canoe trip, be sure to involve everyone going on the trip. Most freeze-dried food companies will send you a meal planner on request.

If you don't use freeze-dried food, be careful in planning the menu not to include a lot of foodstuffs requiring storage on ice, as there isn't a lot of room for ice chests in a canoe, there is little ice in the backcountry, and an ice chest loaded with food, ice, and water can be a problem when portage is required.

Most canoe and backpack shops will be glad to help you plan your first menu for canoe camping. After that you will probably be able to tailor the rest for yourself.

A FEW COMFORTS

One person's luxury is another's necessity—like the little goose-down pillow my mother considered indispensable to a good night's sleep on a camping trip. Strictly speaking, none of the items of equipment and supplies that we'll consider in this section is advisable if you're intent on traveling fast and unencumbered. All, however, add to the comfort of a camping trip, and some you'll probably think essential, depending on your particular tastes and inclinations. Think about them, anyway, when you plan your own trip, striking a balance between what you're actually likely to use and enjoy and what will merely weigh you down and never come out of the pack.

Lighting the Night. On a camping trip, you soon adopt, almost unconsciously, the natural rhythm of the day: get up when it's light, go to bed when it gets dark. You don't really need anything very elaborate in the way of lighting, therefore. If you feel like sitting around after dinner (and the insects cooperate), simply build up the fire a little. For undressing in the tent, a folding candle lantern provides adequate light. One rectangular design, elegantly brass-plated, with isinglass windows, seems to have been around since the Civil War. Backpackers favor a newer, cylindrical type that originated in France and telescopes down to under 5 inches for packing; note however, that this French lantern *doesn't stand;* it must be hung from one of the tapes usually sewn into the tent peak, but it seems not to produce enough heat to be dangerous even for nylon (the older, rectangular lantern can stand *or* hang). Half a dozen 4-inch candles should see you through a two-week trip, but the supermarket variety tend to soften into surrealist curves and loops in hot weather; sticklers can use, instead, a harder candle designed especially for the purpose. Considering the vulnerability of tent floors, especially nylon, put something solid and fireproof under any candle lantern: a flat rock or a metal tackle box; if the candle burns down or the lantern tips over, it could make a hole in a tent floor in seconds.

Since time immemorial in our family, the last camping activity of the day has generally been a word game played in the darkened tent while the players, one by one, drop off to sleep (game's end, rarely more than fifteen minutes). Books all around are just as sleep-inducing, and the candle lantern provides enough light for those few minutes before drowsiness triumphs (a relief from cards, too, on a rainy day when you're stuck in the tent). Even paperbacks I don't mind losing I pack in plastic bags to be sure they last the trip. For the after-lights-out trip out of the tent for a final cup of water or whatever, a flashlight is handy, and I keep one within reach. Roll it up in a sleeping bag when you're traveling, to protect it from damp, and that way it will wind up in the tent, where it belongs. For more light in such situations (and an effective nightime signal in emergencies), you might consider one of the sealed, plastic, 6-volt models that promise both to stay dry and to float, if they have to, and are not too heavy. If you'll remember to check or replace bulbs and batteries before setting

out, you needn't bother to carry spares on a two-week trip.

If you must have the sort of brilliant lamp that will illuminate a whole camp site when hung from a tree branch, several of the stove makers will provide it (Bleuet and Coleman, for instance). It's a matter of taste, but that's more light than I want. A more serious objection is that they're bulky, unyielding objects that don't fit into a pack very well: in daylight, you can identify the users because they're carrying their lanterns along the portage trails in their hands, generally with several other bits of gear they haven't yet managed to lose. And the big lamps mean just that much more fuel that has to be carried, a further nuisance. Leave the lamp at home and use the dark for sleeping, I'd say.

While it is not necessary to have a lot of light in a camp, many canoe campers prefer the luxury of a gas lantern. (Coleman Co.)

First Aid, Repairs, and Personal Care. On a canoe trip, first aid begins with prevention. You don't have to be a bred-in-the-bone woodsman to handle your canoe, in and out of the water, with care and caution, treating rapids, falls, and sudden storms with common-sense respect. The same unhurried carefulness applies to the few other possible canoe-camping hazards—ax or saw, fire, unknown plants that may or may not be edible, animals. You have a double motive for taking care of yourself. Apart from your own discomfort, if you hurt yourself you may spoil the trip for the others you're traveling with, perhaps even, in remote country, endanger them.

For minor, day-to-day scrapes, your first-aid kit should include the following items: adhesive bandages in several sizes; gauze pads; a roll of gauze bandage and another of elastic bandage (useful for sprains); iodine rather than Mercurochrome (stronger when needed, doubling as a water purifier); perhaps also some zinc-oxide powder (mild, good for open abrasions, bad burns); Unguentine (an old-time burn ointment, still more effective than the newer sprays); tweezers and possibly a small pair of scissors (but your sheath knife will do); and aspirin. You can buy these ingredients and a few others in a variety of kit forms from most outfitters, saving you the trouble of assembling them and providing a compact case to carry them in. For canoeing in places like the Everglades and some other parts of the South, where poisonous snakes are common, you should probably add a snake-bite kit. Remember, though, that most snakes are *not* poisonous and, like other wild animals, are as nervous of you as you probably are of them; resist the impulse to smash anything that slithers across your path—it's simply in a hurry to escape. Let it!

The old-fashioned bandanna handkerchief is big enough to bind a wound, tie a splint, or make a sling, and has many other uses.

No matter how tough you think your skin is, on a bright day on the water a periodic application of suntan lotion is in order. (For myself, the object is preventing suntan/burn—one reason for long pants and sleeves plus an antisun lotion on the few exposed places.)

In summer in areas where the mosquitoes are thick, the first line of defense is a breezy campsite, on a point or island (as I suggested earlier). The smoke from your campfire will repel the few hardier insects that can cope with the wind. Out on the water, the breeze from your movement will carry off any mosquitoes that try to follow. As a further protection, once the tent is up make a point of keeping the mosquito netting zipped shut and go in and out as little as possible. When everyone's in for the night, use your flashlight or lantern to find any mosquitoes that have come in with you and knock them off with a judicious use of insect repellent. *Don't* try to use the same stuff to clear the whole campsire; apart from the huge quantities of insecticide it would take and the possible health hazards to you, it really doesn't work. Bear in mind, too, that mosquitoes and flies have their own insect predators: the mosquito hawk, which looks like a treble-size mosquito; a black wasp (name unknown to me) that bears a striking resemblance to an oversize housefly and lives by eating them; and dragonflies, which relish mosquitoes and all kinds of flies and can do wonders in making a swampy campsite tolerable to humans. Keep your spray off these insects. They're on your side.

Wet, shady portages will probably be the one place where normal precautions against mosquitoes won't work. Properly chosen clothes help, but for such occasions you'll want a good insect repellent as well.

The ones that work best are those with the highest percentage of N, N-diethyl-meta-toluamide, commonly called DEET. Use insect repellents with 50 percent or more DEET. Keep in mind that insect repellents will take the finish off canoe paddles, fishing lures, watch crystals, fishing rods, etc. Use it with care and wash your hands well before handling such items as named above.

In the Far North, you may have to resort to a head net, perhaps even gloves.

The secret of finding a particular article in any of the several packs you're likely to carry is *association*. That's why I carry in my tackle box one tool whose real purpose is first aid: a pair of alligator-jaw pliers with a wire-cutting edge. While the pliers serve mainly to extract a deep-swallowed hook from a fish's mouth, you'll need them if you ever have the misfortune to hook yourself. The problem is a hook that's gone in barb deep. In that case, don't try to pull it out again; that will make the wound worse. Instead, push the hook on through on it's own curve until the barb comes out on the other side; then use the pliers to cut it off. And of course, after pulling out what's left of the hook, sterilize and bandage the double wound.

Again working by association, I stow everything that seems like a toiletry in a cloth, drawstring bag ("ditty bag" is the old-fashioned term) and keep it with the cooking kit: toothbrush and toothpaste, hand soap, medicines that have to be taken regularly, comb and brush, nail clippers, nail brush, etc. That's the place, too, for whatever you use as shaving equipment, if you feel like bothering (guides, the real pros in the canoers' world, do)— including, in that case, an unbreakable steel mirror (no bad luck). Those with a not-too-heavy beard and strong feelings about frequent shaving can use a light, battery-powered shaver. If you're a stickler about washing your hands before lunch, you might want in a pocket a small tube of one of the new concentrated liquid soaps made for the purpose, with a spare in the ditty bag. (I've tried those and found them so effective in cold water for grease, soot, and general grime that I now regard them as more needful than luxurious.) And don't, finally, forget the toilet paper, squeezed flat to save space, in a plastic bag to stay dry, and packed where it's easy to find—in the cooking kit, let us say (association again!). If you run out, you can imitate our forefathers by substituting a nonhairy leaf, such as maple.

To repeat what I've suggested in earlier chapters, waterproof cloth tape is good for so many kinds of quick repairs—the canoe, paddles, all fabrics, even your boots—that a roll belongs somewhere in your kit. (The same kind of nylon used in tents is also available in the form of adhesive tape, but it's harder to come by and relatively a lot more expensive than the hardware-store variety.) In addition to the bow and stern lines on the canoe, a 50-foot length of medium nylon rope is useful for such things as tying down the tent against a storm, drying wet clothes, and hanging the food pack out of bears' reach; you might carry it with the tape. Twine will do some of the same jobs and can be used for resewing a ripped pack or tying shut plastic food bags; it will also replace a broken bootlace, if you forgot to bring an extra pair. Elastic tie-downs with hooks at either end are inexpensive and do well for battening the tent or tying into the canoe anything meant to stay there.

HUNTING AND FISHING

Canoeing and hunting go hand in hand today as they did 150 years ago. In the fall there are those who set out after deer, squirrels, waterfowl, moose, and caribou by canoe. It is a very practical way to getting where the game is and away from areas of heavy hunting pressure.

As for fishing, I've never thought of my canoe trips as primarily fishing trips, in the sense that that was their chief purpose. But fishing for me is a part of the whole that canoeing is, and one I wouldn't willingly leave out.

Fishing gear is so much a matter of personal preference—and of what you're fishing for and where—that I can't offer much in the way of specific advice. There are, however, some general pointers to keep in mind. As with every other kind of equipment, your tackle can easily balloon to unwieldy proportions unless you limit it to essentials. Keep the lures down to a few you like and are sure of, so you can fit them (along with a spare line, a few extra leaders, perhaps a reserve reel) into a flat, light tackle box. If you choose the box and what goes in it with care, you can tie it under a canoe seat with webbing straps and it will always be handy when you're ready to go fishing. A big tackle box, on the other hand, with several trays, is awkward to fit into a pack, can't be tied into the canoe without spoiling the balance on portages, and will make a general nuisance of itself.

PACKS AND PACKING

If you're a hiker planning your first canoe trip, you probably have one or more of the rigid, rectangular aluminum pack frames, with separate, fitted nylon pack bag, that are generally favored for hiking. You *can* use a pack of that type for canoeing, but it won't be satisfactory. It's designed for carrying a fairly light, compact load (up to 40 or 50 pounds) over long distances. As a canoer on a trip of a week or two, your requirements are the opposite: a comparatively heavy, bulky load on the short distances of a typical portage (as much as a mile is exceptional). Moreover, because the hiking pack is designed to carry the weight high up on

When carrying fishing tackle on a canoe trip, keep your gear compact and take only what is needed. (The Coleman Co.)

the back, centered at shoulder level, it won't stand up in the canoe but has to be laid flat, taking up undue space for the weight and awkward to get in and out. Although hiking packs are now the most widely available type from outfitters and sporting-goods stores in all parts of the country, *don't buy one* if canoeing is your primary purpose. What you need is a Duluth pack, which will cost you about half what a good pack frame and bag currently sell for. Or outfitters in the U.S. and Canadian canoe country will rent you the packs you need, at modest rates.

The Duluth Pack. This is the type of pack nearly all canoers use. Essentially, it's a big canvas bag shaped something like a Manila mailing envelope, usually with flat seams at the sides and bottom, and a large, square flap that straps down over the top. North of the border, a pack of the kind described may be called a Canadian, canoe, or Hudson's Bay pack, but I'll stick with the American term. By whatever name, the great advantage of a Duluth pack is that it will carry *a lot*, in sizes and shapes that would be awkward to fit into a pack of any other type; it seems as if there's always room for one more item that has to be squeezed in. It evolved from the North American fur trade, and enthusiasts claim that over the centuries it's transported a greater tonnage of furs, trade goods, and supplies than any other nonrigid container that men have mounted on their backs. A good one will probably last you as long as you live.

The most usual dimensions for a Duluth pack are 24 inches wide by 28 inches high. In that size, there will be three straps on the flap closed with buckles on the front so that the pack can be tied down tight whether it's half full or loaded to capacity. Wide (2¼-inch) leather or webbing shoulder straps on the other side also attach to buckles so that their length can be adjusted to fit big or small people. The bigger Duluth packs are also provided with what's called a *tump strap* (or *head strap*), an American Indian idea for making big loads easier to carry: the canvas strap goes over the forehead and transfers some of the weight from back and shoulders to neck. (Great World makes an elegant leather tump strap that can be lashed to any pack not already equipped with one.) For my own use, I prefer a pack with leather shoulder straps, because they're more durable and more comfortable (you

can get or make foam-rubber pads for the straps if you have tender shoulders, but you don't really need them). In heavy-duty canvas (18-ounce), a 24 × 28-inch pack with tump strap and hand-riveted shoulder straps will cost you a little more. A pack the same size in 15-ounce canvas, with machine-riveted webbing shoulder straps, will cost a lot less, and smaller sizes are proportionately less expensive (suitable for children or for carrying the cooking kit). With a 6-inch set-out at sides and bottom, the Duluth pack offers a rectangular interior space and an even greater carrying capacity than the usual envelope-flat design, but that's probably more than you'll need (or want to carry) for any but a very long canoe trip. The biggest Duluth pack now available, appropriately called a Paul Bunyan Special (28 inches wide by 30 inches high with a 6-inch

The canvas Duluth packs have trump straps, leather shoulder and closure straps, and will last through a lifetime of canoeing. (J. Wayne Fears)

set-out), has plenty of room for all the sleeping bags, air mattresses, pajamas, the tent, lamp or lantern, and other night-time conveniences. It's a handful, though, and if packed with anything heavy (food, for instance) it's just too weighty for convenient handling. The 18-ounce canvas, with tump strap and leather shoulder straps, is much more appropriate for a pack of this size.

In the north-midwestern canoe country on both sides of the border, you can buy Duluth packs from just about any canoe outfitter. Waters, Inc., in Ely, Minnesota, has an unusually complete line with several exclusives. You can order direct from the leading manufacturer, the Duluth Tent and Awning Company. Elsewhere, though, packs of this type are harder to come by, though canoe outfitters that handle them can be found in the Adirondacks, New England, and some other eastern states. Another Duluth-type canoe pack is the Superior pack

made by CLG Enterprises. These packs are of high quality and come in several convenient sizes.

Although the Duluth pack is the one most generally used by canoers, two other systems have their proponents. A relative newcomer to the field of packs for canoeing is the Portage Pack made by Grade VI. This pack reflects a rational blending of the carrying characteristics of mountaineering backpacks with the necessary simplicity and versatility of the traditional Duluth pack. It is made from ballistic cloth, coated with rubber or urethane to make it waterproof. It has a waistbelt and anatomically contoured, padded shoulder straps. It is designed to allow ample portage yoke clearance while giving a comfortable carry.

Another system that is being used a lot is the internal-frame mountaineering backpack, which is made by Coleman, Gregory, Camp Trails, Diamond Brand, and Himalayan. Unlike backpacks

The Superior pack is a high-capacity Duluth-type canoe pack.
(CLG Enterprises)

The Grade VI is a unique canoeing pack with the features normally associated with a backpacker's pack. (Grade VI)

with external frames, this internal-frame pack rides better in the canoe and can make the carrying of gear on a portage very easy.

Finally, if you carry photographic equipment with you, the best special purpose pack is the waterproof, almost indestructible Pelican camera case. It is the choice of professional photographers when canoeing. It is also a good case for storing other valuables you don't want to get wet.

Segregate your cooking equipment in a pack of its own. For myself, I use a canvas Norwegian mountain pack with a European-style attached aluminum frame. The canvas is waterproof, there are a couple of big side pockets that hold a liter each

of fuel for the stove, and the frame is made so that the pack will stand by itself for loading and unloading, but the main reason I use it is size. The dimensions (about 20 inches high by 14 inches wide by 10 inches deep—expandable, with a drawstring top) are right for my particular set of cooking equipment, with room over for such small items as the first-aid kid. A small Duluth pack would, however, do about as well, particularly the type with the setout (the smallest of these is 20 inches high by 17 inches wide). If you're traveling with a child, the cooking kit is a good one for giving him the feeling that he's useful on portages: his size and not too heavy.

*Proper packing can make
setting up camp easy.
(The Coleman Co.)*

BALANCING THE LOAD

One of the major reasons that canoes don't respond properly when they are loaded with gear is that the load is not balanced. A poorly loaded canoe will not steer correctly and it can make canoeing hard work. A canoe that is bow-heavy is difficult to steer even in smooth water, and one that is stern-heavy will shift directions even in a gentle wind. If most of the weight is on one side, then the canoe will be tippy on that side.

The most comfortable place for a passenger (and the best from the balance standpoint) is in the middle of the canoe, using the padded yoke as a back rest. To give him room and trim the canoe properly, you'll have to move the packs forward and back, again compensating for one weight with another. The same principle applies if the two paddlers are of different weights, as they probably will be with a husband-and-wife team (move a pack forward or back, toward the lighter partner).

Occasionally, you'll meet conditions in which there's some advantage to trimming the canoe to bow or stern. For example, if the wind's coming at

A properly loaded canoe will steer effortlessly, making canoeing much more fun. (Jim Henry)

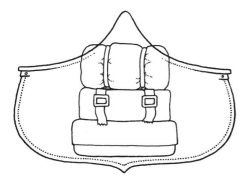

A properly loaded canoe will have the heaviest items on bottom and will be centered from front to back and side to side, with little of the load projecting above the gunwales. (Jackie Aher)

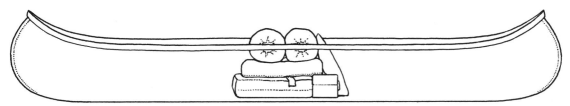

an angle off the stern, it will help you hold the course if you have a little more weight back there; and vice versa. But wind is so variable that it's hardly worth trying to keep up with: by the time you've shifted the load around, the wind will have changed. You'll just have to fight it out! In getting through swift water with a pole, it will be easier to hold the canoe straight, in alignment with the current, if you trim it a little heavy at the downstream end. In other words, in poling upstream, you want the canoe high at the bow, slightly down at the stern. When you use a pole to let yourself down rapids (*setting* is the canoer's term), the canoe should be loaded heavy in the bow so that it rides up somewhat at the stern (the person handling the pole can accomplish this by moving forward, toward the center thwart).

As we noted earlier, the canoe should be fully afloat before being loaded, and if the water is shallow and rocky near the loading place, it's advisable to hold the canoe out from shore and step into the water to set the packs in; teetering on a submerged rock may damage the canoe bottom, and it will certainly add an ugly gash or scratch. For the same reasons, I prefer to position the packs upright in the canoe, leaning against a thwart; it's easier to get them in and out, and there's less chance, therefore, of damaging the canoe in the process (or of dropping a pack). Even though the tops of the packs are above the gunwale line, the center of gravity will still be low if you've been careful to put heavy items well down in the packs—meaning that the canoe will be stable-riding, won't tip from side to side in wind or waves. In stormy weather or in descending a rough, difficult rapids with a course requiring a sequence of sharp turns, you might want to increase the canoe's stability still further by laying the packs down flat so that they're below the gunwales. But I'd say that if you're that close to the limits of what you and the canoe are capable of, shifting the packs won't give you much extra margin. It's the sort of wild water you'd inspect first from the bank, then run with an empty canoe—or not at all.

With everything loaded into the canoe, I take a last look around the camp site before shoving off. Partly it's simply a traveler's instinct for checking the dresser drawers for a forgotten shirt before locking the hotel-room door: have we left some wood by the fireplace for the next guy, whenever he comes? any telltale bits of foil or glass or plastic that we could just as well take away again? a wisp of smoke curling up from a fire that's not quite dead? That final inspection has a more general function, of course. All that carefully chosen equipment and food has the purpose of allowing you to travel freely, dependent only on yourself, and that freedom is diminished in some degree by whatever you leave behind or lose. Beyond that, it's a moment of farewell to the spot of earth, water, rock, and trees where you've spent a night or two, where you've eaten, slept, swum, fished—*lived*. It's a moment of anticipation as well: of the day's travel about to begin, of whatever new and fresh the remainder of the trip holds for you. Of all these feelings of departure and arrival, your loaded canoe, waiting for you at the water's edge, is the exact and concrete symbol. So, satisfied, you go back to it, help your partner in, grab your paddle, and shove off to another day. And *bon voyage!*

6 Traveling Free

When I was still quite small and the laws were a lot less protective than they have since become, the Fourth of July began early in January, when the catalogs came through the mail from the fireworks companies. For what now seems like weeks, my father and I studied them with the utmost seriousness, discussing choices, quantities, costs, making lists and revising them. When at length we settled on our order, and the carton of fireworks in due course arrived, every day I'd get it out, take everything out and look at it, study it, imagine what it would be like, and then carefully pack it back. The Fourth of July, when it finally came, was an all-day festival of sound and light that began with strings of explosions at dawn, reached a raucous climax sometime in the afternoon, and wound down in darkness to rockets, the glowing pastels of Roman candles, and the cool light of sparklers whirled and tossed. All those weeks of planning and anticipation were part of the final day and made it all the grander when it came.

A canoe trip is much like those boyhood Independence Days of mine, particularly if it's your first and you're doing some or all of the outfitting for yourself: weeks of pleasurable thinking, planning, and imagining, the results of which will all be compacted in the week or two of the trip. That, in effect, is what we've been doing so far in this book—planning a canoe trip—but the first steps are, of course, where to go and when, for how long, and with whom.

PLANNING A CANOE TRIP

If you're thinking about going on your first canoe trip, you *can* do all the planning, make all the arrangements, on your own. The chief purpose of this book is to help you do just that. Nevertheless, you'll probably feel more comfortable if you supplement that help with specific information on the many kinds and levels of canoe travel that are possible in various parts of the United States and Canada. In addition, there's a good deal of in-person assistance to be had from national canoeing and wilderness associations and from local or regional canoeing and outing clubs, which offer everything from a chance to meet and talk with experienced canoeists who have "been there" to local canoeing maps and canoe-trail guides to training programs and organized canoe trips of anything from a weekend to a month or more. And, finally, at the entrance points to much of the best North American canoe country, there are outfitters who offer as much or as little as you want or need in the way of general planning and who, in most cases, can furnish most of the equipment you'll need, from a single rented sleeping bag to a complete outfit; and similarly with food and other supplies. Outfitting is a business, of course, but the canoe outfitters I've known are in it first of all because they love canoeing and the canoe country, and making sure you have a successful trip is their first concern. In this inflationary age, the costs of such services are still on the modest side for the value given.

Once the canoeist starts looking seriously for information and practical help, he discovers that the sources for both are so numerous as to be overwhelming. What we'll be doing here, then, is finding our way through this thicket, identifying some of the kinds of information and professional outfitting services that are available, with examples of what you can expect from each. From a canoeing standpoint, the most useful material about the canoe country is firsthand, local, and specific, meaning that much of it is available only in the areas concerned (or through the mail) or from a great variety of local, state, and provincial government agencies.

In the final chapter of this book, we'll be looking at some of the major U.S. and Canadian canoe areas that are especially good for distance canoeing—the *where* of the planning equation—but there are traveled canoe trails in every state and province. Information about the possibilities is available, often without charge, from a great variety of government agencies (see Appendix 5 for sources), and there are also books to be had about much of the canoe country, from historical or broadly descriptive works to detailed itineraries (see Appendix 3 for recommendations). Once you've decided, in general, where you're going, you'll want to provide yourself with some of this material and get detailed, large-scale maps of the area. The U.S. and Canadian governments publish excellent maps based on aerial surveys that cover their respective countries (the most complete series are at scales of 2 or 4 miles per inch), and for the major areas there are maps geared specifically to canoeing, obtainable from private or state and provincial government sources.

MAPS AND MAP SOURCES

Once you've decided in general where you're going for a canoe trip, your next step in planning is to get detailed and accurate maps. You'll study them in figuring out your route, matching distance and difficulties to available time, and you'll rely on them religiously for finding your way on the trip itself. Since the matter of what maps to get and where to find them is a little complicated, we've postponed specific discussion until now.

For the Boundary Waters Canoe Area, the map problem is easily solved. The BWCA was carved out of the Superior National Forest, and the Forest Service publishes an excellent map that you can get by writing to the supervisor in Duluth (see Appendices). The scale (1:250,000, or about 4 miles to the inch) is ideal for over-all planning and, although a little small, is adequate for use on the trip itself. The map shows portages and all geographic features with great exactness. In addition, commercial maps designed for canoeing are published in the area and cover both the BWCA and its sister Quetico region across the border—a total of about 14,500 square miles of canoe country in fifteen overlapping maps. These commercially produced maps are to a scale of a little over 2 miles to the inch, about right for canoe travel, are very accurate for portages and other features of the canoe routes, and are printed on a parchmentlike, waterproof paper for which you'll be intensely grateful the first time you have to consult one on a rainy day. The maps are available from the publisher or from outfitters in the area (see Appendices for addresses).

In a few other parts of the country there are Forest Service maps, comparable to the one for the BWCA, for canoe routes that lie within national forests, but for most you'll have to start with maps produced by one or another state or local government agency (listed in the Appendices along with Forest Service sources). These are good enough for planning, but for actual travel will generally have to be supplemented with topographical maps from the U.S. Geological Survey. Since thousands of these have been published in several different scales, figuring out which you need and actually getting them into your hands is rather a job in itself. The first step is to order the free index maps for the states you're interested in from the central map office in Arlington, Virginia, or Denver (see Appendices).

From the index maps, you discover that the entire country is mapped to two different scales: 1:62,500—or about 1 mile to the inch (what the U.S. Geological Survey calls a 15-minute quadrangle); and 1:24,000—2,000 feet to the inch (7½-minute quadrangle). The 4-mile-per-inch series is on the small side: every inch represents an hour or more of paddling. The 1-mile-per-inch maps typ-

Maps and the knowledge of map reading are essential in wilderness canoeing. (J. Wayne Fears)

two map offices at the price most dealers charge. However you do it, don't order without first studying the appropriate index maps; it's a complicated matter.

From the canoeing standpoint, Canada is rather better off for maps than the United States. For the two major canoe areas in Ontario, the Quetico and Algonquin parks, excellent planning maps, showing portages, are available free from the park headquarters or from the Ontario tourist office in Toronto (see Appendix 4 for addresses). Both are to a scale of 1:250,000, which by now you know works out to about 4 miles to the inch—a little small-scale for actual travel but usable, once you adjust, since the maps are exceptionally accurate. There are similar maps for some other national and provincial parks that are good for canoeing, and, as we noted in the previous chapter, the provincial governments supply booklets describing other canoe routes, with route plans that will do for planning.

As in the United States, for a trip that's at all complicated, you'll probably want to supplement these planning maps with more detailed ones to a larger scale. The American set of 2-mile-per-inch maps for the Boundary Waters Canoe Area also covers the Quetico, but elsewhere you'll need the maps published by the Canadian federal government in Ottawa (see Appendix 4 for address). There are two separate systems of interest to the canoer: one to a scale of 1:250,000, which covers most of the country, though not always with maps in completely final form; and a large-scale system to a scale of 1:50,000 (1¼ inches to the mile), still only about half-finished. The first step in ordering the 1:250,000 maps is to write for the index map (one covers the whole country); for the 1:50,000 series, you need to start with an *index of the index maps* (there are eighteen, not corresponding to provinces or territories), get the index map for the region you're interested in, and *then* order specific maps. Generally speaking, since systematic mapping of Canada is a comparatively recent undertaking, the available maps are more up to date than their American counterparts.

One other Canadian map system will be ideal for canoeing, when completed: a 1:125,000 series, which (you guessed it!) works out to about 2 miles to the inch. So far, however, only a few maps are available in this scale, covering a large part of Ontario and scattered quadrangles elsewhere.

ically show quadrangles about 13½ miles square, with the consequence that you may need ten or fifteen maps to cover a trip of only a week or two, making a cumbersome bundle to carry and protect from weather. (One solution practiced by a number of serious hikers and canoers is to trim off the extraneous parts of the series of maps needed for a trip, then stick them together with rubber cement or transparent tape to show the intended route in a continuous strip that won't be too bulky and can be folded, with care, to fit a map case.)

Each state map index lists libraries and dealers that attempt to stock all the available maps for their region, and if you live near one of them you'll be able to examine or buy the maps you want in person. Or you can order the maps from one of the

A clear-plastic map case is essential for protecting your maps in the course of a canoe trip. (Folding them to fit the case so that the route will be visible takes a certain amount of forethought.) Even in a case, however, maps printed on ordinary paper (all except the commercial maps for the Boundary Waters Canoe Area) will be subjected to moisture and dirt and will wear at the creases. You can prevent that by treating the maps, as some canoers do, with the kind of spray varnish you can get from art-supply stores or most hardware stores; put on several coats and let each dry thoroughly before spraying the next. Apart from making the maps last long enough to get through the trip or preserving them for the next time—considering the nuisance of getting them in the first place—I like to save my maps as a kind of visual summary of a trip I've enjoyed. Perhaps you will too.

There are a couple of map accessories that are moderately useful. A *map measurer* is an instrument with a revolving wheel geared to a gauge that converts map distances to inches, centimeters, miles, or kilometers, according to the scale of the map. They're handy in the planning stage, once you have your maps, particularly for a long trip, in which distance (and time) may be critical. They're available from map stores and a few outfitters. A large-frame *magnifying glass* will also be handy at the planning stage, if you see through middle-aged eyes. Maps at a scale of 4 miles to the inch or more cram so much detail into a small space that I find them hard to follow without optical help.

The Superior pack has a convenient water-repellent map case on its cover. (CLG Enterprises)

I think of a *compass* as, first of all, an accessory to a good map. The best way to keep from getting lost on an unfamiliar lake is to follow the map closely all the way, identifying each point, island, and indent as it comes along. Even so, however, there will be times when it's difficult to relate what the map shows to the particular waterscape in front of you, and in such situations a compass can be decisive. If you're going to use a compass, I'd recommend one like the Silva Huntsman, which has a safety-pin arrangement for clipping onto your shirt so that it will never be buried in a pack if you happen to need it.

With accurate maps, you can figure your route to fit the available time and do so as closely as your inclinations demand. In the flat-water midwestern lake and river country, you can expect to travel 10 or 15 miles per day without pushing, and going down a good-sized river with a moderate current will be about the same. Either way, you'll have time for hearty, leisurely breakfasts, exploring, picture taking, and perhaps a little fishing along the route and still be able to make camp at the end of the day with plenty of time to set up, cook dinner, swim, and fish. A lot of portages may slow you down somewhat. Even quite modest rapids take up time, too: the whole route should be inspected and worked out from the bank before you attempt it, and I like to study the entrance point from the water as well, back-paddling and holding off till I'm sure. The suggested average daily distances can, however, be doubled, if you have to, without undue exertion. Conversely, in planning the route, it's well to build in some leeway for the day you're windbound on a big lake or a strong head wind holds you to 5 or 6 miles instead of the 10 or 15 you expected; and if an all-day rain sets in, I'd rather stay in camp than travel in it. In addition, if there are children in your party, they'll be grateful for a day or two when there's nothing to do but laze around camp, try a little casting from the shore, perhaps go off by themselves to explore the stretch of lake or river that, for the moment, is theirs—and yours.

In general, you'll enjoy the trip more if you don't lock it into an ironclad schedule. Allow for serendipity—finding what you didn't know you were looking for. Let yourself go off in a different direction if it looks inviting. More than in most other forms of travel, you're *free* when you travel by canoe: you can go wherever inclination leads.

If the canoe trip is your summer vacation, you'll probably be taking it in the traditional months of July or August. Even in the far South, heat's not likely to be a real problem, though in the smaller rivers low water levels may be if the weather's dry; farther north, you'll be escaping from midsummer city heat to springlike sunny days and cool nights. In the leading canoeing areas July and August are also, of course, the peak travel months—meaning that in wilderness country on any given day you may be sharing the lake or river with two or three other parties. They're also the months when flies are most numerous, though by late July the mosquitoes should be past their peak. If you crave solitude and the best fishing, you might try to go as early as mid-May, ahead of the crowd; in lake country, the big muskies and lake trout, which by midsummer will have retired to the cool depths, will still be up near the surface, where you can take them by casting. Since the water levels are generally higher, the rivers faster, spring canoeing is for the more experienced canoeist—and the mosquitoes will be at their fiercest. Finally, if you can manage it, there's much to be said for a September or early-October trip in Maine or Minnesota. The insects will have vanished with the first frost, the leaves on the hardwoods will be starting to turn, and solitude, if you want it, will be real, not relative. As in the northland spring, the days will be sunny and brisk but at night you'll want warm pajamas and a better-than-summer-weight sleeping bag, and it will help to pitch the tent near the fire and leave a well-built blaze before you go to bed—though, as always, with care for the possibility of wind-driven sparks.

ORGANIZING YOUR GROUP

Travel in any form with other people is an intimate kind of experience: like marriage, it can bring out frictions and personal oddities that in the ordinary course of things would never reveal themselves—and a canoe trip is particularly so. As a group, you're free of the world, but precisely because of that you're dependent on each other. That's one reason canoeing is so fine for families: you're used to living at close range with each other and know or can imagine what to expect in a great range of situations. Other kinds of groups should be considered with care; physical stamina is less important than how you'll get along together in the day-to-day intimacy of canoeing and camping. Particularly for canoers of limited experience, a party of two or three canoes (four to seven or eight people) is a commonsense safety precaution: if emergencies *do* come up, you'll be able to help each other, but the larger group also means more variety, more fun. I'd avoid a much bigger group, however. With too many people, you'll find it hard to fit into most campsites, and the more there are, the greater the chance that some will be constantly lagging behind, on portages or in the canoes— gnawingly tedious for everyone else—or discover after you start out that a canoe trip isn't what they wanted to be doing after all.

If you're planning a canoe trip for a youth group—Scouts, Y, church—the size of the party may be a problem: you don't want to leave anyone out. You'll find it more satisfactory for all concerned if you break it down into groups of eight or ten, each with an adult leader, that can travel more or less independently, even if they're following roughly the same route at the same time. (That's the rule in some areas, such as the Boundary Waters country in northern Minnesota, where a no-charge permit is now required: parties no larger

If you're traveling in a group (here, Brabant Lake, northern Saskatchewan) in calm weather on a big lake, leadership is less important than it will be when descending rapids, where it is sensible for the most experienced team to go through first, setting the course for the rest to follow. (Saskatchewan Department of Tourism)

than ten, each with an adult who's responsible.) Whatever the group, as a practical matter one person will have to take charge of general planning and getting together whatever equipment and supplies are needed, simply to make sure nothing vital gets forgotten. That makes sense on the trip itself, too. Among the voyageurs, the leader of the party was known as the *bourgeois* and had the authority of a ship's captain, not in the Captain Bligh sense but as a matter of respect and trust, based on experience and judgment. A modern canoe trip is likely to evolve its own bourgeois—someone with the sense to say no and make it stick when everyone else wants to run a dangerous rapids or ride out a sudden storm; who'll make sure the tent's pegged down tight, the food safe from animals, the fire really out before you leave. Indian tribes and bands seem usually to have developed a similar kind of leadership, reflecting not submission to power but a recognition of wisdom and responsibility. It's a working model for the kind of primitive society in miniature that a party of canoeists becomes for the days or weeks of its trip.

With several canoes in the party and marked differences in skill and experience, leadership needs to be more formal. In fast water, the most

One responsible person should serve as the leader on any canoe trip. (Vermont Travel Division)

practiced twosome takes the lead and determines the course, which the others follow—*and no argument!* The number two pair brings up the rear, assisting any weaker paddlers in between who have difficulty. Make the descent one at a time, with intervals of 20 or 30 feet, back-paddling while you wait for the one ahead to start on down. The same general rule applies in storms: the lead canoe sets the course, determines when and where to pull out, and the rest follow. Mutual adjustment is in order. The strongest paddlers should set a pace that's within reach of everyone, but the novices will probably have to push to keep up.

CANOE ORGANIZATIONS

A liking for associations and interest groups is one of the traits that sets Americans apart from other nations. It's not surprising, therefore, that in the United States there are a great many national and local organizations concerned in one way or another with canoeing; the Canadians lag in this respect. Even if you're not by nature a joiner, there are practical reasons for hooking up with one of these groups. At the least, you'll be in touch with a clearing house for useful information about canoeing techniques, equipment, places. Several of these organizations sponsor group canoe trips during the summers in various parts of the country, an effective nad not too expensive way for a beginner to learn the ropes under trustworthy leadership, the only drawback being that if the trip is oversuccessful and too big, the experience will be more like summer maneuvers at Fort Bragg than a vacation. In addition, some local groups organize training sessions in white-water technique, an indispensable safety factor for most river canoeing even if hell-for-leather rapids shooting doesn't happen to be your idea of fun. You can learn a good deal about such matters from books, but unless you can afford a smashed boat or two as part of the instruction fee, serious learning begins in the front end of a canoe with a master canoeist in the stern. Apart from these formal benefits, there's more than a little to be said for the chance to get together periodically and simply talk with others who share your interest in canoe and paddle.

Of the several national American organizations, the long-established American Canoe Association is the one most relevant to general or distance canoeing. As a member, in *Canoe*, the interesting bimonthly magazine sponsored by the ACA, you have access to an up-to-date source of information on the multifarious state and local publications, a fair number of ACA pamphlets on techniques and canoe routes, and the large number of affiliated local clubs. A few of these local groups (notably the Minnesota Canoeing Association) are sufficiently strong and well organized to rival the national one in influence, activity, and general usefulness.

The American Whitewater Affiliation overlaps with the ACA in interest (with an obvious difference in emphasis), and like it produces publications for its members. As the name implies, it's a federation of local clubs. Although kayaking (and rafting) have a larger place in Whitewater's sun than canoeing as such, what the various affiliates actually go in for depends on where they are; some are connected with the American Canoe Association as well as the American Whitewater Affiliation.

In Canada, the Canadian Canoeing Association is the organization corresponding to the ACA, but as in most other areas of Canadian life there are really two groups, one English-speaking (this one, based in Ontario), the other French, the Fédération Québécoise. Perhaps because the provincial governments do such a thorough job of providing information about canoeing, there is not, in Canada, the multiplicity of strong local canoe clubs to be found in the United States.

Although their primary concerns are elsewhere, two other organizations interest themselves in canoeing. Besides its *New England Canoeing Guide*, the venerable Appalachian Mountain Club publishes John Urban's *White Water Handbook*, a sensible, brief manual of the canoe and kayak techniques needed for getting through rapids. Headquartered in Boston, the AMC has chapters throughout the East, several of which double as local canoe clubs. The West Coast equivalent of the AMC is the Sierra Club, based in San Francisco but with regional chapters that cover nearly all of North America. Although best known as a ferocious defender of what's left of the wilderness heritage (and a publisher of superb illustrated books dedicated to the same goal), the Sierra Club each year sponsors dozens of what it calls outings for its members: wilderness expeditions under experienced leadership at fairly modest rates that cover transportation and outfitting and leave the anxieties of group planning to someone else. Many of these are hiking or climbing trips (or depend on horse or burro power) and some are aimed at exotic portions of the globe, but several each year are family-oriented canoe trips down wild western rivers or through parts of the Canadian canoe country. For a novice canoer who wants the security of an organized group and informative leadership, the Sierra Club canoe trips are a good bet—and generally easier to find out about and join than the more casual group trips of the local canoe clubs and similar organizations.

Canoe travel forms an important part of the program of the Boy Scouts and the YMCA—provided you're young enough. Locally, both organizations sometimes provide instruction in canoeing technique (worth asking about). Don't, however, let yourself be talked into leading (or co-leading) a Scout or Y trip unless you're a proficient canoeist to begin with, already know the intended area, and possess a naturally winning way with kids in numbers. For those who are past the summer-camp stage of life, the American Youth Hostels are worth getting acquainted with. The hostels themselves are hard to find outside New England, but in cities as far west as St. Louis if an AYH branch is active at all there's a good chance that canoeing is one of the things it's involved in. In some places the AYH chapter is also *the* local canoe club.

Several organizations primarily concerned with conservation have, at least, interests in common with canoers and have played a part in the creation of the Boundary Waters Canoe Area and the national scenic waterways, for which we can all be grateful. Even if you're not a fanatical conservationist, you may well be led, through some aspect of canoeing—photography, the observation of and curiosity about plants and animals along the canoe-and-paddle routes, simple reverence for water and landscape—to the Wilderness Society, the National Audubon Society, or the Izaak Walton League. Depending on the terrain, strong local Audubon chapters will sometimes take to the water in pursuit of birds to watch—and do so by canoe.

OUTFITTING SERVICES

One index of the quality and popularity of a canoeing area is the number of outfitters it supports and the range of services they offer. By that standard, the Boundary Waters/Quetico region is preeminent, with dozens of long-established and reliable outfitters at the Minnesota entrance points to the south and in Ontario north of the Quetico Park. Other areas well provided with outfitting services are Maine, the Adirondack region of New York, Algonquin Park in southeastern Ontario, the Delaware River basin, and the Missouri Ozarks.

In general, in the eastern half of the continent, the minimum you can expect from a canoe outfitter is a canoe rental service, with auxiliary equipment such as cartop carriers or trailers additional (in such crowded areas as eastern Pennsylvania, rates may be higher on weekends). Most canoe renters are dealers as well. Particularly for the Boundary Waters/Quetico and Algonquin Park, *complete outfitting* is available, meaning that the outfitter supplies enough food for a trip of a specified length, with rental tents, sleeping bags, cooking equipment, and other basic equipment at a fixed rate per person per day. This is certainly the easiest and least expensive way to handle your outfitting if you're making your first trip, and the costs are surprisingly modest, all considered.

While some outfitters offer only complete outfitting, most also do *partial outfitting*: you can buy some or all your food from them and rent, at quite nominal charges, any equipment you don't happen to own. Even if you're well equipped for canoe camping and bring some of your food with you from home, you'll find it advantageous to do business with an outfitter simply for the sake of the contact. He can advise you on your intended route, current conditions, any special hazards, and it's well for someone to know where you're going and how long you plan to be out, in case you run into trouble, even in such areas as the Boundary Waters and the Maine wilderness, where registering with the local rangers is required. The outfitters' general advice and checklists of equipment and supplies help you make sure that you don't forget anything vital to the trip.

Most outfitters can also provide you with a *guide* if you want one, and, in a few places, that may be the only basis on which they'll work with you. In the major canoe areas, few people use guides any more—with systematic preparation and the help of a competent outfitter, you don't really need one—but in several respects it's an ideal way to make

Hiring an outfitter is often the easiest and least expensive way to make your first canoeing trip.
(Don Wick)

your first canoe trip. A good guide will know the route and the area as thoroughly as you know your own house, will do as much of the mere work as you'll let him, and will make certain you get to the spots where the fishing's best, if that's what you're after; even an experienced camper will probably learn a few things about canoeing, the canoe country, and the general lore of the woods. In the old days, the North Woods guides were generally full-time professionals, often Indian or part Indian—spiritually, direct descendants of the voyageurs and the original wilderness men. Today, they're more likely to be college students or young teachers, free for the summer; but the tradition continues.

In the American Southwest and the Canadian Northwest, "outfitting" has a meaning rather different from the one that applies to the east. In these areas, the big rivers—much of the Colorado, some of the steep tributaries of the Mackenzie—are *not* canoeable but can be run in big, inflatable rafts (heavily built wooden dories are also used on the Colorado). Outfitters in California, Nevada, and Edmonton, Alberta, organize such expeditions, trucking or flying their parties to the starting points, retrieving them, providing guides, camping gear, supplies—in effect, package tours through regions that by any other means would be absurdly dangerous or simply impossible but, in rafts or boats, with skilled leadership, are both safe and exciting; in the nature of things, the groups tend to be big—several ten-man rafts. The Edmonton outfitters will make similar arrangements for canoe travel on rivers where that's possible; otherwise, in the Northwest Territories, the canoer is pretty much on his own.

Somewhat closer to civilization, if your time is limited and your ambition is remote wilderness canoeing, flying in may be the solution. Canadian outfitters in the Quetico region, for example, can arrange to fly you to your starting point, fully equipped, in a light float plane and pick you up again at the end. Because these bush planes are small, the canoes are generally strapped on under the belly, across the pontoons, passengers and their equipment squeezed into the cabin; the ride, unless you're a born aerophobe, is no scarier than in any other light plane, and the seat-of-the-pants bush pilots who do the flying can be relied on to get you safely in and out of the lakes and rivers that make a patchwork of the Canadian North. From, say, Atikokan, north of the Quetico in western Ontario, you can get to the headwaters of the Albany River, flowing northeast 300 miles into James Bay, to the Hayes, Nelson, or Churchill rivers, each of which feeds Hudson Bay proper, or to literally hundreds of other famous and historic canoe routes than are still part of the canoer's heritage.

On a smaller scale, similar fly-in arrangements are useful in the roadless canoe country of northwest Maine. You can, for instance, get to the headwaters of the St. John River by plane, and that's the way to do it if you want to take the river whole, from its source. The alternative is several days of arduous poling up shallow rivers that are on the wrong side of the watershed from which the St. John flows.

For the adventurous and experienced canoeist who has felt the call of the vast wilderness distances, there remains one further possibility: The Hudson's Bay Company's *U-Paddle service*. "The Bay" (as it likes to call itself) has dozens of posts dotted across the Canadian wilderness south, west, and north of Hudson Bay, nearly all of them on lakes and rivers that include the great canoe routes of the past and present. You can rent an aluminum canoe at most of these posts, paddle it downriver to the next outpost, leave it there, and return

home. The likely starting and stopping points are the mining and oil towns scattered across the North, bearing such romantic names as Yellowknife, Nelson House, Fort Chipewyan; many are accessible by the scheduled planes of Northward Airlines, Pacific Western, or Canadian Pacific (which can also arrange charters to points off their routes).

Obviously, any of these remote trips will take a lot of planning. For a start, The Bay has to know *in the fall* if you're going to want a canoe during the summer. The reason for this is that the canoes are hauled in by road, and many of the likely starting points can be reached only over frozen winter roads that vanish with the spring breakup around the middle of May. In addition, although many of the Hudson's Bay stores sell clothes and camping equipment (and a sufficient range of food to allow for resupplying along the route), they're *not* in the rental business; most of the camping equipment you need will have to fly in with you, and you'll have to make your own arrangements. And finally, the distances are considerable: any canoe trip you make will run to hundreds of miles and several weeks, and skill, experience, and long-term preparation will have to be in proportion. Cautions aside, though, as I study the maps, and the possibilities fill my imagination—my canoe parting those solitary waters, unlimited except by strength and ingenuity—I'm ready to start packing, and the only real question is *where*. You may feel that call yourself; when it comes, answer.

ON THE MOVE

If you have to travel any distance to get to the starting point of your trip, the chances are that you'll do so by car—either loaded with camping gear (if you're doing some or all of your own outfitting) or allowing time to pick up food and equipment from your outfitter if you've arranged things that way. In either case, *don't* try to start out by canoe late in the day, even if the vacation time you have is limited. You won't get very far with a late start, you're quite likely to wind up trying to make camp in the dark (tough on the best of dispositions), and being tired to begin with increases the risk of an accident that could ruin the trip. Instead, you and your car can probably pull into a campground

Here, a desirable campsite along the Mackenzie River, Northwest Territories: a compact, open, windswept point on an island, free of mosquitoes and flies, where after a long day's paddling, even a rock makes a comfortable pillow while dinner cooks.

in the area for the night. Or treat yourself to a hotel or motel and a good dinner in town. Whatever the formula, work it out so that you can start fresh, fairly early in the morning, with nothing else on your mind but the trip itself. (I try to reverse the procedure at the end of the trip: a motel with plenty of hot water for scrubbing and shaving, a change into going-home clothes, and a good dinner topped off by a night in a real bed—civilized touches that seem doubly luxurious after a stay in the wilds.)

Once you're under way, it's well to set a rough objective for each day's travel and then stick to it. It may be a lake where you've heard that this year's fishing is particularly good (there's always one) or an island in an otherwise populous river with an attractive and secluded campsite. A few canoers seem to like to paddle hard for thirty or forty minutes at a stretch and then break to lounge and smoke, like the voyageurs, while the canoe drifts.

It's a matter of one's personal style, I guess. My own is to keep going fairly steadily and let the rest periods fall where they may. It may be no more than a cup of clear, cold water all around to sample the newest lake (hang a cup from a pack strap for the purpose so it will be handy without having to rummage through a pack).

As you travel, keep your eyes open for animal life in the water and along the shore: a beaver swimming a log back to his lodge; a bear or moose come down for a drink, as curious about you as you about him; a huge, ungainly looking eagle's nest silhouetted against the sky at the tip-top of a solitary tree. Those are moments for setting the paddles silently in the bottom of the canoe, for passing the field glasses around and digging out the camera for some pictures. In the North in spring and early summer you'll see, as well, a profusion of water-bird young—loons, several species of ducks and geese, gulls, perhaps, with luck, the great blue heron of the upper Midwest and southern Canada. If you sight a duck swimming erratically ahead of the canoe, it's probably a parent playing hurt to lead you elsewhere; look around for the string of ducklings hiding along the shore. Or perhaps even, if they're still very small, they may be concealed among the feathers on their mother's back. Gulls, which seem to like to nest on a rocky outcropping in the middle of the lake, will swoop at you with raucous cries if they have young to protect and you approach too close; since they nest in groups, you may find yourself with several white-feathered dive bombers darting and screeching around the canoe, not just a pair. They won't in fact strike if you paddle over to peer into the nest, but the mock assault is unnerving enough so that you may not want to find out.

It hardly needs repeating that in this season of cubs and calves, bears and moose should not be approached. Both will run from man in most circumstances, but with their young nearby they may be running *at you*. If you chance on either at uncomfortably close range, the old woodsmen's rule (which I've never had to test) is to stand still and talk soothingly until it decides to leave. Sudden movement on your part may be taken as a threat.

Fishing doesn't combine very satisfactorily with traveling. With two paddlers and a passenger trying to troll, you'll be moving a little fast to catch anything. For casting, you need to drift along close to shore, taking several casts into each shallow little cove. Save the serious fishing for early morning and after dinner, the fishes' natural feeding times, with perhaps a few practice casts when you stop for lunch.

Seeing animal life along the waterways can be the highlight of a canoeing trip.
(We-no-nah Canoes)

The passenger, if there is one, is the natural navigator and map reader; otherwise, the sternman had better keep the map handy in its case, perhaps tucked into the straps of a pack where he can glance at it from time to time without having it blow away. In lake travel, your primary concern is finding your way from one portage to the next, and if it's a good-sized lake, with deep bays and islands that may be hard to tell from mainland, that can be tricky. A compass, which I rarely use, is not much help; you can orient the map accurately enough by the sun. The key element is your own adjustment to the scale of the map so that you can relate its two dimensions to the physical features you actually see. That may take you a day or two, like arriving in Paris equipped with your college French courses, when everyone seems to talk too fast to follow. At first you'll do well to keep a close watch on the map, identifying each island and shoreline indentation as you pass so that you'll know constantly exactly where you are.

On a river, following the route is no problem, but the map helps you anticipate rapids, falls, and other hazards. Since a rapids or waterfall is made by a sharp drop in the riverbed, you often can't see it from upriver, and if the wind's behind you, you may not hear it, either. Since the river will often be narrow as well as steep at a rapids, the current is generally slower along the banks, perhaps eddying back, stronger in the middle. If the rapids is short and easy enough so that you can see the whole length from the canoe, you may feel confident enough to run it without scouting from the shore. If not, look for a portage trail on either bank—signs of the wear of human feet; often an ax or paint blaze; perhaps, in a park, a sign of some kind. If there's a clearly defined portage, you'd better use it, but bear in mind that rapids feasible in spring high water may be too shallow for safety at other times, and one that looks easy enough at the start may be blocked by boulders or choked with deadwood farther down. If you have to cross the river to reach a convenient carrying place, work your way back well upstream along the bank, so you'll be able to stem the swift midriver current without being pulled dangerously close to the fall. On a big river with a powerful midstream current above a drop of several feet, you may need half a mile or a mile of leeway for a safe crossing. *Don't take chances.* Even a comparatively gentle river will impose harsh penalties for carelessness or misjudgment.

At any portage, it's a sensible precaution for one canoeist to unload while the other holds the canoe steady in the water. If you're using a one-man carry for the canoe (see Chapter 3), you may want your partner to help you get it up or at least stand by just in case, then go ahead of you with a pack to scout the landing at the other end and help you get the canoe down and into the water. If you've chosen your packs with carrying in mind, you'll probably be able to make the portage in one go, particularly toward the end of the trip, as packs get lighter and it's easier for one person to carry two of them, one on top of the other (or canoe plus pack, the system most guides use).

On a long portage, you may need a rest part way, but try to do it without setting down the pack or canoe: it saves the energy required to get it up again. With a pack, look for a big rock or fallen tree where you can half sit while you take a breather. With the canoe, look for a natural canoe rest that will support the bow while you let the stern down to the ground—two trees growing close together in a V, a crotch or limb at the right height. When you're carrying the canoe, especially on a trail that's rocky or slippery with mud, don't hurry: take deliberate, wide-braced steps; if you come to a log across the trail that's too high to step across easily, let the canoe down on it, get across and then slide the canoe over along the gunwales until you can pick it up again. Unless there's something interesting to see at the beginning of the portage, I prefer to get the carrying over with and do my resting at the other end: travel is faster that way, with less waste time.

In lake country, the portages are generally clearly marked on the maps and at both ends of the trail, but matching those indicators with the physical geography isn't always so easy. The portages that exist today are mostly connecting links in voyageur and Indian trade and migration routes that have existed for centuries: near points between two lakes, rarely steep, often running beside a connecting stream—geological facts. Guided by the map, look for a low point in the horizon, a break in trees that indicates a stream, quite possibly with a portage trail beside it.

When you stop for lunch, all you should need to take out is the pack with your lunch foods in it—

probably, as I suggested earlier, the cooking pack, since it's small and light and will have the stove in it, if you feel like a hot drink. Be sure to pull the canoe halfway up out of the water so it won't drift away—easy enough to do loaded by lifting one end and letting the other float while you draw it up. If it's windy, though, or waves are breaking hard against the shore, you'd better unload the canoe completely and carry it up above the waterline: the chop might damage the bottom of the half-floating canoe even if it doesn't drift it away. With a soft bank and a calm day, you can use a painter line to moor the canoe, fully afloat, to the nearest tree, but make sure it's solid, not a half-rotten stump that may break or uproot if the wind comes up suddenly.

7 Emergencies

Canoeing is generally considered a safe sport; however, there are times when, due to poor planning, severe weather, or carelessness, emergencies do occur. Those who have considered these possibilities ahead of time are prepared for them. Those who haven't usually get into trouble. A canoeing emergency may be as minor as losing a paddle or as major as losing the canoe and all its contents to unforeseen rapids. Suddenly the occupants are left in a survival situation. Let's start with the most likely, least dangerous emergency.

LOST PADDLE

As I suggested earlier in discussing rapids, when your mind's on something else you can knock a paddle out of the canoe and lose it that way—because of its shape and length, it will tend to stick out past the gunwales when you put it down to do something else. Be careful to lean it on a thwart (so you can retrieve it again quickly) with the handle well inside the canoe, whether you're lifting the canoe over a rock or a beaver dam or landing to investigate a portage- or campsite.

Any time you have to pole the canoe with your paddle or hold it in position, save wear on the blade by turning the paddle upside down and pushing with the handle—as I've already said. In rapids, however, there's not always time to make the switch, and in a shallow, stony—but navigable—stream, you may be scraping the blade across jag-

ged rocks at every stroke. Either situation will leave gouges in the blade, perhaps split it. In fast water, prying the canoe over or around a submerged rock may produce enough stress to break the paddle at the throat. For minor repairs of all kinds, I carry a roll of cloth tape in my pack and it will probably hold a split paddle together well enough to finish your trip. Much poling with the canoe handle may roughen the grip enough to make it uncomfortable, a potential source of blisters. In that case, a little careful whittling with your knife will smooth it out again.

The obvious precaution against loss or damage to a paddle, of course, is simply to carry a spare. So that it will be out of the way and won't get forgotten on a portage, tie it to the back thwart and rear seat, blade wedged into the stern. Use light twine and bow knots so that you can release the paddle quickly if you have to—or use an elastic shock cord of some kind. The weight of the paddle won't have much effect on the balance of the canoe when it comes to portaging. On a trip of up to two weeks, one spare paddle ought to be enough, though on a longer trip it would make sense to carry two, tied in at bow and stern. Be sure the spare has the same size blade as your regular paddles.

LOST CANOE

On the first night of nearly every canoe trip I've made in the past few years, while the lapping

Emergencies can occur when least expected on a canoe trip. (J. Wayne Fears)

waters lull me to sleep in my tent, I have a sort of half-waking dream of water rising, floating the canoe, and carrying it away. Fresh waters are not tidal, of course, but the strong winds and high waves of an overnight storm can produce the same effect if you've left your canoe too near the water; a river with many tributaries can rise a foot or two after a heavy rain, and the release of water from an upstream dam will make an even greater difference. As a precaution, carry the canoe well up the bank for the night and turn it over; that will keep it from filling with water if it rains and make it less vulnerable to being knocked about by a sudden gust of wind. Leave your paddles under the canoe, where they're handy and less likely to be floated away in the downpour.

When you land to have lunch or look over a possible campsite, everyone wants to jump out and see for himself—with the result that no one re-

Cloth tape can be used to mend a paddle or canoe. (J. Wayne Fears)

members the canoe until it's drifting gently away from shore. Don't forget! Always lift the canoe half out of the water (or more), even if you're only stopping for a few minutes. If it does get away from you and you're sure of your strength as a swimmer, strip quickly and swim for it—from the bow, you can fairly easily swim it back. Or climb into the canoe and use that spare paddle to come home in style. If worse comes to worst, don't panic. Wind and current will eventually lodge the canoe against the shore again like any other piece of flotsam, and you'll be able to retrieve it, though probably at the cost of some rough and time-wasting walking. Don't let it happen in the first place!

CANOE SPILL

To the noncanoeist, the possibility of tipping over is probably the biggest single source of anxiety. It needn't be. As I suggested earlier, a canoe may *feel* tippy, but that's because it's responsive. Even in the trough of good-sized waves, it can heel far enough to take in several gallons of water and then pop upright again without going over. Still, not to tempt my luck, I wouldn't start out in a loaded canoe against waves of more than a foot or a foot and a half, and if they came up beyond that while I was out, I'd head for shore.

Canoe spills can happen to even the most experienced canoer. Knowing what to do next is critical.

U.S. law now requires an approved life jacket or flotation pillow for everyone in a canoe. The law also specifies that your life jacket must be within easy reach (not put away in a pack) but doesn't say you have to wear it. You'll put life jackets on your children and wear one yourself in fast water. No matter how good a swimmer you are, clothing and boots make the going tough, and getting dumped in rapids can give you a bang on the head at the same time. Even without injury, water no colder than 50 degrees will rather quickly exhaust you.

If you do capsize in deep water, the fundamental rule for a canoe is the same as for any other small boat: *stay with it;* and hang onto your paddles. The canoe will right itself and, even full to the gunwales, will still support you in the water: the older, wood-and-canvas types have the buoyancy of their materials, while those built of synthetic or aluminum achieve the same effect with sealed flotation tanks in the bow and stern. Holding on to the canoe, you and your partner can then—slowly!—swim it to shore. When you've reached a place shallow enough to stand, empty the remaining water, and carry the canoe on up—taking it out full could wreck it. After a ducking like this, a wood-and-canvas canoe will be heavy for days with the water it's soaked up, but the newer materials, of course, don't present this problem.

The rules for surviving a spill in rapids are rather different from those that apply in the middle of a lake. The immediate threat is not gradual loss of strength from a prolonged float in cold water, but a sudden bang on the head, which may have the same effect. Get over on your back, feet pointed downstream to fend off rocks, head up so you can see where you're going; control your direction by sculling with your hands at your sides. It may be possible to grab the upstream end of the canoe as it goes past and ride it down, but on the whole it's best to keep an eye out for it and steer clear—with its weight and momentum, a canoe can be as dangerous to you as a rock, hit head on.

Unless the water's very cold or you're far from land, getting back into a capsized canoe from the water simply isn't worth the effort. Although tricky, it can be done, however. The first step is to get out as much of the water as possible. Treading water at either end, the two canoers rock the canoe back and forth, sideways, to slosh some of the water out over the sides, then swing it completely over, as high as possible, to dump most of what remains. They then move to the middle of the canoe on opposite sides and one holds it steady while the other climbs in and then helps his partner over the side. To get in, you need a strong kick so that you can lunge for the opposite gunwale while at the same time flopping torso and legs over the near gunwale; even with help, not easy to do without taking in more water. A less athletic and perhaps easier method is to climb in over one end while your partner steadies the canoe from the other end. The canoe will be safe enough to paddle even if still half full of water, but slow—water's *heavy.* Even if you've lost your paddles, you should have the spare (one reason for tying it in). Failing that, it's possible to paddle with your hands, from a crouching position at bow and stern, where the canoe is the narrowest; but most assuredly not my idea of fun!

Even if you manage to capsize, you're not likely to lose your canoe or your paddles, which are equally floatable. The more serious risk is dumping your gear into water too deep for retrieval by diving or dragging. One answer to that unpleasant possibility is to tie in your packs. My father did just that on our first canoe trip, forty years ago—for the first few portages—but never again. The nuisance is considerable, and in lake-and-river flat-water canoe travel, with reasonable canoe sense, it shouldn't be necessary. On the other hand, if you're traveling a fast river with a succession of rapids that you expect to run rather than portage, tying things in makes sense. At the same time, your canoe can take on a fair amount of water without in fact being in danger, and your packs can get nearly as soaked that way as if they'd been spilled overboard. My personal compromise, therefore, is to use packs that shed water efficiently—and then double that precaution by sorting everything *in* the packs into sturdy plastic bags, tied shut. That way, the contents will be proof against prolonged wetting and probably buoyant enough for quick rescue in the event of an overturn.

HYPOTHERMIA

A major danger in turning over in a canoe during the winter or in cold water is hypothermia—the loss of body heat. Cold water is much more dangerous than cold air, as water drains heat away from the body twenty times faster than air. If you fall from your canoe into a cold lake, within two minutes your skin temperature will drop to within 3 degrees of the water temperature. If you have a weak heart, it could result in a heart attack. Numbness will occur quickly, because as your skin temperature falls, your body protects the vital organs by cutting back the blood supply to your legs and arms.

After the initial shock, your body begins to slow down. Your brain becomes confused from the decrease in oxygen. Delirium is followed by unconsciousness when the body temperature reaches 90 degrees Fahrenheit, and death, usually from heart failure, when the body cools to 85 degrees Fahrenheit. A person in 32-degree water will be unconscious in about fifteen minutes, in 40-degree water in thirty minutes, and in 50-degree water about sixty minutes.

A person who is swimming or treading water cools faster than one who remains still. Swimming and treading water increase the cooling rate by about 35 percent. Therefore, do not swim unless there is absolutely no chance of rescue and you are absolutely certain you can make it. If you are hanging onto your canoe, get as much of your body out of the water as possible. Anytime you are canoeing in cold water or during the winter, make sure that you are wearing a good PFD—one that will keep your face above the water if you should lose consciousness.

If a member of your group should become a hypothermia victim, move him to an area sheltered from the wind. Remove all wet clothing, handling the victim gently. Apply heat to the person's trunk by using a warm bath or heated blankets. If this is not immediately available, the victim should be embraced by a warm person and the two covered with a sleeping bag. If the victim has no pulse, administer CPR. In the case of mild hypothermia, shelter and dry clothing may be all that is needed. If the victim is conscious, he may be given warm, nonalcoholic beverages.

LIGHTNING

During the summer, sudden thunderstorms can produce dangerous lightning, and lightning can be a killer either on water or on land. The best defense is to make it a practice to watch the weather. When you see or hear an approaching thunderstorm, get off the water and seek shelter in a low area under a thick growth of short trees. Do not stand or camp under natural lightning rods such as large trees.

ILLNESS AND INJURY

As with our everyday life, any number of illnesses or injuries can occur on a canoe trip, especially on one of a prolonged nature into remote backcountry. The first precaution is for everyone on the trip to pass the Red Cross basic first-aid course. Next, anyone with any special medical conditions should know his limitations and be prepared with his doctor's guidance. The group leader should know of these special conditions and what to do if a problem should occur.

A good first-aid kit and the ability to use it properly is a good safety measure for any canoe trip in the backcountry. (ICS Supply Co.)

LOST OR STRANDED

Occasionally we hear about canoers getting stranded or lost and having to be rescued. This doesn't happen often, but it could happen to any of us. Strandings can be caused by many things, including bad weather, a lost or damaged canoe, an injured or sick canoer, getting lost on a side trip, or making a wrong turn.

The first precaution is to file a trip plan with some responsible person or agency before any canoe trip, including a one-day float on a stream near your home. Include in the float plan the names, addresses, and phone numbers of all on the trip. Indicate when and from where the trip will start and when and where it will end. A route of intent should be included. With this information, in the event you get into trouble, help won't be long in coming.

Those going on trips into the backcountry should have a knowledge of wilderness survival, including how to provide shelter, fire, and signals. Chances are you will never need to use these skills, but if you should, you will be glad you took the time to learn.

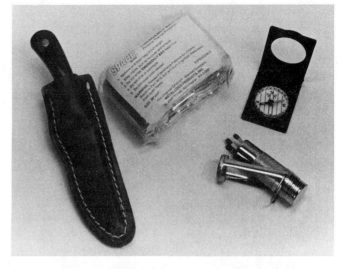

Every canoer should have on his person at all times a knife, space blanket, compass, and matches in a waterproof container. (J. Wayne Fears)

Stay calm and think. The first survival skill you will need is the ability to admit that you are lost or stranded. With this accepted, stop, sit down, and think. Convince yourself to avoid panic and stay calm. Accept the challenge and prepare to make the best of your adventure. If you have informed friends or family of where you were going and when you planned to return, chances are someone will begin looking for you soon. In fact, most lost or stranded people are found within a few hours after they are reported missing, and even in the more remote areas of the United States, 99 percent of these people are found within seventy-two hours.

Once you have gotten over the initial shock of being stranded or lost, look around you and evaluate your situation.

Signaling. Since people will be looking for you soon, your first concern should be preparing to let people know where you are. In most lost cases, a fire is the best signal device. At night it can be seen for miles from the air and a fair distance on the ground. Before dark the smoke can be seen from the air as well as from forest-fire towers which watch over most of the woodlands. Not only does a fire serve as a good signal, but it also keeps you warm, gives you a somewhat reassuring feeling,

and can be used for cooking if you happen to have food with you. More about fires later.

Other signal devices you may want to consider include a whistle, which can be heard farther than the human voice and will last long after a shouting person becomes hoarse. A small mirror or shiny object can be seen for miles by an airplane during the day. Also, a plane can spot a blaze orange PFD, white T-shirt, or even light-colored skin if the person is in an open area. A brightly colored canoe can be easily seen in an open area. Other signal devices include small aerial flares for night use and blaze orange smoke signals for day use. These handy devices may be obtained from backpack and sporting goods stores or ordered from outdoor catalog houses.

If all else fails, locate an opening in the woods and make a large X with logs, rocks, or with whatever is available. All airplane pilots know the X as a signal for help.

Any combination of these signals or, if available, the use of all of them, is the first step toward being found.

Firemanship. Except for a few experts, there are few among us who can start a fire without matches. Despite what many survival books say, there is no substitute for dry matches in a survival situation. Make it a practice to carry a waterproof match container with you at all times in the backcountry.

With this taken care of, let's get down to the second common misconception, which is that most outdoorsmen with matches can build a fire. Search and rescue officials find many lost outdoorsmen who are cold and without fire. In many cases, they'd had matches but exhausted the supply just trying to get a fire started.

Take the time to learn an old Boy Scout skill—build a fire with just one match. Learn what makes good tinder—a bird nest, bark from a river birch tree, pine lighter, or cedar bark. Don't assume you know this. Go out, find them, and use them to build a fire. In a damp situation, don't forget that dead standing wood, limbs, etc., are usually drier, as are the dead lower branches of evergreen trees. Take the time now to become a fire-building expert. It may save your life.

Shelter. One of your first considerations should be shelter. If it were a cold winter's evening, shelter would be a must. The easiest shelter to make is a lean-to, especially if you have a small space blanket with you. If you don't have one of these small cigarette-pack–sized blankets with you, consider roofing a lean-to with pine straw, loose bark, or whatever you can find. The overturned canoe can be used as a shelter. Use your imagination. To keep your mind occupied and off your problems, see how good a shelter you can make.

Other quick shelters can be made from blown-down trees and rock overhangs. Common sense and a little ingenuity can do a lot to build an adequate shelter. It goes without saying that many times it is not necessary. You be the judge of that.

Food and water. Many outdoorsmen think that food and water are not the most important needs in a survival situation. Far from it. It has been proven many times that most people can live for up to three days without water and easily three weeks or more without food. So don't panic and think you are going to die from the lack of food or water the first night. Odds are great that you will be found long before the need of either occurs. However, since you are canoeing, water is available.

As a final precaution, I like to have a few indispensables on me, just in case—matches in a waterproof container, a compass, my knife in its sheath on my belt, and a space blanket or sheet of plastic that folds up to handkerchief-size and in a pinch will make a tent, a screen against wind, or an oversized bucket for collecting and carrying water.

With proper planning, good equipment, and the use of common sense, chances are good that you will spend a lifetime canoeing without suffering any serious emergencies.

8 Canoe Country

Canoeable waters are, quite literally, everywhere. There is not a major city on the continent more than a day's travel from attractive, often challenging, lakes and rivers; and in most cases the distance is even less. These are the waters the canoeist can turn to for a day or weekend of relief from the pressures and anxieties of a densely urban life, for the fresh and refreshing perspective that is one of the rewards of slipping from behind the steering wheel of a car and gripping one's means of propulsion, a paddle, in one's two hands. Yet the canoe country we've been heading for all through this book is something more, grander, bigger, generally more remote. That is the landscape we'll be exploring in the present chapter.

The major canoe areas are as various as the North American continent itself, but in a canoeing context they have several things in common. For one, all are big enough for extended canoe trips, from at least a week to a succession of weeks or even months—the kind of long-distance canoeing that was once a normal and indispensable means of travel in much of the central and northern United States and Canada. In addition, the great canoe country is also in some sense wilderness country, which is to say that it's comparatively remote from the most tightly packed urban corridors; unless you're exceptionally lucky in where you happen to live and work, you'll probably not be able to set your canoe on one of the major water systems for a casual weekend: you'll undertake such a trip only with the thorough advance planning that, in effect,

we've been doing in this book. Conversely, the canoeing regions I've picked *deserve* that kind of preparation: all, in their different ways, are worth crossing a continent to experience, even if the chance comes only once in a lifetime.

Finally, all the canoeing waters discussed are within the capacity of canoeists of moderate ability and experience, properly equipped. And all are reasonably accessible: you won't have to mortgage your back teeth to get there, and, in most cases, you'll be able to count on local outfitters for some or all of your equipment and supplies, and for seasoned advice and other services.

These common characteristics of the canoe country—my standards, if you like, for selecting the areas described—require some comment.

Most of the values we connect with wilderness are positive: land where plant and animal life, earth, water, air, light exist in something like a natural balance; where men intervene on comparatively even terms, with a minimum of those material props that most of us twentieth-century humans unconsciously depend on. Ironically, in most of the United States, wilderness in that positive sense is an artificial and quite sophisticated arrangement, expressed in state and national parks and in wilderness areas, with their sharply defined boundaries and multiple exclusions—of lumbering, mining, hydroelectric dams, homesteading, private property of all kinds, whether for summer cottages or for vacation lodges and hunting and fishing camps. In the little more than a century

Canoe country may be found in all parts of North America. (J. Wayne Fears)

since Yellowstone, the first of the national parks, was created, we have learned that any area penetrated by railroads, highways, airplanes ceases to be wilderness; where difficult access and physical remoteness are not enough to preserve the fragile natural balance, limits on human numbers and increasingly complex rules for their behavior, with the means of enforcement, do the job.

All this is at odds with the strictly human value of wilderness: the freedom to go where one will, unimpeded by outside regulations and the pressures of human society, with no limits but one's own strength, skill, endurance. Yet the canoe traveler can hardly complain. You cannot canoe a river that has been blocked by log booms or turned into a series of lakes by dams. You cannot pitch your tent on the lawn of someone's summer cottage or on land that has been stripped bare by logging or turned into a slag heap by strip mining.

Wilderness in the original sense—wild land still virtually unpeopled, unregulated—has not disappeared from our continent. Across its northern third sprawls a nearly limitless land, where hunting and fishing remain the serious means of livelihood they have been since the earliest men wandered the earth, and on the vast lakes and endless rivers, the canoe is still the natural mode of travel that it was when the Indians taught the first European explorers the use of paddles: the northland frontiers of the Canadian provinces, the Alaskan interior, above all the Northwest Territories, where a relatively small number of Indians, Eskimos, and whites cluster in settlements scatttered across almost a million and a half square miles, and population densities are reckoned not, as elsewhere, by the square mile but in hundreds of square miles.

Sooner or later, if you come to care deeply about canoeing, you will want to paddle your vessel into those northern waters. The rewards are commensurate with the actual remoteness, the personal challenge: not least, the possibility of living in something like a balance with the natural world, not set apart from it by all our civilized dependencies. There is no real alternative if you are to travel that land even for a few weeks of the northern summer. Living *with* that world—not against it and the unrestrained forces that play across it unpredictably, not with the preposterous notion that you will somehow conquer it—is simply a matter of survival, natural in the fullest sense. In the process, you may learn also a few other fundamentals the northland's peoples have not yet forgotten. It is a great teacher, that land; demanding but just.

The canoe country of the Far North is not necessarily in itself more difficult or demanding than some you can find nearer to home. Within easy reach of most American and Canadian cities, you can, if that's your taste, paddle rivers (or big lakes and tidal bays) that reach or exceed what the whitewater people call "the limits of navigability"— what's humanly possible in an open canoe propelled by paddles. In the northern wilderness, remoteness, the huge scale of the landscape and the waters that fill it, and the scarcity of people are simply an extension of the conditions you face wherever you set your canoe, answering to the same skills. The moment of bravado or misjudgment that wrecks your canoe or sinks food, clothing, or tent in heavy rapids may, in the Far North, leave you weeks away from help rather than days or hours, but the difference is not fundamental.

Nevertheless, as I said at the outset, all the canoe country I'll describe in this chapter is within the ability of experienced canoeists of moderate ability, properly equipped. You needn't be an Olympic slalom medalist or a flat-water racing champion to make any of these possible canoe trips successfully and pleasurably. You *do* need to have mastered the basic paddling skills outlined in earlier chapters, practicing them in varied and increasingly demanding conditions, where possible under the eye of more experienced friends or in company with a local canoeing or outing club. Strengthening your canoeing muscles and learning to use them effectively are only part of the preparation for a canoe trip. Experience is also a state of mind, a level of judgment: knowing what you and your canoe are capable of and recognizing the limits when you reach them; knowing, for instance, when to portage around a rapids instead of attempting to run it, when to head for the lake shore before those scattered whitecaps build up to ocean-size surf that can swamp you.

To be properly equipped for a canoe trip means that your canoe and paddles will be adequate for the waters they'll have to negotiate, the loads they'll carry; that clothing, food, tent and sleeping bags, cooking equipment, first-aid supplies will suit the geography, climate, and probable weather. Some of these items are basic, the same wherever you travel. Others depend largely on the particular locale of the trip; to reduce them to checklists, you'll need to inform yourself as fully as possible about where you're going. The notes that follow are a first step. They should be fleshed out with books about the region, preferably with the focus on canoeing; with descriptions of the canoe routes, whether in guidebooks or the many pamphlets on canoeing available from state, provincial, or national government agencies, with the firsthand reports of other canoeists who have been there and of local canoeing outfitters; and with large-scale, detailed maps, which you'll study with care.

With the analytical precision that their language seems to encourage, the French-speaking canoeists of Quebec speak of the preparations for a canoe trip as "moral, physical, and material" and attach greatest importance to the first. By that they mean not only that you'll inform yourself about where

you're going, what to expect; you'll travel with confidence in your own strength and skill balanced by caution in the face of the unknown, the unpredictable, that is likely whenever we venture away from the familiar routine of daily life. It's a good point. The right equipment for the particular canoe trip is important, of course, but what counts, finally, is your own state of mind, both in your preparations and on the trip itself. Wherever you travel, under whatever physical conditions, every canoe trip is first of all an interior journey. Its most important events take place in your mind.

In what follows, I'll indicate in general what's available for the main canoe routes in each region in the way of background information, guidebooks, maps, and outfitters. Sources for all such material and the addresses of selected suppliers and outfitters are given in the Appendices.

MID-CONTINENT

Through the heart of north-central North America stretches a vast region of connected lakes and rivers, flowing generally north to Hudson Bay and the Arctic Ocean: the finest, most varied, most extensive canoe country on earth. Bear with the superlatives. It was here, as a child, that I got my first exposure to canoeing and canoe travel, here that I return, in imagination, as to a touchstone for the thousands of miles of canoeing I've done since then.

The preeminence of this central canoe country of the continent is programmed into its geology. Across it, like a great bowl curving gently upward around the rim, lies the Canadian Shield, the most ancient exposed rock on earth, its surface glacier-scoured into gentle mountain shapes and etched with the wild rivers and tranquil lakes left behind by the retreating ice sheet. The Shield covers much of Quebec, Ontario, and the Northwest Territories, holding Hudson Bay in its immense embrace and extending below the Canadian border into northern Minnesota, Wisconsin, Michigan and, in New York, the Adirondack Mountains. Along the southern edge of this region, extending west from Lake Superior for 200 miles on both sides of the Minnesota-Ontario border, something over two million acres have been set aside primarily for canoeing: the Boundary Waters Canoe Area in Min-

North America's best-known canoeing area is the Boundary Waters Canoe Area in northern Minnesota. (Minnesota Department of Natural Resources)

nesota and, adjacent to it in Ontario, Quetico Provincial Park.

Boundary Waters-Quetico. The border-lakes country has formed a natural highway probably for as long as it has held human inhabitants—which is to say since roughly nine thousand years ago, when the first people to leave a trace, ancestors of the later Indian tribes, arrived, at the end of the last ice age. Montreal-based fur traders, in the eighteenth and nineteenth centuries, using big freight canoes, followed these immemorial waterways to reach the great lakes and rivers of the Northwest, crossing the mountains to the Pacific and the Alaskan interior, descending the Mackenzie River to the Arctic Ocean—distances, paddled for the sake of beaver pelts, that make most modern canoe trips seem tame by comparison. Their long-established trade routes eventually determined the international boundary in the border-lakes country, leaving the main route open to traders of both nations.

For the French-speaking voyageurs, who manned the trade canoes, the border-lakes country was *le beau pays*—beautiful country, certainly, but also gentle country, soft country, easy in its currents and portages, rich in food of all kinds free for the taking; a description one appreciates fully only after traveling, as they did, the harsher country stretching to the north and west. For the modern canoeist, part of the attraction of the Boundary Waters-Quetico area is the knowledge that the routes he paddles, the portages he makes, the campsites where he pitches his tent have been imprinted on this land by thousands of years of Indian and voyageur history.

For those who care about canoeing or about wilderness and its preservation, the more recent history of the border-lakes country is equally instructive. For a century on both sides of the border, it has been subjected to various forms of exploitation—for iron ore and other minerals, lumber, water power, marginal homesteads, vacation homes, and fishing camps. Repeatedly, it seemed that the border lakes were destined for irrevocable change—to be logged over, mined out, built up. That did not happen. That it did not has been due largely to the perceptions of a few men who over the past fifty years succeeded in communicating their ideas to the two national governments: the perception simply, that whatever value

wilderness may have lies not in what it may produce but in its very existence.

The practical expression of that idea—the preservation of the border-lakes country—has been a series of compromises. In 1909, Superior National Forest was set aside in the northeast corner of Minnesota and in the same year Quetico Provincial Park was created. On both sides of the border, logging, mining, and existing private property were to be regulated but not abolished. In the mid-1920s, the nucleus of the Boundary Waters Canoe Area was outlined within the national forest as a roadless area, though logging roads continued to be cut, away from the lake shores. It was not until thirty years later that the Boundary Waters Canoe Area took its present form, confirmed by the Wilderness Act in 1964, for which it had been the working model: a million acres set aside for canoeing, from which not only roads but airplanes have been excluded (earlier, fly-in fishing parties had begun to exhaust the more remote lakes—canoe travelers can keep no more fish than they actually eat). In the years since, the encroaching summer cabins and fishing camps have been brought up, dismantled, and removed, and their traces have disappeared under the renewed growth of black and red pine and birch. Consciously and deliberately, the land was returned to something like its original state.

Today, the two parks together embrace what is estimated as 2,500 miles of canoe routes, though, since all the waters are connected, the possibilities are really beyond numbering. The lakes are comfortably scaled to the size of a canoe and its human occupants: a big lake, such as Saganaga, Basswood, Crooked, or Lac La Croix, which formed the voyageurs' main line along the border, may be as much as 3 or 4 miles across at its widest point, 20 or so miles long (with the wind blowing and the waves rolling, that can, of course, seem an ocean from the seat of a canoe); most are considerably smaller. The Laurentian Divide crosses the Boundary Waters Canoe Area about 35 miles west of Lake Superior. East of that point, the waters flow into the Great Lakes, to the St. Lawrence, and ultimately to the Atlantic; west of there, the flow is west and north through Lake of the Woods and Lake Winnipeg to Hudson Bay.

The connecting streams are generally narrow, shallow, and rocky, expanding here and there into short stretches of river broken by small rapids and, along the border, by spectacular waterfalls—Basswood, Curtain, Rebecca. Canoeing these waters rarely involves as much as a full day of solid paddling. The natural rhythm of border-lakes canoeing alternates an hour or two of paddling with, typically, a quarter-mile portage along a well-worn woodland trail beside one of the connecting streams or around a waterfall. As a boy, I thought of the portages as something of an ordeal, toiling under a heavy pack in the sharp clarity of the midsummer northern sun, but now I welcome them. Just as the paddling begins to seem tedious, you reach the next portage and a chance to stretch the legs, pause by a waterfall to take some pictures, perhaps gather blueberries or the tiny, sweet wild strawberries. Since the portages do come up several times in the course of a day, you'll plan your gear accordingly, to fit into as few packs as possible, with no loose odds and ends to dangle from hands and catch on shrubs and tree branches along the trail. Two people on a two-week trip should be able to fit *everything* they need into a pair of medium-sized packs, plus a smaller cooking kit—meaning not more than two portages per person on any trail, and if you're feeling strong you'll double up the packs and make the portage in one go.

From the American side, the town of Ely is the most central to the Boundary Water Canoe Area and is also within a day's paddle of the Canadian border and the Quetico (most Americans spend at least part of their trip in Canada). Other possibilities are Crane Lake to the west and, to the east, Grand Marais on Lake Superior, at one end of the Dawson Trail, a road that leads north through Superior National Forest almost to the border, with the entrance points to the BWCA on either side and to the Quetico at the terminus. From the north, Atikokan on the edge of the Quetico is the usual Canadian base town, within easy reach of entrance points on Nym or French Lake. Ely and Atikokan can be reached by plane, train, or road (Ely is about half a day's drive north of Duluth). All four towns are generously served by outfitters, Ely particularly so; most will provide either complete or partial outfitting and can also arrange for a guide, a service that makes an easy initiation for the inexperienced but is far from necessary. Both the U.S. and the Canadian park authorities or any of the outfitters will supply, free for the asking, planning maps for their respective areas; for the trip itself, you'll want the more detailed commercial maps.

The canoeing season in the border-lakes country extends from about mid-May to mid-October. If it's solitude you crave, you'll go early or late, when it's quite possible to make the entire trip without seeing another canoeist. The spring fishing is likely to be particularly good, with cold-loving lake trout up on the surface, which by midsummer will have retreated to the depths; a light frost will often have put an end to the mosquitoes by late August or early September, and a little later you can expect as a bonus, a display of autumn colors hardly less gaudy than in New England. (In the summer months, the mosquitoes live up to their northland reputation, but if you're suitably prepared—with an insectproof tent, mosquito repellent—and choose your campsites judiciously, they'll not trouble you.) Through most of the season, you can expect warm and sunny, not hot, days, interspersed with rain in a three- or four-day cycle; cool nights may make you put on a sweater or warm jacket in the evenings and get the breakfast fire going in a hurry in the morning, but will rarely go below the capacity of a medium-weight sleeping bag.

On our family canoe trips in the 1930s, it was unusual to meet more than one or two other parties in the two or three weeks we were out on the lakes. Several years ago, traveling the same routes with two of my sons, I saw dozens. The country did not *feel* crowded: the blue-gray smoke from another campfire at the opposite end of a lake is not a crowd. Nevertheless, the change is an index of the area's growing popularity and of a new hazard, still potential, for country that has survived so many others: overuse. The Canadians and Americans have treated it in accordance with their rather different national styles.

The 150,000 or more canoeists who enter the Boundary Water Canoe Area every year must have permits issued either by their outfitters or by the Forest Service. (In Ely the handsome Voyageurs' Center has a fine exhibit of the area's natural history, worth perusing when you get your permit.) There's no charge. It's simply a means of keeping track of numbers—and of making sure each party has a responsible leader and is not overlarge (ten, currently, is the maximum)—but the same system could also be used to ration use of the area if that ever becomes necessary. In the BWCA now one is required to camp at one of hundreds of official campsites, each equipped with a permanent grill for wood-fire cooking and, usually, a rustic toilet at a short distance—a way, apparently, of concentrating the leavings in a comparatively few places and making them easy to clean up. For the same reason, canned and bottled foods are illegal, a rule enforced with fines (freeze-dried foods in their foil or plastic packages have become the norm), and other cans (aerosol insect sprays, for instance) must be carried out. Resident hydrologists, assisted by computers, monitor the water quality as one means of determining if any of the lakes are becoming saturated with people; so far, the water seems to be as good as ever. At the start of each portage trail, an unobtrusive sign, identifying the portage and giving the distance, has replaced the older ax blazes; rangers walk the trails periodically, clearing fallen wood, filling in the wet spots. Although on paper the system sounds overregulated, in practice it's tactful and doesn't seem restrictive; given the alternatives, one accepts it.

Across the border in the Quetico, the Canadian system is a little more easygoing than the American "management" approach, relying on fees to keep the numbers of users within bearable limits. There's a modest charge for the permit to bring a canoe in and another for camping. There are no official campsites in the park; terrain, personal preference, and a camping history going back to Indian days determine where you'll set your tent. Portages are marked by blazes, as they've always been, not by signs. Visitors are encouraged to carry out any nonburnable refuse, but there's no law compelling them to do so.

Elsewhere in Ontario. Although the Boundary Waters-Quetico area comes close to being the ideal canoe country, Ontario—with what are said to be 250,000 lakes and 20,000 miles of rivers within her borders—offers limitless alternatives. The best of these for family canoeing is Algonquin Provincial Park in the southeast corner of the province, midway between Ottawa and Georgian Bay. Older as a park and bigger (2,910 square miles), Algonquin, like the Quetico, is a region of connecting lakes and rivers sculptured by the last ice age in the southern rim of the Canadian Shield. The water routes are more loosely formed in Algonquin, how-

ever: portages of a mile or two, almost unheard-of in the Quetico, are commonplace. Nor does the canoe reign supreme: there are summer camps and lodges; two highways and a railroad cross the park, though not near the main canoe routes. Being close to several of the biggest Canadian and American cities means that the park is heavily used but is also an advantage: if you live in the northeastern United States or Canada's populous southern tier, you're no more than a long day's drive, at most, from this very attractive canoe country, a welcome time-saver for anyone limited to a two-week vacation. The usual entrance points are by way of Whitney, Ontario, and the park's East Gate, near the midpoint of the southern boundary, or via Dwight, Ontario, and the West Gate, in the southwestern corner. There are semiofficial outfitters inside the park just past both these entrance points and a few others in the adjacent towns. Those who want to get a little farther away can go in by way of South River, Ontario, near the park's northwestern corner, and here again outfitting services are available. All the outfitters provide both complete and partial outfitting; Northern Wilderness Outfitters also offers organized trips for the young and inexperienced, with the aim of developing canoeing skills.

A descriptive planning map (scale: 3 miles to the inch) is available from any outfitter or from Ontario's Department of Lands and Forests. Detailed travel maps in the several Canadian topographic series can be ordered from the national Map Distribution Office in Ottawa (see Appendices).

Ontario's Ministry of Natural Resources publishes booklets detailing dozens of the province's other canoe routes. Most of these are in southern Ontario, easy to get to, comparatively short, and not too demanding. Of particular interest are the several in the North Georgian Bay Recreational Reserve, which includes a number of provincial parks and the historic French River, a link in the voyageurs' water connections with the West and still beautiful and comparatively unspoiled.

In a quite different category are the river systems of northern Ontario that flow northeast into Hudson Bay or James Bay (the narrowing southern extension of the former): the Missinaibi, Albany, Attawapiskat, and Winisk. Each is several hundred miles long and requires from two to four weeks, depending on your starting point. All, too, are big, fast, and thickly sown with rapids, particularly in the upper stretches. I consider them within the ability of medium-level canoeists who are properly cautious (you'll inspect the rapids, and portage or line any you're not dead sure of), but they require thorough preparation and, for safety, are best attempted with parties of two or three canoes. The logistic problems are considerable. There are few sources for supplies or emergency help along the way; except for the Missinaibi (which ends at Moosonee, with scheduled air service and a branch rail line), you'll need chartered bush planes to get in and get out again.

For the Missinaibi, the natural place to start is Mattice, which is on the Trans-Canada Highway and the Canadian National Rail Way as well as the river, about 200 miles from James Bay. The Albany, which has its source in Lake St. Joseph, about 250 miles north of Thunder Bay on Lake Superior, was one of the lesser fur-trade routes linking Hudson Bay with the Far West and North. Although you can, therefore, canoe there from several places farther west, the most promising jumping-off place is the village of Osnaburgh House, near the end of a gravel road running north from the Trans-Canada Highway and just east of Lake St. Joseph, roughly 500 miles from James Bay. The best way out from Fort Albany, at the mouth of the river, is a charter flight to Moosonee to the southeast, thence by train or scheduled plane. Paralleling the Albany to the north is the Attawapiskat. Lansdowne House, on Attawapiskat Lake, is something like 300 miles from the river's mouth and as yet beyond the reach of any road; you'll need a chartered bush plane to get there and another to return at the end of the trip (or else arrange to fly to Moosonee and proceed from there).

Finally, for the Winisk River, the put-in point is the village of Webequie on Winisk Lake, about 250 miles from the river mouth at Winisk on Hudson Bay. To fly to Webequie, the nearest charter point is at Nakina about 250 miles to the south or at the slightly larger town of Geraldton 40 miles farther down (both can be reached by road, train, or plane).

Upper Midwest. Wisconsin, Michigan, and central Minnesota all have extensive lake and river systems which historically were significant canoe routes and still have their attractions. Nearly all, however, are so thick with summer cottages and motorboats, so broken up by dams, that they can't be seriously compared with the great wilderness canoeing to be had in the nearby Boundary Waters Canoe Area. Nevertheless, all three states offer a good many short, challenging stretches of whitewater river which make effective training grounds for the wild rivers of the Far North. There are also a number of longer rivers flowing through rural or semiwilderness country, affording a week or more of fairly easy canoeing for experienced beginners and their families—preparation for more demanding canoe trails elsewhere. All three states publish useful free guides to their best-known canoeing rivers, and descriptive leaflets for several individual rivers are available locally; in addition, for Wisconsin there are three comprehensive regional guidebooks, detailed and professionally produced.

In our grandparents' time, the exact Minnesota source of the Mississippi River was a matter of considerable controversy, and it was leaders of the first generation of American sport canoeing who finally solved the problem. Modern canoeists can retrace their explorations. The attractive headwaters—meandering northeast before the river swells and swings southward—are narrow, shallow, and swampy, flowing through quite wild country and crossing several good-sized lakes. The distance for this section, from Lake Itasca to Ballclub Lake, is about 100 miles, but the whole upper portion of the river as far as Anoka just north of Minneapolis (a total distance of 370 miles) is frequently canoed.

In Wisconsin, probably the best river for extended canoe travel is the Wisconsin itself, which rises in Lac Vieux Desert on the border of Michigan's Upper Peninsula and flows generally southwest about five hundred miles until it empties into the Mississippi. Campsites, mostly in state parks, occur at regular intervals. All considered, the most interesting, least spoiled sections are above the town of Merrill. The river as a whole is generally easy, interspersed with dams (mainly in the central portions), reservoirs, and fair-sized lakes, some fast water, big riffles, and a few rapids that prudent canoers will prefer to portage. The Wisconsin Dells, where the river flows deep and swift through a series of canyonlike channels, are of great inherent beauty much vulgarized by tourism (the backwash from the motorboats speeding sightseers through the Dells is the most serious hazard the canoer will face on the Wisconsin).

Canoeing the Platte River in Michigan. (Michigan Travel Bureau)

The Wisconsin River connects with a number of worthwhile shorter canoe routes. The Kickapoo (yes, there really was an Indian tribe by that name), a tributary, joins the Wisconsin not far from the Mississippi—125 miles of easy canoeing through hilly country that can be stretched to a week's trip; a canoe-rental agency at La Farge will shuttle you to the starting point and pick you up at the end. The Fox River, flowing northeast from the town of Portage, has the interest of being a connecting link in the voyageurs' route that led from Sault Ste. Marie south through Lake Michigan, Green Bay, and Lake Winnebago to the Wisconsin River, the Mississippi, and points south (there was a long and arduous carry at Portage—as the name suggests). Near Lake Winnebago, the Fox joins the Wolf River, which in the 65 miles below Post Lake offers

several days of semiwilderness canoeing spiced with frequent rapids and falls.

Although Michigan is sprinkled with French and Indian place names that recall the voyageurs (from Detroit to Sault Ste. Marie), the state has no long canoeing rivers comparable to the Wisconsin. Several rivers in the northern part of the state are, however, good for pleasant trips of up to two weeks, covering 1 or 200 miles. The Menominee, which forms the boundary between Wisconsin and the Upper Peninsula before emptying into Green Bay, has the recommendation of avoiding the few towns in the sparsely inhabited region east of the Iron Mountain ski resort—from a canoe, it *seems* wilderness. To the east, on the Lower Peninsula, the gentle Au Sable, flowing into Lake Huron, is much traveled by canoers. The Big Manistee and Mus-

Canoeing the popular Ausable River in Michigan. (Michigan Travel Commission)

kegon both wander more than two hundred miles through attractive country east of Lake Michigan before falling into the lake.

NORTHEASTERN UNITED STATES

Geography did not endow the American Northeast with the limitless waterways that made the canoe the Pegasus of the Indians and voyageurs in the center of the continent and in the Canadian North. It is perhaps that smaller scale, however, that has made the region synonymous with canoeing as a sport since its inception little more than a century ago. Quite apart from their intrinsic attractions, the modern paddler will be drawn to the lakes and rivers of western Maine and New York's Adirondacks by the knowledge that he is following in the paddle strokes of Thoreau, the painter William Remington, and other canoeists hardly less noble. Although of more regional interest, the big

rivers of New England and the Middle Atlantic states provide varied and often challenging waters for distance canoeing in the backyard of several of the biggest American cities. It is no coincidence that two of the leading American canoe builders, Old Town in Maine and Grumman in New York, are long established in this section of the canoe country.

The canoeist headed for the waters of the Northeast has no excuse for venturing unprepared. In its sober detail and comprehensiveness, the AMC River Guides, published by the Appalachian Mountain Club, are models of what such a book should be. There are also useful free canoeing guides for Maine, Vermont, New York, and Pennsylvania published by the states (see Appendices). The Maine wilderness, the Adirondacks, and the Delaware Valley are served by knowledgeable canoe outfitters (names and addresses in Appendices).

Dozens of Maine rivers offer a day or two of

paddling ranging in difficulty from easy to barely canoeable. Among them, the Allagash Wilderness Waterway, with its lovely Indian name and its Thoreau associations, is unique in providing distance canoeing of considerable variety for the experienced canoeist of moderate ability. A narrow band of much-regulated wilderness that the state in 1966 carved from the surrounding millions of lumber and pulpwood acres, the waterway begins west of Mount Katahdin, northern terminus of the Appalachian Trail, in a series of lakes feeding the north-flowing Allagash. Telos Lake, the official starting point, is accessible from Greenville, Millinocket, or Patten by way of private paper-company roads (advance permission required). The Waterway ends 92 water miles north, just below the 40-foot Allagash Falls, but in practice, having portaged the falls, one continues the few miles farther downstream to the village of Allagash and the juncture with the parallel St. John River, making a trip of a week or a leisurely two; several alternative approaches to the system's headwaters may be used to extend the trip, but they're hard work (upstream stretches, long portages).

Since high spring water following the mid-May breakup and low water in late summer are both inimical to enjoyable canoeing, the best season for the Allagash is from about June 15 to early August (also the peak period for mosquitoes and black flies). Camping along the route is at official campsites only (grills, toilets), which may be crowded. State-licensed guides are encouraged but not required and are unnecessary for first-timers who've prepared for the trip with reasonable thoroughness.

No other New England river matches the Allagash's combination of distance canoeing with country that approximates wilderness. The Connecticut River, however, has several characteristics that recommend it to the average canoer. Its 400-odd miles are canoeable from near the river's source on the New Hampshire-Quebec border to the mouth at Old Saybrook, Connecticut, on Long Island Sound—a three- or four-week trip, if that's your pleasure, that breaks readily into shorter segments. The country along much of the route, while not wilderness, has the scenic attraction of New England's half-mountainous hills alternating with lovingly tended farmland, and even in populous areas the river can seem quite secluded; many of the riverside villages possess great charm and are worth visiting. Finally, unlike other New England rivers, the Connecticut has a long season: for most of its length, it carries enough water for good canoeing through late summer and into the fall.

The upper half of the Connecticut, forming the Vermont-New Hampshire border, is best, varying fast water and easy rapids with longer sections of gentle current and lakelike reservoirs (the Hartland Rapids, 6 miles below White River Junction, are serious, though, and must be portaged). The most practical starting point for paddling this section in its entirety is on the Vermont side just below the village of Canaan, and the water levels should be satisfactory from late May or early June onward, after the spring runoff (earlier, high water may be troublesome). Apart from the one big rapids, the main hazards are dams and their attendant portages; most of the latter are short and pleasant enough, but at Bellows Falls, 200 miles downriver, the portage is a long one down a village street, and you may want to arrange there for someone to truck you over it, or end the trip at that point.

In Massachusetts, the Connecticut River has good possibilities for carefully selected day trips but cannot be recommended as a whole (the human, industrial, and agricultural effluvia, which make the water unsafe to drink farther north—like virtually every other New England stream—here become noxious to eye and nose as well as intestines). From Windsor Locks in Connecticut to Long Island Sound, the river is broadly meandering, moderately attractive, and mercifully unbroken by dams. For the river's whole length, state and private campsites occur just about frequently enough to be practicable.

In northern New York, the large area of wilderness enclosed by Adirondack Park is recurringly threatened with final disappearance by road building, summer homes, large-scale real estate development, the several famous and long-established resort hotels that rim its lakes—yet it survives. The canoe routes at the heart of this region form a kind of Quetico in miniature sculptured in a final outcrop of the Canadian Shield: a system of scenic, stream-connected lakes winding among mountains that rise to 3,000 or 4,000 feet. The main route between the towns of Old Forge and Saranac Lake is good for five or six easy days by canoe and can be stretched with a number of variants or side trips; the devel-

A scenic float in New Hampshire. (Dick Smith)

oped campsites along the way are numerous and attractive. If your imagination is excited by a sense of the past, you feel the presence not only of Thoreau and Remington but of the early canoeing writer George Washington Sears ("Old Nessmuk") and J. Henry Rushton, one of the first canoe builders of the modern sporting era, whose designs are still unsurpassed. The foot trails that in places link the waterways are known as *carries*, not portages, the traditional American term still used in parts of Maine as well.

The Hudson River has its source as a narrow, east-flowing stream in mountains a few miles south of Long Lake, the main axis of the Adirondack canoe country. The upper river is a revelation if you know only the grandiose, much-polluted sections near New York City—swift and wild in the 75 or so miles above Glens Falls, demanding spring water conditions and skilled canoemanship, then widening out but still attractive as it turns south toward Troy, another 35 miles.

New York and Pennsylvania share two important distance-canoeing rivers, quite different in character in the two states: the Delaware and the Susquehanna. The Delaware's East and West branches rise near each other in the Catskill highlands and come together at Hancock, New York, to form the New York-Pennsylvania line. The river is canoeable from Hales Eddy a few miles up the West Branch from Hancock, pleasant and surprisingly unspoiled as far as Trenton, New Jersey, a distance of 210 miles that makes a good and quite varied ten- or twelve-day trip. Throughout the route, easy stretches alternate with fast water and riffles and occasional serious rapids that, in the upper section, should be portaged by those who haven't had a lot of practice in white water (below Port Jervis, New York, the river is wide enough to offer routes around most of the hazardous rapids); between Hales Eddy and Port Jervis, the river is best reserved for the high-water conditions of May and early June. The scenery along the route is generally attractive as far as Trenton, spectacular in the Delaware Water Gap around East Stroudsburg, Pennsylvania, where the river slices through the Appalachians. Considering how much of the river's banks is privately owned, the camping possibilities are pretty good (on the Pennsylvania side between Easton and Point Pleasant, there's a state park formed around a 60-mile stretch of the old Delaware Canal paralleling the river—a pleasant bit of safe water, incidentally, in which to introduce young children to the art of canoeing).

Canoe-oriented maps of the Delaware are published by the Delaware River Authority. There are several places to rent canoes within reach of Philadelphia on both sides of the river. One, at Point Pleasant in Bucks County, Pennsylvania, has the distinction of being a comprehensive canoe outfitter comparable to those that serve the Quetico-Boundary Waters area, Algonquin, and the Allagash: complete or partial outfitting with food and camping equipment in addition to canoes, plus trip-planning advice and delivery or pickup service at the start and/or finish of your trip.

Winding more than 400 miles in a nearly endless series of loops, the Susquehanna can be rewarding for the canoeist who can manage his logistics without the kind of outfitting help available on much of the Delaware. The river is generally swift and shallow, with few natural obstructions. Although the dark valleys and rugged mountains along its course have been battered since the eighteenth century by coal mining and various other industries, the country, like an aging *grande dame*, retains much of its inherent beauty. It is really two widely separated rivers. The North Branch of the Susquehanna has its source in Lake Otsego at Cooperstown, New York, not far from the headwaters of the Delaware; 300 miles downstream, at Shamokin Dam, Pennsylvania, it is joined by the West Branch to form the broad waterway that empties into Chesapeake Bay 125 miles farther down. At fairly regular intervals throughout its known history, the cramped tributaries of this system have combined in devastating floods.

The narrow upper section of the Susquehanna's North Branch is best run in the high water of spring: after June 1, the flow is likely to be inadequate, the going tough on your canoe. Below Binghamton, New York, the river widens to make a pleasant week's trip to the coal town of Wilkes-Barre 135 miles distant, or on to Shamokin Dam 60 miles farther. The West Branch flows through similar country no less attractive, with mountains of considerable grandeur, the towns fewer and smaller (here, too, coal mining has left its marks). The more interesting section is the 115 miles between Clearfield and Lock Haven; allow about four days, about the same for the shorter distance and slower current between Lock Haven and Shamokin Dam. Below the confluence of the two branches, there are half a dozen power dams to portage around, and the broad, slow-moving river hardly repays the week's paddling to the Chesapeake; on the other hand, if you do continue as far as the bay, the shores opposite the river mouth—with several marshy streams flowing in, and abundance of waterfowl, fairly good fishing, and pleasant camping in a Maryland state park at Elk Neck—are worth exploring.

SOUTHEASTERN UNITED STATES

The Indians around Chesapeake Bay and in the subtropical swamps farther south built intriguing dugout canoes in a variety of forms burned and chipped from single logs or from several joined together. So did the white trappers and fishermen who succeeded them. The Southeast as a whole, however, was never the natural canoe country that produced the sophisticated bark-covered canoes developed in the northeastern quarter of the country and in most parts of Canada. Here and there, particularly in the mountains of Virginia, West Virginia, and Tennessee, white-water enthusiasts have searched out sections of wild rivers that are good for strenuous trips of a day or two. The hair-raising rapids of the upper Potomac, for instance, are not much more than an hour's drive from downtown Washington, and the country around Harpers Ferry is as splendid to look at as when the young Jefferson first saw and described it, but the river itself and its banks have suffered shamefully from every form of pollution.

The scattered stretches of white water are not the whole story of canoeing in the Southeast, but everywhere in the Appalachian states dam building and pollution, particularly from mining, have taken their toll of the longer rivers, and those that remain are threatened by overuse. Virginia and Tennessee have both taken steps to establish scenic river systems, sections of several rivers that have some chance of being preserved for canoeing and fishing and are of at least local interest. In Virginia, the South Fork of the Shenandoah—winding northeast through a lovely valley between the Blue Ridge Mountains and the lesser Massanuttens to the west—is a possible five- or six-day trip throughout the year: close to 100 miles between Port Republic and Front Royal, with some fast water but generally easy.

Below the meeting of the two forks at Front Royal, parts of the broad expanse of the Shenandoah proper are also worth trying as far as Harpers Ferry, where the river joins the Potomac. The historic James River, rising in the mountains south of the Shenandoah, is potentially important for distance canoeing, but its future depends on legislative wisdom to preserve and restore it.

In western Tennessee, the Buffalo River is comparable to the Shenandoah: 110 miles between Henryville and its confluence with the Duck River near the Tennessee, year-round canoeing of modest difficulty, comparatively clean water flowing through pretty country. Both the Buffalo and the Duck are described and mapped in leaflets available from the state's Game and Fish Commission. The Green River, flowing 370 miles through the middle of Kentucky between McKinney and the village of Basket on the Ohio River, offers several possibilities for easy trips, notably in the protected sections in and near Mammoth Cave National Park. There are canoe renters in the area.

One of the greatest canoeing adventures in the Southeast lies on the Georgia-Florida line—the Okefenokee Swamp. Here the venturesome canoer will discover a world of water and exotic plant and animal life unlike anywhere else he is likely to dip his paddle.

Most of Georgia's Okefenokee Swamp lies within the 300,000 acres of a national wildlife refuge. It is not the stagnant waste that its name implies: the waters *flow;* the swamp is the focus of several important canoeing rivers that can carry the traveler east to the Atlantic or southwest through Florida's panhandle to the Gulf of Mexico. The swamp itself is set aside for canoeing in an experiment in controlled and limited use that may well be the future of American wilderness waterways, if they are to survive. Parties of not more than ten canoes make advance reservations; the park authorities assign dates that will ensure their having their chosen route to themselves (see Appendices for address). The half-dozen water trails are clearly signposted, a feature you'll be grateful for in this featureless wilderness of narrow channels winding among cypress trees and islands of clustered vegetation that may float away with the current, but detailed maps

The New River in North Carolina is a National Wild and Scenic River.
(North Carolina Tourism Division)

and some skill with a compass are also necessary. Most camping will be on wooden platforms built for the purpose, and a suitable frame tent should be chosen with that in mind: there is not much solid ground in this country, whose Indian name means "trembling earth." Possible trips through the interior of the swamp range from two to six days, the latter a 50-mile circuit; the constricted channels, often shallow and thickly laced with roots, make for slow going.

The Okefenokee is canoeable throughout the year. From about October through April, you can expect pleasantly cool weather, occasionally chilly, not much rain, a scarcity of mosquitoes, and an immensely varied cast of aquatic birds—the majestic sandhill cranes, for instance, which have their summer nesting grounds north of the Arctic Circle, spend the winter here. Alligators, on the other hand, sluggish and somnolent when it's cool, are more likely to be seen during the summer months. With luck, you may see other animals with fearsome reputations—black bears, several species of

The Okefenokee Swamp has 13 canoe trails that vary in length from 12 to 55 miles. (J. Wayne Fears)

poisonous snakes, wildcats, or wild hogs—but they're not likely to threaten you: like other wild creatures, they'll recognize you as the ultimate predator and treat you accordingly.

The Okefenokee forms the headwaters of both the Suwannee (the "Swanee" of Stephen Foster's song) and the St. Mary's rivers, which flow in opposite directions through Georgia and Florida. A short portage in the southwestern corner of the wildlife refuge links one of the swamp canoe routes with the Suwannee for a 250-mile float to its mouth on the Gulf, a leisurely two- or three-week extension of the Okefenokee trip, if you have the time; the upper 106 miles, designated by the two states as an official canoe route and ending at Suwannee River State Park, is generally wild, undisturbed by motorboats, with numerous campsites—but the whole river is attractive. Two tributaries permit longer variants on the Suwannee trip, and both are

official canoe routes: the Withlacoochee for the 56 miles from just east of Valdosta, Georgia, to the Suwannee, at Suwannee River State Park; and the Alapaha, running 83 miles from Willacoochee, Georgia, to Statenville near the Florida line, thence another 25 miles to the Suwannee. Both offer good camping and are punctuated minor rapids that may be difficult in the high water of late spring.

From its source in the Okefenokee Swamp to its mouth in the Atlantic, the St. Mary's River forms part of the boundary between Georgia and Florida, a distance of about 100 miles. The upper 60-odd miles is another jointly designated canoe trail, but you can, if you like, continue through the tidal lower portion to the ocean. Nearly every bend in the river encloses a bar of pure-white sand that offers good swimming and makes a pleasant natural campsite.

Swinging in a great arc north and east of the Okefenokee Swamp, the Saltilla River is among the loveliest rivers in the area for canoeing. The best section is the 149 miles between Waycross and Woodbine, Georgia, designated by the state as a canoe trail, with abundant campsites similar to those on the St. Mary's. The river is canoeable for nearly 100 miles above Waycross, but the season must be chosen with care: in summer and fall, low water makes the river a tedious succession of snags to avoid or pull over, while in the spring it may become a raging torrent. In its final miles below Woodbine, the river swells into St. Andrew's Sound, where it empties into the sea, broad and tidal, with swampy shores, and the canoer faces increasing competition from motorboats.

Except for the upper Saltilla, the advice about the canoeing seasons given for the Okefenokee applies equally to the surrounding rivers, and in the unobtrusive silence of your canoe you have a good chance of encountering a comparable range and variety of wildlife. There are several places in the area where you can rent canoes, but there are no general outfitters.

Information on the Okefenokee Swamp is available from the U.S. Fish and Wildlife Service, and on Georgia rivers from the state travel agency. Florida, which prides itself on its sailing and motorboating waters, has also interested itself in canoeing, and the result is a system of canoe trails, mostly in the northern half of the state, that currently includes twenty-two rivers; all are described and mapped in the *Guide to Florida Canoeing Rivers*, a booklet available from the state's Department of Natural Resources.

You'll find state and federal agencies helpful in planning a specific trip. Check particularly on the current state of the water: the waterways are generally in good shape, but you may have to purify what you drink or cook with or else provide yourself with containers to carry what you'll need for the duration of the trip.

Florida holds one other intriguing prospect for the canoer. If you've seen the Everglades only from the causeway west of Miami or the front seat of an airboat (that particular noisemaker is banned within the boundaries of Everglades National Park), consider the advantages of traveling *through* this tropical wilderness of mangrove swamp by canoe. You'll come across patches of wild sugarcane and banana trees among the mangroves, cypresses, and sawgrass; wading the shallows you'll see egrets, storks, spoonbills, possibly flamingos, several species of heron, and other remarkable shore birds you're not likely to encounter anywhere else. A well-marked 100-mile inland waterway leads through a series of sheltered bays, river mouths, and narrow channels from Everglades City at the north end of the park to Flamingo on the south coast. (Motorboats are also allowed, but the nature of the route restricts their size and speed, so they're not likely to be a nuisance.) You can make the trip in a week from either end (current is not a factor); or add a couple of days for side trips. Cleared campsites on solid ground occur frequently enough for leisurely travel, though most are off the main route. As in the Okefenokee Swamp, the channel markers are helpful in finding one's way, but you should carry a compass, the detailed navigational charts produced by the U.S. Coast and Geodetic Survey, and the careful description of the route by the park naturalist William G. Truesdell, *A Guide to the Wilderness Waterway of the Everglades National Park* (order from the Everglades Natural History Association or the University of Miami Press).

Before we leave the Southeast: In case you read James Dickey's novel *Deliverance* (or saw the movie) and wondered what river he had in mind, it's the Chattooga. It rises on the slopes of 4,900-foot Whiteside Mountain just over the North Carolina line from Georgia, then furnishes about 30 miles of the boundary between Georgia and South Carolina before vanishing into a series of reservoirs. Although short, it's wild white water nearly all the way, with several rapids that are extremely dangerous. The Chattooga is part of the National Wild and Scenic Rivers System, and there is an outfitting service operating on the river.

All of the southeastern states have rivers of interest to canoers, and with a little research, some interesting rivers with little canoeing traffic can be discovered.

THE CENTRAL MIDWEST

Illinois, Indiana, Iowa, and Ohio have all made official efforts to encourage canoeing, and all four states publish pamphlets on their canoeable rivers. Nevertheless, the pickings are slim. Too many of the rivers that in their natural state would make for interesting canoe trips have been swamped by urban growth. Of those that survive, the Fox and Spoon rivers in Illinois (the latter the inspiration for Edgar Lee Masters) offer easy, short trips in rural surroundings. Indiana's Sugar Creek is 90 miles of fairly fast water; the Wabash, whose 450 miles form much of the border with Illinois, has quite a number of possibilities for trips you needn't feel nervous about making with small children or the family dog.

It's only as you travel south and west of these much-developed states that you reach canoe country bearing serious comparison with, say, Algonquin or the Allagash: the Ozarks. The region's borders are elastic, but within it are the southern third of Missouri, below the Osage River, and the northern quarter of Arkansas. This is highland country with mountains rising to 2,000 or 3,000 feet, deeply slashed by rivers that all, sooner or later, find their way into the Mississippi.

Some of the best of these have been dammed into great rambling sources for power or drinking water such as Lake of the Ozarks, formed from the Osage, but strong canoeing and conservation organizations in the two states have managed to preserve dozens of others. The area's history since World War I has been one of small farmers driven from their land by poverty, of the gradual return of something like wilderness. One regrets these human losses, but for canoeists the unpeopling of the Ozarks is mostly gain.

The centerpiece of Ozark canoeing is the Ozark National Scenic Riverways in southeast Missouri, the first (1966) area to gain such protection under a complex program that can only rejoice canoeists and wilderness lovers everywhere. The riverways, administered by the National Park Service, embrace more than 100 miles of the Current River, close to 50 of its tributary the Jacks Fork River. Much of the Current River route lies in the shadow of high limestone bluffs, thickly grown with hardwoods, with many big cold-water springs along the banks, some waterfalls, and water-hollowed caves to explore; riverside campsites are frequent. The fishing is pretty good; among the wildlife are many varieties of water fowl, beavers returning to the area after long absence, and at least a few wild turkeys. While the water in the springs and in the

river itself is generally clean, there are enough exceptions so that precautions are advisable.

The Current is an all-year river, though the winter weather can be quite chilly and in midsummer the park gets crowded. The Jacks Fork may be too shallow in summer to be practicable. The 105 miles of the Current within the park, between Montauk Springs and the Hawes campground, make a pleasant five- or six-day trip, enlivened by some fast water and riffles but with no sections that require highly developed white-water skills. You can continue the voyage on down into Arkansas (34 miles to the state line), but below the park the motorboat traffic becomes increasingly heavy.

Two other Ozark rivers offer relaxed semiwilderness canoe travel comparable to the Current: the Gasconade, a tributary of the Missouri (250 miles) and the Meremec, which flows into the Mississippi (193 miles). These and other Missouri canoe routes are all covered in *Missouri Ozark Waterways*, a very competent guidebook by Oz Hawksley, published by the Missouri Conservation Commission (well-drawn two-color maps for all the rivers, too). A map-brochure for the Current and Jacks Fork rivers is available from the park headquarters in Van Buren. At Akers Ferry, a few miles below the northern entrance to the park, there is a competent canoe-rental agency that will provide a shuttle service to any put-in or take-out point along the Current.

Southwest of the Current in Arkansas is another fine canoeing river on a somewhat grander scale— higher bluffs, bigger bankside caves, a generally faster, more strenuous current that on occasion can rise to dangerous flood, wilder, less traveled, less peopled: the Buffalo.

With the right water conditions, the Buffalo can be canoed between the villages of Boxley and Buffalo City, where it meets the White River—a distance of about 150 miles for which you'll want to allow a couple of weeks (why hurry?). Low water, beginning in early June and getting worse as the summer progresses, may make it necessary to start farther down. Provided there's enough water to float a canoe in the first place, the upper section between Boxley and Pruitt (about 30 miles) has several shallow rapids that require a fair degree of skill; look them over before you attempt them and line or portage if in doubt.

WESTERN UNITED STATES

When you turn your mind to water sport in the great West, quite possibly the first image to form is of the Colorado River in its plunge through Grand Canyon: clumps of elephantine inflatable rubber rafts lashed together, steered through cascading falls by powerful outboards or professional oarsmen while the paying customers cling to the grab loops. Personally, I'd as soon take a two-week tour through Disneyland in a wheelchair, but each to his pleasure.

There are some grand and awesome rivers in the mountain states and along the West Coast, but too many of them are like that stretch of the Colorado: splendid to look at, photograph, explore on horseback or possibly on foot, but navigable (unless the likelihood of geting your irreplaceable body smashed is your idea of fun) only with the kind of elaborate mechanical assistance that has turned climbing in the Himalayas into a branch of indus-

The Snake River in Grand Teton National Park is one of America's most scenic float trips.
(Wyoming Travel Commission)

trial technology. Or else the big western rivers have been swallowed by the gargantuan reservoirs that supply water and power to places like Los Angeles, Denver, and Phoenix; or their banks have been sprinkled with towns and industry; or, since many of the rivers have their sources in high mountains and drain country that was either half desert to start with or has been made so by overgrazing and modern strip mining, they offer few months in the year when they're not either in murderous spate or too nearly dry to paddle. Nevertheless, when all these subtractions have been made, there remain a number of important western rivers that, seen through canoer's eyes, are both wild and beautiful, exciting but not suicidal.

Near the top of any western canoer's list is that part of the Rio Grande that forms the border between Texas and Mexico. Texas paddlers, an intrepid and well-organized bunch, speak of the Rio Grande with the same kind of reverence and affection that Downeasters use for the Allagash, and with reason. The river is unlike any other that can be traveled for extended distances by canoe: coursing deep canyons that very nearly rival those on the Colorado, through arid, mountainous country that feels as remote from homely human activity as it is in fact; a land rich with history, from Indian cliff dwellers to Cortez and his dogged search for the fabulous cities of gold, from the first great herds of longhorns to the badmen from both sides of the river for whom the river was more gateway than barrier.

The canoeing from Presidio to the archetypal Texas frontier town of Langtry is good all the way, a distance of about 250 miles; the best of it, wildest, most isolated, is the 90-mile section near the middle, within the boundaries of Great Bend National Park, the only segment that can easily be taken separately from the whole in this almost roadless country. You'll need at least two weeks for the run from Presidio to Langtry, twice that if you take time to explore the many interesting side canyons that slash the river's rocky banks. The current is generally swift, interspersed with fairly difficult rapids; get local advice and equip yourself with detailed U.S. Geological Survey maps so you know where the tough ones are, then be sure to go ashore and inspect them, lining or portaging when in doubt; this is harsh country, and misjudgments won't get off lightly. The camping along the river

is good; purify the water and plan to carry big jugs that you can fill from the occasional reliable spring. The best season extends from fall through about the end of February; the flood levels of spring can be dangerous, and in the summer, low water and excessive heat make the going tough.

The Rio Grande is as big as its name, and there are other wild and remote sections farther upstream, in particular the 150 miles or so north of Santa Fe, New Mexico, now part of the National Wild Rivers System. Only short and carefully selected segments of the upper Rio Grande are within the capacity of canoe and paddle, and the approaches involve steep trails descending banks several hundred feet high. In between these canoeable sections are fearsome rapids that can be outright killers, beyond the reach even of the gasbags that ply the Grand Canyon.

Farther north, in Montana, two other major rivers deserve the attention of the canoe traveler: the Missouri and the Yellowstone. The Missouri has the distinction of being the longest American river. Its upper reaches, cutting deep canyons through the living rock, are still wild and remote and can be enjoyed by canoemen of quite modest experience. As preparation for canoeing the upper Missouri, there's no better first step than a reading of the journals of Lewis and Clark describing their expedition up the river to the Pacific coast: it is so little changed since that time.

The upper Missouri River from Fort Benton downriver to the Fred Robinson Bridge (U.S. Highway 191) was designated a component of the National Wild and Scenic Rivers System in October 1976. This 149-mile segment of the Missouri is the only major portion of the river to be protected and preserved in its natural, free-flowing state. You will enjoy scenic vistas that remain much as first described by Lewis and Clark in 1805–06. Detailed information on this interesting float can be obtained from the Bureau of Land Management in Lewiston, Montana.

Within the park to which it gave its name, the Yellowstone is hazardous, but its course from the Montana line to its confluence with the Missouri has several possibilities for pleasant, fairly easy trips. Probably the best is that between Livingston and Billings, again a week or so (160 miles). There is a useful guidebook for the whole river, privately published (see Appendices).

Canoeing in Montana's Glacier National Park is an ideal summer day trip. (Montana Travel Promotion)

In this same general area, Wyoming's Green and North Platte rivers, flowing in opposite directions, on either side of the Continental Divide, provide a few days' paddling each. The Green rises in a series of small lakes south of Yellowstone Park—a transplanted fragment of the border-lakes country, complete with portages—and can be followed for about 100 miles south, when it disappears into the Fontanelle Reservoir; or cross the reservoir, with its motorboats, and continue the 150 miles to Dinosaur National Monument in northeastern Colorado. West of Laramie, you can put in three or four days on the North Platte, paddling north from the Wyoming-Colorado border, before the way is blocked by a series of dams and reservoirs at Fort Steele, a distance of 67 miles.

The three coastal states all have short stretches of daredevil white water but few attractions for the purposeful distance canoer who doesn't happen to live in the neighborhood. Oregon has the Rogue in the southwestern part of the state (difficult and treacherous for open canoes); the Deschutes, a tributary of the Columbia (attractive and not unduly demanding in the 100 miles north of Bend); the John Day, flowing north to the Columbia through the arid moonscape west of the Cascade Mountains (about 150 miles below the village of Service Creek, easy but restricted by water level to late fall and early spring). Paralleling the coast, the Willamette (natives accent the second syllable) is longer and easier than any of these but is punctuated by a series of good-sized towns and shadowed by a heavily traveled interstate expressway before it empties into the Columbia amid the southward-thrusting urbanization of Portland.

WILD WATERS OF THE FAR NORTH

Canada is the natural homeland of the canoe. Before the first Europeans sailed up the St. Lawrence, her immense system of rivers and lakes served the thinly scattered Indian and Eskimo populations as routes for fishing and hunting, migration, warfare, and, in some cases, trade over considerable distances. With few exceptions, the earliest explorers followed these routes, borrowing the Indians' skills. The canoe-borne fur trade spawned by the pathfinders, in time settling the country and shaping it into a nation, is an inland epic to rival the transocean voyages of the Vikings and the Polynesians. In parts of the Canadian Far North, the canoe of necessity holds its own against other forms of transportation, though it's more likely to be driven by a multihorsepower "kicker" than by a set of paddles. The modern canoer can discover these historic routes for himself, sometimes in a quite literal sense.

In traveling this north country, you'll use essentially the same canoeing and camping skills that serve you in other parts of the continent. The routes described—a few selected from the nearly infinite number of possibilities—are ones that I consider within the ability of canoers of moderate skill and experience: enough experience, to repeat, to recognize the rough waters that may be dangerous *for you*, enough skill to act on that judgment. There is, however, a very real difference in scale. Even such rivers as the Mackenzie and the Yukon, which are generally easy canoeing, require an extra dimension of those who would travel them: their sheer size demands endurance; the few settlements occur at intervals of 100 or 200 miles, and since they're the natural starting and stopping points, any canoe trip on them will be a three- or four-week expedition rather than the week or two that would be sufficient elsewhere. This is not the circumscribed and protected wilderness that canoeists experience in southern Canada and most parts of the United States. The northland is wild because people and their means of livelihood, their industries, have still hardly penetrated; or where they have come, they have not stayed. Preparations for such a trip must be made accordingly, starting months in advance.

To begin with, there's the canoe itself. Starting points for many great northern canoe trips can be reached by a road such as the Alcan or Mackenzie highway, so that it's feasible to cartop your own canoe there and use it on the trip (the road, gravel-graded, is likely to be an adventure in itself). The canoe should be chosen for toughness and carrying capacity: you'll be heavily loaded on a long trip, and an extra margin of freeboard will help keep you dry and safe when the water's rough. If the route includes rapids and/or much portaging, a 17- or 18-foot canoe with a hull designed for maneuverability is probably as big as you'll want; if long stretches of straight paddling are going to predominate, think seriously about a 20-foot canoe, though you may have less use for it later unless you return to the North. Where flying in or flying out is necessary, however, using your own canoe will be a big expense and a substantial nuisance. In that case, your best bet will be a one-way rental. Remember, though, that since the canoe may have to be tractored in over a winter road that ceases to exist when the spring thaw comes, early planning is essential: make your reservation in early fall for a trip the following summer.

The chances are that on any route you pick you'll never be more than a week or two from a settlement where you can replenish your food. You needn't, in other words, carry all you'll need for the trip. You can count on standard canned goods (including canned butter, bacon, and those great canned Canadian jams that inexplicably are unobtainable in the United States), such staples as flour, sugar, and coffee, sometimes fresh or frozen meats, vegetables, and bread. On the other hand, to save weight and bulk, you'll probably want to take a fair amount of freeze-dried food and supplement that with systematic fishing. In addition, as a cushion against accident or delays caused by bad weather, you should keep your basic food supply about a week ahead of actual need; for example, if you figure a week's travel between supply points, carry enough food for two weeks.

The northern summer weather is not as cold as you might think. Even within the Arctic Circle there will be bright, warm days in July and early August when the temperature is in the 80s. There will also, of course, be days (and nights!) in the 30s. Clothes and sleeping gear should match this considerable range: the sort of three-season clothes and sleeping bags I've recommended for less northerly climates, supplemented by long underwear, a jacket that's both warm and windproof, and heavy pajamas. Warm, waterproof gloves provide insurance against wet days when the temperature hovers in the mid-30s and you make the uncomfortable discovery that the hands are the most vulnerable parts of a canoer's anatomy.

The size of your party may be an important consideration. The easier trips through the North are practical for two people reasonably experienced in canoeing and camping. For mutual safety in emergencies, the more difficult routes are best attempted by parties of two or three canoes with an agreed-on leader, even though the larger party complicates planning and logistics and limits campsites to those with room for two or three tents.

Sources of information for the regions described below are listed in the Appendices. The provincial governments of British Columbia, Alberta, Saskatchewan, and Manitoba all publish materials on their canoe routes: guidebooks in the case of Alberta and British Columbia; separate booklets, including maps, on numerous Saskatchewan routes; detailed canoeing maps for Manitoba. For Quebec, the same job is admirably done by the *Guide des rivières du Québec*, compiled by the province's canoeing association and published commercially by Éditions du Jour in Montreal. There is not as yet anything comparable for the Northwest Territories, but there are several accounts of canoeing there (including my own *Ultimate North*) and of travel generally.

Quebec. In canoeing, as in most other things, *La Belle Province* goes her own way. This is an effect partly of geography, partly of history. The European fur trade, with bases in Montreal and the city of Quebec, had exhausted the easily accessible sources by the end of the seventeenth century. This was the practical motive that pushed the traders west, but Montreal, with its ocean-going link to Europe, remained the eastern terminus of those immense waterways, and French-Canadian voyageurs supplied the strength and skills that drove the canoes along the trade routes—in the process, scattering French place names across what was to be the northern United States and all of Canada, west to the Pacific, north to the Arctic Ocean. But where the western waterways were connecting veins and arteries in the growth of the future provinces of Ontario, Manitoba, Saskatchewan, Alberta, British Columbia, in Quebec they were barriers, not highways. Except for the Ottawa River—the boundary between Quebec and Ontario and the first link in the chain of trade and communication laid through the Great Lakes and the Quetico region to the farthest west and north—Quebec's major rivers flow north into the James and Hudson bays and never had the importance of the rivers farther west; or they drain into the eastern St. Lawrence and lead, if anywhere, to Europe; or north to the icebound Hudson Strait and Ungava Bay at the mouth of Hudson Bay. Yet the characteristics that made Quebec's big rivers unrewarding for the

The Ottawa River, Quebec: the start of a difficult portage on the upper river, in La Verendrye Provincial Park. (Gouvernement du Quebec, Direction Generale du Tourisme)

early explorers and traders are precisely the ones that make them attractive to modern canoeists: their size, extent, direction, and remoteness.

To the outlander acquainted only with Montreal or Quebec, the sheer size of the province is difficult to take in: more than 1,200 miles from south to north, nearly 1,000 east to west; from the small farmers along the St. Lawrence, living in conscious continuity with *paysans* ancestors in central France, to the Indians and Eskimos of the sub-Arctic tundra, whose second language is not English but French. In this huge area, innumerable wild rivers invite the canoeist, but there are serious qualifications. Some of the biggest long-distance rivers are so thick with murderous rapids and high waterfalls—the Rupert, which leads to James Bay,

or the Kaniapiskau, emptying into Ungava Bay in the Far North—as to be impractical for all but the most skilled, daring, and persistent canoemen. Or they suffer from mammoth hydroelectric and logging operations, such as those spreading across the eastern shore of James Bay. In addition, the provincial government so far seems more attuned to the interests of hunters than canoeists, though the young canoe-kayak association attempts to fill that gap (besides the general guidebook mentioned earlier, it can provide descriptive notes and maps for quite a number of routes, exactly the kind of first-hand information a canoer likes to hear). The three routes I've chosen to describe are *comparatively* accessible and (for well-prepared moderate canoers like me) feasible. They'll also give you an idea of the possibilities in three distinct regions of Canada's biggest province.

Easiest to get to is the upper section of the Rivière des Outaouais (the Ottawa, to English speakers) about 150 miles due north of Ottawa. The river's source is the Lac des Outaouais east of La Vérendrye Provincial Park, which you can reach by rough logging roads that lead northeast from near the park entrance. (La Vérendrye, with Laurentides Provincial Park farther east, is one of the areas where canoeing is officially encouraged by the provincial government.) The river flows generally west through La Vérendrye, linking a series of big lakes, to Lake Timiskaming on the Ontario border, a distance of 330 miles. Except for the first 40 miles, where there are some fairly difficult rapids (they can be portaged), it's easy and varied travel through nearly uninhabited wilderness, with good camping. What more can a canoeist ask? From Lake Timiskaming, you can, if you like, continue to Ottawa or the St. Lawrence, but this long stretch of voyageur water is urban and uninviting. (For crossing La Vérendrye or canoeing within it, get a permit at the park headquarters, Le Domaine, a few road miles beyond the turnoff to Lac des Outaouais.)

A number of important south-flowing rivers drain the North Shore of the St. Lawrence. Among them, the Moisie is particularly intriguing and not too tough. Not the least of its interest is the means of getting to it. You can drive along the North Shore to Sept Îles or the village of Moisie (at present, the end of the road) near the mouth of the Moisie, or, if you have plenty of time, you can take the weekly ship from Rimouski, at the base of the Gaspé Peninsula, across the St. Lawrence from Sept Îles. (Rimouski is accessible by road or rail.) Either way, you then avail yourself of the Quebec, North Shore and Labrador Rail Way, which runs north from Sept Îles, to reach your starting point, mile 19 on the branch line to the towns of Wabush and Labrador City (be very clear about your destination when you buy your ticket). That particular point is within easy reach of the Moisie River, which runs 265 miles from its source nearby to the St. Lawrence, an attractive three-week trip. Since the mouth of the river is swampy, arrange in advance to be picked up by truck at the bridge that crosses the river between Sept Îles and Moisie. Except in the river's upper reaches, where there is a lengthy

series of moderate rapids, the trip is demanding but feasible, the country wild and virtually uninhabited. For a longer and more strenuous trip, you can continue on the branch rail line to Wabush, thence through a series of lakes to the Rivière aux Pékans and down it to the Moisie.

Schefferville, the northern terminus of the Quebec, North Shore and Labrador (an eleven-hour trip) gives access to several north-flowing wild rivers in the Ungava Bay basin—the Swampy Bay River, for instance—but they're generally too hazardous to be attempted by any but the hardiest canoers unless provided with local guides.

In the great drainage basin of James Bay, there's one river the Quebec canoe association, little given to superlatives, describes as "a paradise of canoe camping": the Mégiscane. It's also relatively easy to get to. You can drive as far as Senneterre, about 35 miles north of La Vérendrye Provincial Park, use the train from there 70 miles east to Monet near the source of the Mégiscane (or take the train all the way from Montreal or Quebec). The Mégiscane flows north and west about 200 miles through a series of lakes, emptying into Lac Parent at a point only a few miles from Senneterre. It's a small, energetic river with frequent rapids (about half will have to be lined or portaged) but no falls. It also provides access to several much longer routes. From Lac Parent, for example, you can travel north down the Bell River to the Nottaway (difficult and hazardous, with several big falls), then to James Bay. Or from near Monet you can cross over into a different watershed, traverse the big Gouin Reservoir, and from there paddle down the St. Maurice River 235 miles to Trois Rivières on the St. Lawrence, midway between Montreal and Quebec. (The best section is the 135 miles above La Tuque, wild, much used by canoeists and not difficult except for portages around five big rapids; farther down, the river is quite industrial and may at times be blocked by dangerous log booms.) For the energetic canoer, there are several other good possibilities using the Mégiscane as a starting point.

Across the Prairie Provinces. Like a great hand spilling toward Hudson Bay, the Canadian Shield supports half a dozen mighty river systems that flow generally east and north: the Albany (mentioned earlier in this chapter); the Assiniboine and Red, feeding the south end of Lake Winnipeg, linked by that big and always treacherous lake with the Hayes and Nelson rivers; the Saskatchewan, with its two large branches rising in the Rockies; above all, the Churchill. These rivers, with their immense drainage basin, formed the main highway that led from Montreal west and north by way of the Great Lakes and the border-lakes region. They connected, in turn, across two divides, with the headwaters of the Columbia River and the fearsome Fraser, falling into the Pacific; and with the Fond du Lac, Athabasca, and Peace rivers, draining through a series of huge lakes into the Mackenzie River and, ultimately, the Arctic Ocean.

All these lakes and rivers are set in remote and generally wild country that has changed remarkably little since they first floated the big birch-bark canoes of the voyageurs. Although they differ greatly in character and difficulty, collectively they're a Promised Land for modern canoemen. Given the unique conjunction of history and geography, the best introduction to this vast region is Eric W. Morse's *Fur Trade Canoe Routes of Canada, Then and Now*. Morse has traced the routes through the accounts of the early explorers and the records of the fur traders (often the same people). More importantly, he has paddled many of the routes for himself and set down what he observed with exactly the concrete attention to rapids, currents, and portages that his fellow canoers will appreciate when they set out to follow.

The Saskatchewan River proper is formed by the meeting of two large branches in central Saskatchewan. The upper part of the South Saskatchewan, from its beginning near Grassy Lake, Alberta, to a big reservoir just over the Saskatchewan border (Lake Diefenbaker), makes a fairly easy trip that you can take in a leisurely ten days. The river course stays away from the few towns in the area, but there are enough access points along the way so that you can break the trip or get additional supplies if you need them. By starting at Fort McLeod, Alberta, on the Oldman River, a tributary, you can lengthen this trip by 160 miles (above Fort McLeod, the Oldman is canoeable but difficult, with rapids rated from moderate to impossible). The South Saskatchewan is worth picking up again outside the city of Saskatoon, Saskatchewan, for another easy 200 miles as far as Nipawin; or, if you're ambitious and have plenty of time, you can continue to Cumberland House, a voyageurs' cross-

roads for several historic routes to Hudson Bay. The North Saskatchewan, which flows through Edmonton, Alberta's capital, and joins the South Saskatchewan east of Saskatoon, is more populous, less interesting.

Till near the end of the eighteenth century, while the French traders from Montreal and their Scottish and English rivals and successors pushed into the Canadian interior to procure the furs at their ever-receding source, the Hudson's Bay Company stayed put, operating from one or another base at the mouth of one of the rivers emptying into Hudson Bay: Fort Churchill, Fort Nelson, York Factory (on the Hayes River), Fort Albany. From as far west as Lake Athabasca and the modern site of Edmonton, the Indians brought their furs to these points to exchange for guns, powder, shot, cloth, metal tools, the rum or brandy, and the glass beads that were staples of European trade everywhere in North America. The Indian canoe routes led east down the Saskatchewan River to Cumberland Lake, then northeast to the Grass River and a meeting with the Nelson halfway down to Hudson Bay; or through Moose Lake, avoiding treacherous Lake Winnipeg, to the Carrot River or the Bigstone and Fox rivers, both connecting with the lower Hayes. Later, with inland outposts at Norway House northeast of Lake Winnipeg and Cumberland House on Cumberland Lake, the Hudson's Bay traders made the Hayes their main route, partly solving the problem of crossing Lake Winnipeg by using heavily built boats with sails, manned by rugged boatmen from the North of Scotland.

None of these routes was entirely satisfactory. The Nelson is a big, rocky river with a torrential flow of water for canoes and small boats to negotiate, rapids and falls (and, today, dams on the lower river). The Moose Lake connection with the lower Hayes involved a long and difficult portage across a height of land. The Hayes, tedious and mud-banked in its lower section, is broken by 50 miles of rapids halfway up, and the crossing of Lake Winnipeg that it leads to, with its threat of fierce and sudden storms, is hazardous for canoes and boats no matter how big or stoutly built. Yet for the modern canoer these routes retain the attraction of their history, and parts of them, accessible by road or rail, make good, extended trips that are not excessively difficult. Long since abandoned and now established as a national historic site, York

The Churchill River: Nistowiak Falls in north-central Saskatchewan, one of the many hazards to be admired and portaged on this grand but strenuous river. (Saskatchewan Department of Tourism)

Factory, with its links to the seventeenth century, serves as a magnet at the end, pulling the adventurous canoer into the past.

One interesting trip along a part of the historic route can be made starting from Cumberland House, today at a road end, from there northeast through Namew Lake and the Goose River to Grass River and its confluence with the Nelson at Split Lake about 325 miles downstream. Hudson's Bay stores at both ends make possible one-way canoe rental. From Split Lake you can fly out or connect with the Churchill branch of the Canadian National Rail Way. A variant on the same route, about 75 miles shorter, starts from Cranberry Portage, which you can also reach by road. Another possibility is to fly in to Norway House northeast of Lake Winnipeg (scheduled service). From there you can follow the traditional main track to York Factory down part of the Nelson, the Echimamish, and the Hayes rivers as far as Oxford Lake, returning from there by plane and avoiding the toilsome lower section of the Hayes; or continue on to York Factory, again about 325 miles. (To get back, you can fly the whole way by prearranged charter, or only as far as Gillam, a station on the Churchill rail line.) An alternative near the start would be to follow the Nelson to Cross Lake, thence to Oxford Lake via the Carrot River or else through Utik Lake to the Bigstone and Fox rivers, joining the Hayes about 90 miles above York Factory and bypassing the long stretch of rapids on the Hayes.

Cumberland Lake was a junction not only for the Hudson's Bay traders but for the Montrealers headed up Lake Winnipeg for the Saskatchewan River and the west—or for the arduous connection with the Churchill by way of Amisk Lake and the Sturgeon Weir River. Traveling up the Churchill to its source, the intrepid voyageurs crossed the northern divide (over the 12-mile Methye Portage, one of the longest and steepest on the entire route) into waters that carried them ultimately to the Arctic and across the mountains to the Pacific coast and into Alaska at a time when it was still a little-explored extension of Russian Siberia. The Churchill remains, as it was when the voyageurs paddled it, one of the grandest watercourses on the continent, a 1,000-mile succession of large and beautiful wilderness lakes periodically narrowing to wide, fast river thick with rapids.

For canoers who feel the pull of the Churchill—and the more you know of it, the more you will be drawn—Sigurd Olson has captured its history and present state in *The Lonely Land*, which is, among other things, an account of his own trip down the river. It is not an expedition for the inexperienced or the imprudent. Between Churchill Lake and the river's mouth at Fort Churchill on Hudson Bay there are well over 100 major rapids, some of them miles long, the exact number depending on water conditions in any given year and month; fewer than half can be run by even the most expert canoeists. But there are portages around most of these danger spots, kept up by the Indian hunters and fishermen who are still the river's chief inhabitants. With careful preparation, good maps and due caution along the way, the Churchill offers experienced canoeists possibilities for several exciting trips of from two to six weeks.

Two hundred miles north of Saskatoon, Saskatchewan, the headwaters of the Churchill at Buffalo Narrows on Lake Churchill can be reached over a long stretch of northland gravel road. From there it's about 300 miles and at least twenty rapids that will have to be portaged—three weeks—to the village of Missinipe on Otter Lake, the next access point by road, on the north edge of Lac La Ronge Provincial Park. (Or you can cut 50 miles from the start of the route by putting in at Île-à-La Crosse on the lake of the same name.) You can start (or continue) from Missinipe or, a little farther east, from Pelican Narrows, another road end, connected with the Churchill by the historic and fairly easy Frog Portage (or paddle to the same point from Cumberland House, though the rapids in the connecting Sturgeon Weir River are difficult and tiring). From Missinipe it's still more than 600 miles to Fort Churchill, but it's possible to fly out halfway along (or resupply) at South Indian Lake; from Fort Churchill, one gets back to civilization by scheduled plane or by the train, which has its terminus there. Since there are Hudson's Bay posts at all of these access and exit points, their rented canoes are advisable, particularly on the lower half of the river (they're also the *only* places on the river where you can count on buying food, a further reason for careful planning).

For less experienced canoers or those who are short of time, the Saskatchewan Department of Natural Resources has worked out a number of shorter and easier routes, with some circuits, centering on Lac La Ronge, all designed to give the modern voyageur, for a week or two, an authentic taste of the mighty Churchill. The routes are described in individual booklets and shown on the province's laudable canoeing maps.

If, like the voyageurs, you were to paddle *up* the Churchill to its source instead of down and carry canoe and packs across the back-breaking Methye Portage to the Clearwater River, you would enter an entirely new system of waterways, draining north and west 2,000 miles to the Arctic Ocean: the vast Mackenzie River system, second only to the Mississippi-Missouri in North America. The *if* in that sentence is, admittedly, a big one for most of us. Yet the route is followed, the portage made, since there is in fact no other way of getting to the Clearwater. And it is appropriate that so radical a change in geography, with all it implies of history and human culture, should be marked by the harsh climb up and over the Methye Portage.

From the portage, the Clearwater flows about 85 miles west to Fort McMurray through a beautiful narrow valley. Apart from its remoteness and physical attractiveness, the river has the interest of having served as a funnel through which passed nearly all the early explorers of the far Northwest— a kind of pantheon of North American canoeing. There are some bad rapids in the upper half of the Clearwater but the portages around them are fairly clear, well documented. Access is by gravel road to La Loche on the lake of that name 8 easy water miles from the start of the portage.

Before we turn to the Northwest, two big southern tributaries of the Mackenzie are worth noting: the Athabasca and the Peace. Historically, their importance was that several heroic expeditions traveled up them to their sources in the Rockies, thence over high passes and down the western slopes to the Pacific. The modern voyageur will reverse the procedure.

From high mountains near Jasper, the Athabasca offers about 650 miles (three or four weeks) of isolated semiwilderness canoeing as far as Fort McMurray, Alberta—modern towns where the few roads cross (access points for shorter trips), not many other evidences of a human presence. The current is fairly strong most of the way, with dangerous rapids near Fort McMurray, the present end of the road north from Edmonton, at the confluence with the Clearwater. Beyond Fort Mc-

Murray there are no hazards, and the Athabasca, once a highway for barge traffic to Lake Athabasca and Fort Chipewyan 200 miles north (there being no road) is now virtually deserted.

The Peace River, rising north of the Athabasca, is comparable in size, character, and difficulty. For a not too difficult two- or three-week trip, you could pick it up at the town of Peace River at the start of the Mackenzie Highway, or farther north at Fort Vermilion. From where the river empties into the Slave River, you're half a day's paddle from Fort Chipewyan (fly out), a couple of days south of Fort Smith (scheduled plane service or road north to Great Slave Lake and a connection with the Mackenzie Highway for a return to the starting point).

THE FAR NORTHWEST

The Mackenzie River is the great axis of the Northwest. Around it, like spokes on a wheel, its tributaries offer limitless possibilities for long-distance canoeing at every level of skill and experience.

The Mackenzie itself is easy canoeing, assisted by a fairly strong current that periodically boils up into a big riffles or short rapids. Given its size (a couple of miles across in places), its hazards are more likely to come in the form of storms driven by the prevailing north wind, which will tie the canoer down for a day in an average summer week. The half-dozen settlements occur at intervals of a 100 miles or so. Apart from them and an occasional distant barge or team of prospectors, you'll see no people. In a shrinking world, it is a last frontier, and that is one of its attractions; another is the chance to share, if only in a limited way, with much support from the civilization to the south, in the life of the Indians and Eskimos for whom the river, with its trapping, hunting, and fishing, is still the natural means of existence. Since World War II, the frontier in the form of the Mackenzie Highway, gravel-graded and arduous but passable in all seasons, has pushed north to Fort Providence at the beginning of the Mackenzie, now another 160 miles downriver to Fort Simpson. In time it will extend the whole length of the river, to its Arctic delta. The transformation will be slow, but the river and its people are worth seeing before it comes.

The river distance from Fort Providence to Inu-

Camsell River, Northwest Territories: rapids on Marian Lake, near the start of the river-and-lake system connecting two giant lakes of the Far North, Great Slave and Great Bear. (Information Canada Phototheque, Paul Baich)

vik in the delta is close to 950 miles. With cooperative weather, you can paddle it in three or four weeks—or take twice the time, if you can, and explore the settlements, the attractive side rivers along the way. A good shorter trip would be from Fort Simpson to Fort Norman (fly out), about 300 miles, with rugged northern mountains on both sides of the river. Or start from Fort Good Hope near the Arctic Circle (regular but infrequent plane service) and travel down to Aklavik or Inuvik (on opposite sides of the delta). From either of these half-Eskimo towns, you can continue another 100 miles to the edge of the Arctic Ocean itself. Getting back is not easy, but when you've gotten that far the pull of the icebound sea is irresistible.

Fort Simpson, with the beginning of a canoe-oriented outfitting service, is a base from which to explore the steep mountain rivers to the west, particularly the South Nahanni, enclosed by the Nahanni National Park. You can charter a float to a point above the Virginia Falls (316 feet high). The two-week trip down the South Nahanni to the Liard River and Fort Simpson is difficult and fraught with rapids and portages (not least the one around Virginia Falls) but grand.

A comparable but less demanding circuit can be made starting from Fort Norman farther down the Mackenzie, at the mouth of the Great Bear River. A local Indian outfitter can arrange to fly you, with a canoe and supplies, to one of the lakes east of the river (spectacular fishing). From there, you can paddle through lakes and rivers to the swift Great Bear and down it to the starting point.

An intriguing but more difficult trip is the 250 miles of wilderness water between Great Slave and Great Bear lakes: the Camsell River. Like the Churchill River, the Camsell is a sequence of lakes connected by rivers that have their due share of rapids. The start is the Indian village of Rae near the head of the North Arm of Great Slave Lake, on the road to Yellowknife, the gold-boom town that is now the capital of the Northwest Territories. The Camsell empties into Conjuror Bay on Great Bear Lake. From there, unless you've arranged to be met by a chartered plane from Yellowknife, it's necessary to paddle 60 miles northeast to Port Ra-

dium, where you can return to Yellowknife by a scheduled flight. With unlimited time, you can, as an alternative, reach the starting point from Fort Resolution on the south side of Great Slave Lake, going around the lake's superb rocky east end; or return from Conjuror Bay by heading west on Great Bear Lake to Fort Franklin or down the Great Bear River to Fort Norman. Both lakes are, however, big, slow, and tedious for canoers, and even close to the shore they can be dangerous in the periodic storms that blow down from the Arctic.

One other canoe route in this far-northwestern corner of the continent is worth thinking about: the Yukon. Like the Mackenzie, it's big, remote, easy, and wild for much of its length, with settlements just frequent enough to remind even the confirmed misanthrope of the necessity of human society. Again like the Mackenzie, it's been dyed by many layers of history and only since World War II has it begun to be probed by highways of a sort. Indeed, rumors that the Yukon existed across the mountains were the motive that led to the discovery of the Mackenzie toward the end of the eighteenth century. The long-sought Northwest Passage became a reality when traders some years later struggled up tributaries of the Mackenzie to mountain passes, from there to the Yukon River and the Pacific by way of the Pelly River nearly 600 miles up the Liard from Fort Simpson, or the Porcupine, north of the Arctic Circle. In the 1890s, gold added its glamour to these man-killing backdoor routes to Alaska—as it still does.

The 435-mile section of the upper Yukon between Whitehorse and Dawson, in the Yukon Territory, is a popular two-week canoe trip, with gold-built ghost towns to explore along the way as well as the live frontier towns at either end. Whitehorse and Dawson are both easy to get to or from by plane or by loops of the Alaska Highway. Another 300 miles carries you to Circle, Alaska, the last point on the river that's accessible by road. The Bering Sea and the end of the river are still close to 900 miles for those with the time and the inner stamina. Getting back is the difficulty, but there, too, modern canoemen have dipped their paddles. It can be done.

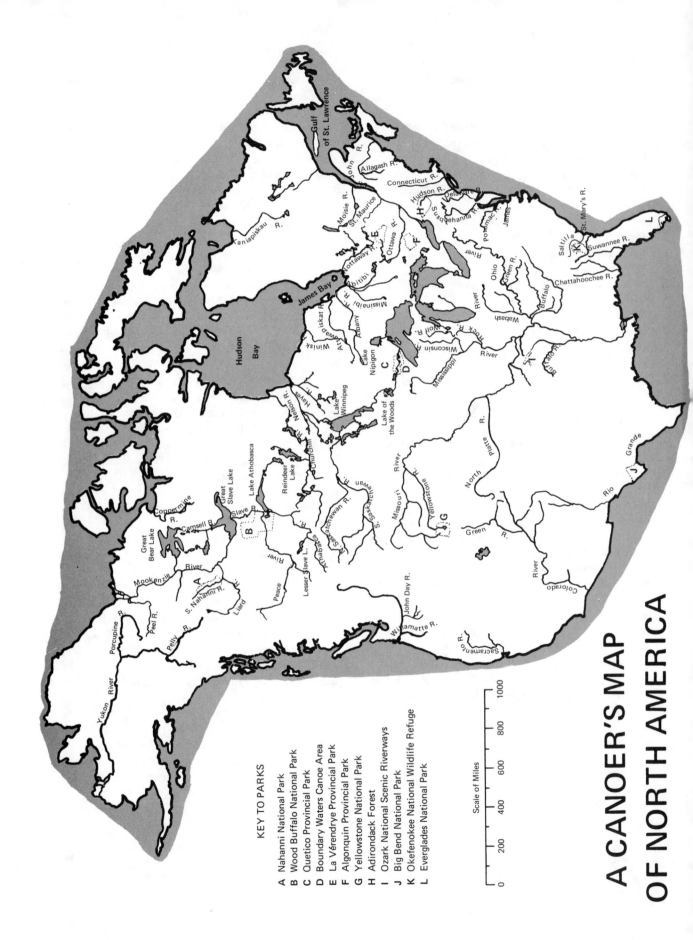

KEY TO PARKS

A Nahanni National Park
B Wood Buffalo National Park
C Quetico Provincial Park
D Boundary Waters Canoe Area
E La Vérendrye Provincial Park
F Algonquin Provincial Park
G Yellowstone National Park
H Adirondack Forest
I Ozark National Scenic Riverways
J Big Bend National Park
K Okefenokee National Wildlife Refuge
L Everglades National Park

Scale of Miles

0   200   400   600   800   1000

A CANOER'S MAP
OF NORTH AMERICA

APPENDIX 1

Canoeing Checklist

DAY TRIP

Canoe
Three paddles (one spare)
Personal flotation device (one per person)
Carrying yoke
Bow and stern lines
Repair tape
Rain suit
Map, waterproof
Compass (on person)
Knife (on person)
Matches in waterproof container (on person)
Space blanket (on person)
Hat with brim
Long-sleeve shirt
Trousers
Belt or suspenders
Socks
Boots, waterproof-treated
Sweater
Underwear for season
Coat or parka in cold weather
Insect repellent in season
Camera and film (in waterproof pack)
Fishing tackle
Sunscreen
Water jug
Lunch

OVERNIGHT TRIP

Tent
Sleeping bag in waterproof bag
Air/foam mattress
Stove
Lantern
Grill, if open-fire cooking
Cook kit
Extra fuel in fuel bottle
Small funnel
Extra clothing in waterproof bag
Personal-care items
Water-purifying kit
First-aid kit
Extra rope
Packs
Food

APPENDIX 2

National Associations

In addition to the canoeing associations, I've included four environmental groups whose goals often parallel those of canoers and who occasionally sponsor related activities.

AMERICAN CANOE ASSOCIATION. Publishes *Canoe* magazine (semimonthly); books and leaflets about canoeing and canoe routes, general information, access to local clubs; races and regattas. Address: 8580 Cinderbed Road, Suite 1900, P.O. Box 1190, Newington, VA 22122–1190.

AMERICAN WHITEWATER AFFILIATION, 1343 N. Portage, Palatine, IL 60067.

CANADIAN RECREATIONAL CANOEING ASSOCIATION, P.O. Box 500, Hyde Park, Ont. NOM 1ZO.

IZAAK WALTON LEAGUE OF AMERICA, 1701 N. Fort Myer Dr., Suite 1100, Arlington, VA 22209.

NATIONAL AUDUBON SOCIETY. Publishes *Audubon* (semimonthly), workshops through local clubs. Address: 950 Third Ave., New York, NY 10022.

NATIONAL PADDLING COMMITTEE. Administers paddling competition for U.S. Olympic team. U.S. Olympic Complex, 1750 East Boulder St., Colorado Springs, CO 80909.

SIERRA CLUB. Bimonthly magazine, environmental news bulletin, discounts on publications (guides to hiking and camping as well as superb illustrated books), organized wilderness trips, some by canoe; collective action on environmental issues. Address: 730 Polk St., San Francisco, CA 94109.

U.S. CANOE ASSOCIATION. P.O. Box 5743, Lafayette, IN 47904.

THE WILDERNESS SOCIETY. Publishes *The Living Wilderness* (quarterly); organizes wilderness trips that include canoeing; information and action on conservation matters with emphasis on legislative issues. Address: 1400 I St. N.W., 10th Floor, Washington, DC 20005.

APPENDIX 3

Books About Canoeing

Books of a general nature are listed here; local guidebooks, pamphlets, and other sources of information about specific regions are grouped in Appendix 5. While some books cannot be purchased directly from the publisher whose address is given, you can write to the publisher for information on where to find the book.

In addition to the books listed below, two catalogs are available which contain ordering information on dozens of books on canoeing and related subjects. They are available from Chicagoland Canoe Base (4019 N. Narragansett, Chicago, IL 60634) and American Canoe Association Bookservice (7217 Lockport Place, Lorton, VA 22079).

GENERAL GUIDEBOOKS

APPALACHIAN MOUNTAIN CLUB. *AMC River Guide: Massachusetts, Connecticut, Rhode Island.* The Appalachian Mountain Club, 5 Joy St., Boston, MA 02108.

————. *AMC River Guide: Maine.* The Appalachian Mountain Club.

————. *AMC River Guide: New Hampshire and Vermont.* The Appalachian Mountain Club.

FISCHER, HANK. *The Floater's Guide to Montana.* Guide to 26 rivers; paperback. Falcon Press Publishing Co., P.O. Box 731, Helena, MT 59601.

FOSHEE, JOHN. *Alabama Canoe Rides and Float Trips.* Detailed guide with maps of 25 float trips in Alabama. Strode Publishers, 6802 Jones Valley Dr. S.E., Huntsville, AL 35802.

GABLER, RAY. *New England White Water River Guide.* Includes 78 maps. The Appalachian Mountain Club.

INDIANA DEPT. OF NATURAL RESOURCES. *Indiana Canoeing Guide.* Guide to 26 streams; maps; paperback. DNR, Division—Outdoor Recreation, 612 State Office Bldg., Indianapolis, IN 46204.

JUNAS, LIL. *Cadron Creek.* Photographic narrative of floating Cadron Creek. Ozark Society Books, Box 3503, Little Rock, AR 72203.

LETCHER, GARY. *Canoeing the Delaware River.* Divides the Delaware into 10 separate canoe day-trips, giving descriptions and accompanying maps. Rutgers University Press, 30 College Ave., New Brunswick, NJ 08903.

MAKENS, JAMES C. *Makens' Guide to U.S. Canoe Trails.* Condensed notes, state by state, on most of the canoeable rivers and lake systems of the United States. Le Voyageur Publishing Co., 1319 Wentwood Dr., Irving, TX 75061.

PALZER, ROBERT J., and JOETTE M. PALZER. *Whitewater, Quietwater.* Guide to river canoeing in Wisconsin, Upper Michigan, northeastern Minnesota, with photographs, maps. Paperback. Evergreen Paddleways, 1416 21st St., Two Rivers, WI 54241, or 1225 Richmond St., El Cerrito, CA 94530.

PARNES, ROBERT. *Canoeing the Jersey Pine Barrens.* 13 river maps, with local lore and history. Globe Pequot Press, Box Q, Chester, CT 06412.

SMITH, KENNETH L. *Illinois River* and *The Buffalo River Country.* Photogenic guides. Ozark Society Books.

CANOEING TECHNIQUE

AMERICAN RED CROSS. *Canoeing and Kayaking.* American National Red Cross, 17th and D Streets N.W., Washington, DC 20006.

BURCH, DAVID. *Fundamentals of Kayak Navigation.* Practical book on navigation under various circumstances. Globe Pequot Press.

FEARS, J. WAYNE. *The Complete Book of Canoe Camping.* Backcountry Press, P.O. Box 217, Heflin, AL 36264.

FOSHEE, JOHN. *Solo Canoeing.* Guide to fundamentals, equipment, and techniques for running solo in an open canoe. Stackpole Books, Box 1831, Harrisburg, PA 17105.

————. *You, Too, Can Canoe*. Covers fundamentals to advanced techniques. Strode Publishers, 6802 Jones Valley Dr. S.E., Huntsville, AL 35802.

GULLION, LAURIE. *Canoeing and Kayaking Instruction Manual*. Teacher's guide for instructors. American Canoe Association.

HARRISON, DAVE. *Sports Illustrated Canoeing*. Harper & Row, 10 E. 53rd St., New York, NY 10022.

JACOBSON, CLIFF. *The New Wilderness Canoeing and Camping*. Covers canoeing, camping, and portaging. Stackpole Books.

————. *Canoeing Wild Rivers*. Advanced techniques for river-running. Stackpole Books.

RUTSTRUM, CALVIN. *North American Canoe Country*. Guide to canoeing techniques. Collier Books, 866 Third Ave., New York, NY 10022.

URBAN, JOHN. *White Water Handbook*. Latest advances in white-water canoeing technique. The Appalachian Mountain Club.

BACKGROUND, HISTORY, TRAVEL

BLEGEN, THEODORE. *The Voyageurs and Their Songs*. History of the voyageurs, with words to 12 of their songs. Minnesota Historical Society Press, 690 Cedar St., St. Paul, MN 55101.

BURMEISTER, WALTER F. *Appalachian Water: The Delaware River and Its Tributaries*. A detailed study, but with notes on a number of attractive canoe runs. Paperback. Appalachian Books, P.O. Box 248, Oakton, VA 22124.

————. *Appalachian Water: The Hudson River and Its Tributaries*. Paperback. Appalachian Books.

GOODRUM, JOHN. *Rivers of Alabama*. Strode Publishers, 6802 Jones Valley Dr. S.E., Huntsville, AL 35802.

MEAD, ROBERT DOUGLAS. *Ultimate North*. Canoeing in the Mackenzie Valley from Alberta to the Arctic Ocean—the land and its people, present and past. Doubleday.

NUTE, GRACE LEE. *The Voyageur*. Paperback. Minnesota Historical Society Press, 690 Cedar St., St. Paul, MN 55101.

————. *The Voyageurs' Highway*. The border-lakes country; paperback. Minnesota Historical Society Press.

OLSON, SIGURD F. *The Lonely Land*. The Churchill River. Alfred Knopf, Inc., 201 E. 50th St., New York, NY 10022.

————. *Runes of the North*. Canoeing in many parts of the North, from Hudson Bay to the Camsell River. Knopf.

————. *The Singing Wilderness*. The border-lakes country. Knopf.

ROWLANDS, JOHN. *Cache Lake Country*. Chronicle of life in the north woods. Norton & Co., 500 Fifth Ave., New York, NY 10036.

SEVAREID, ERIC. *Canoeing with the Cree*. An account of the famous author's boyhood trip from the border-lakes region to Hudson Bay; paperback. Minnesota Historical Society Press.

SUTTON, ANN and MYRON. *The Grand Canyon*. Not canoeing as such, but a splendid introduction to the natural and human history of the Grand Canyon and of the Southwest generally; handsomely illustrated. J.B. Lippincott Co., East Washington Square, Philadelphia, PA 19105.

OUTDOOR SKILLS

BECHTEL, LES and SLIM RAY. *River Rescue*. Information on river safety and rescue. The Appalachian Mountain Club.

FEARS, J. WAYNE. *Complete Book of Outdoor Survival*. Covers all aspects of outdoor survival anywhere in North America for canoers and other outdoorsmen. Backcountry Press.

————. *The Sportsman's Guide to Swamp Camping*. How to travel and live comfortably in a swamp. Backcountry Press.

APPENDIX 4

Sources for U.S. and Canadian Maps

Sources for the two countries' national map systems, with methods for ordering, are given below. In addition, a number of canoe-oriented maps—published locally or by various state and provincial government agencies—are listed in Appendix 5, along with many other kinds of canoeing information.

UNITED STATES GEOLOGICAL SURVEY MAPS

Free index maps for each state show maps available in three different series (7½-minute/1:24,000, 15-minute/1:62,500, and 1:250,000) and list a variety of special maps, including maps of national parks (but *not* maps of the U. S. Forest Service that happen to cover canoe routes, as in the case of the Boundary Waters Canoe Area—see Appendix 5). The index maps also list dealers and libraries in each state that carry a comprehensive stock. For index maps and orders: Dept. of the Interior—U.S.G.S., Branch of Distribution, Box 25286, DFC, Denver, CO 80225.

CANADIAN TOPOGRAPHICAL MAPS

The Federal Surveys and Mapping Branch publishes a free booklet (MDO 79) listing the index maps for the available series (1:125,000, 1:250,000, 1:500,000, 1:1,000,000); the same booklet includes a master index, in map form, of the eighteen index maps in the 1:50,000 series. (For maps produced by other agencies or by the provincial governments, see Appendix 5.) For index maps and orders, write to: Map Distribution Office, 615 Booth Street, Ottawa, Ont. K1A 0E9.

APPENDIX 5

Local Sources of Canoeing Information

Much of the most useful material is published in the area to which it pertains—by state or provincial governments, parks, canoeing and conservation organizations, or enterprising individuals. Many of the publications listed below are free, the rest modestly priced.

Alabama

General information. Alabama Conservation Department, 64 N. Union St., Montgomery, AL 36130.

Alaska

Alaska Canoe Trails. Twelve routes, with maps, mileages, other details. Bureau of Land Management, U.S. Department of the Interior, 555 Cordova St., Anchorage, AK 99509.

The Milepost. A guidebook, revised each year, to road travel in Alaska, northern Alberta, British Columbia, the Yukon Territory, and the Northwest Territories (approaches to the Alaska Highway), all useful if you're trying to get to canoe country in these areas by car. Alaska Northwest Publishing Co., 130 Second Ave. S., Edmonds, WA 98020.

Canoeing in the Kenai National Wildlife Refuge. Maps and general information. Refuge Manager, Kenai National Wildlife Refuge, P.O. Box 2139, Soldotna, AK 99669.

Arizona

General information. Office of Tourism, 1700 West Washington, Phoenix, AZ 85007.

Arkansas

Kenneth L. Smith. *The Buffalo River Country*. Guidebook, with maps and photographs; paperback. Ozark Society Books, Box 3503, Little Rock, AR 72203.

The Float Streams of Arkansas. Division of Tourism, 149 State Capitol, Little Rock, AR 72201.

Maps of the Buffalo River. Buffalo National River, P.O. Box 1173, Harrison, AR 72601.

Maps of float streams in Arkansas. Arkansas Department of Parks and Tourism, #1 Capitol Mall, Little Rock, AR 72201.

Ouachita River Float Trip. Also, separate map. Supervisor, Ouachita National Forest, Hot Springs, AR 71901.

California

General information. Office of Tourism, 1121 L St., Suite 103, Sacramento, CA 95814.

Colorado

General information. Office of Tourism, 1313 Sherman St., Denver, CO 80203.

Connecticut

Connecticut Canoeing Guide. Boating Commission, State Office Bldg., Hartford, CT 06115.

The Farmington River and Watershed Guide. Booklet, separate map. Farmington River Watershed Association, Inc., 749 Hopmeadow St., Simsbury, CT 06070.

Delaware

General information. State Travel Service, P.O. Box 1401, Dover, DE 19901.

Florida

Everglades National Park, Florida. Leaflet, with map. Everglades National Park, P.O. Box 279, Homestead, FL 33030.

Everglades National Park Canoe Trail Guide. Booklet. Everglades National Park.

Florida Canoe Trail Guide. A booklet, with maps, covering sixteen routes; a supplement from the same source describes eight additional canoe routes. Florida Department of Natural Resources, Division of Recreation and Parks, 3900 Commonwealth Blvd., Tallahassee, FL 32399.

William G. Truesdell. *A Guide to the Wilderness Waterway of the Everglades National Park*. University of Miami Press, Drawer 9088, Coral Gables, FL 33124.

Guide to Florida Canoeing Rivers. Office of Communications—DNR, 3900 Commonwealth Blvd., Tallahassee, FL 32399.

Georgia

Wilderness Canoeing in Okefenokee National Wildlife Refuge. Okefenokee National Wildlife Refuge, Route 2, Box 338, Folkston, GA 31537.

General information. Tourism Division, P.O. Box 1776, Atlanta, GA 30301.

Hawaii

General information. Visitors Bureau, Suite 801, 2270 Kalakaua Ave., Honolulu, HI 96815.

Idaho

Canoeing maps and general information. Idaho Department of Commerce and Development, Room 108, Statehouse, Boise, ID 83707.

MAPS: *Salmon River* and *North Fork of the Snake River.* Idaho Fish and Game Department, P.O. Box 65, Boise, ID 83701.

Middle Fork of the Salmon. Map and guide. USDA Forest Service, Middle Fork District Ranger, Challis National Forest, Challis, ID 83226.

Illinois

Illinois Canoeing Guide. Office of Public Information. Illinois Department of Conservation, 524 S. 2nd St., Suite 100, Springfield, IL 62701.

Indiana

Indiana Canoeing Guide. Indiana Department of Natural Resources, Division of State Parks, Room 616, State Office Building, Indianapolis, IN 46204.

Iowa

Guide to the Upper Iowa River. G. E. Knudson, Luther College, Decorah, IA 52101.

Iowa Float Trips. Iowa Department of Natural Resources, Wallace State Office Building, Des Moines, IA 50319.

Kansas

Kansas Streams. Kansas Department of Economic Development, 122-S State Office Building, Topeka, KS 66612.

Kentucky

Daniel Boone National Forest. Canoeing guide. USDA Forest Service, 100 Vaught Rd., Winchester, KY 40391.

Mammoth Cave National Park. Map (park includes part of the Green and Nolin rivers). Superintendent, Mammoth Cave National Park, Mammoth Cave, KY 42259.

Louisiana

General information. Information & Education, Department of Wildlife and Fisheries, P.O. Box 15570, Baton Rouge, LA 70895.

Maine

Maine Canoeing. Development Office, 193 State St., Augusta, ME 04333.

Allagash Wilderness Waterway. Illustrated leaflet, with map. Bureau of Parks & Recreation, Maine Department of Conservation, State House, Station #22, Augusta, ME 04330.

Eben Thomas. *No Horns Blowing; Canoeing 10 Great Rivers in Maine.* A highly personal guidebook. Hallowell Printing Co., 145 Water St., Hallowell, ME 04347.

Massachusetts

The Connecticut River Guide. Detailed description, with maps, of the river from source to mouth. Connecticut River Watershed Council, Box 89, Greenfield, MA 01301.

Michigan

West Michigan Canoe Map. West Michigan Tourist Association, 136 Fulton East, Grand Rapids, MI 49503.

Huron National Forest and *Manistee National Forest.* Maps. USDA Forest Service, Cadillac, MI 49601.

Michigan Canoeing Directory. Recreational Canoeing Association, P.O. Box 296, Montague, MI 49437.

Canoeing in Michigan. Travel Bureau, P.O. Box 30226, Lansing, MI 48909.

Minnesota

Trails and Waterways Map and Brochure Listing. Lists 41 canoe routes for which free maps are available, plus brochures of interest to canoers. Minnesota Dept. of Natural Resources, Information Center, 500 Lafayette Road, St. Paul, MN 55155.

General information. Boundary Water Canoe Area, P.O. Box 338, Duluth, MN 55801.

General information. Voyageurs National Park, Box 50, International Falls, MN 56649.

Big Fork River Canoe Trail. Box 256, Big Fork, MN 56628.

Canoeing Chippewa National Forest. Map. Forest Supervisor, Chippewa National Forest, Rt. 3, Box 244, Cass Lake, MN 56633.

Crow Wing River. Crow Wing Trails Association, Box 210, Sebeka, MN 56477.

The Minnesota River. Booklet, with map. Chamber of Commerce, 112 N. Main St., Le Sueur, MN 56058.

Catalogue listing publications and services relating to outdoor travel and recreation in Minnesota. Dept. of Administration, Minnesota State Documents Division, 117 University Ave., St. Paul, MN 55155.

Mississippi River Guide. Aitkin County Park Commission, Court House, Aitkin, MN 56431.

St. Croix/Nomehagon Rivers. Muller Boat Co., Inc., Taylor Falls, MN 55084.

Superior National Forest (including the Boundary Waters Canoe Area Wilderness). For information on canoe routes or other recreation opportunities, contact Forest Supervisor, Superior National Forest, P.O. Box 338, Duluth, MN 55801, (or District Rangers at Aurora, Cook, Ely, Tofte, Grand Marais, Isabella, Virginia—all in Minnesota).

Superior-Quentico Canoe Maps. Set of 15 detailed maps covering border-lakes routes on both sides of the international boundary; printed on waterproof paper. W. A. Fisher Co., Virginia, MN 55792.

Mississippi

Float trips. Brochures with maps. Mississippi Department of Natural Resources, P.O. Box 20305, Jackson, MS 39209.

Missouri

Canoeing in Northern Missouri. Department of Natural Resources, P.O. Box 176, Jefferson City, MO 65102.

General information. Ozark National Scenic Riverways, P.O. Box 490, Van Buren, MO 63965.

Maps, Current and Jacks Fork rivers. S. G. Adams Printing & Stationery Co., 10th and Olive Streets, St. Louis, MO 63101.

Oz Hawksley. *Missouri Ozark Waterways.* Detailed guide to 37 canoe routes, with maps. Missouri Department of Conservation, P.O. Box 180, Jefferson, MO 65101.

Montana

The Wild and Scenic Missouri River. Bureau of Land Management, Airport Road, Lewistown, MT 59457.

Montana's Popular Float Streams. Introductory notes on canoeable sections of 23 rivers. Also, leaflets on the Yellowstone and Missouri rivers and planning map. Montana Department of Fish & Game, Helena, MT 59601.

Nebraska

Nebraska Canoe Trails. Game & Parks Commission, P.O. Box 30370, Lincoln, NE 68503.

Nevada

General information. Tourism Division, Carson City, NV 89710.

New Hampshire

General information. Travel Office, P.O. Box 856, Concord, NH 03301.

New Jersey

Maps of the Delaware River. Delaware River Basin Commission, P.O. Box 7360, West Trenton, NJ 08628.

New Mexico

Rio Grande Wild River. Bureau of Land Management, P.O. Box 1449, Santa Fe, NM 87501.

Rafting, Kayaking and Canoeing on the Rio Grande and Chama Rivers. C. Carnes, 130 Rover Blvd., White Rock, Los Alamos, NM 87544.

New York

Adirondack Canoe Routes. Descriptive folder with planning map. New York State Department of Environmental Conservation, 50 Wolf Road, Albany, NY 12233.

Canoe Trips. Leaflet with brief notes on 35 rivers. New York State Department of Environmental Conservation.

North Carolina

General information. Division of Travel, 430 N. Salisbury St., Raleigh, NC 27611.

North Dakota

General information. Parks & Recreation Department, 1424 West Century Ave., Suite 202, Bismarck, ND 58501.

Ohio

General information. Office of Travel, P.O. Box 1001, Columbus, OH 43215.

1,000,000 Miles of Canoe and Hiking Routes. Catalog of dozens of route descriptions and maps for rivers in Ohio and elsewhere, available from the same source. Ohio Canoe Adventures, Inc., P.O. Box 2092, Sheffield Lake, OH 44054.

Oklahoma

General information. Tourism Department, 500 Will Rogers Memorial Building, Oklahoma City, OK 73105.

Oregon

General information. Travel Department, 101 Transportation Building, Salem, OR 97310.

The Rogue River. Descriptive map and map of the national forest. Supervisor, Siskiyou National Forest, P.O. Box 440, Grants Pass, OR 97526.

Pennsylvania

Canoe Routes. Notes on the Allegheny, Monongahela, Ohio, Susquehanna, and Delaware rivers. Also leaflets on state park boating and camping. Bureau of State Parks, Pennsylvania Department of Environmental Resources, P.O. Box 1467, Harrisburg, PA 17105.

Paddle Pennsylvania. Leaflet rating many rivers for difficulty and attractiveness. Pennsylvania Fish Commission, Department of Environmental Resources, P.O. Box 1673, Harrisburg, PA 17120.

Canoeing Guide: Western Pennsylvania/Northern West Virginia. From the same source, a large canoeing map of the area covered by this guidebook. Pittsburgh Council, American Youth Hostels, 6300 Fifth Ave., Pittsburgh, PA 15232.

Rhode Island

General information. Parks & Recreation Division, 83 Park Street, Providence, RI 02903.

South Carolina

South Carolina River Trails. Division of Tourism, 1205 Pendleton St., Columbia, SC 29201.

Canoeing the Chattooga. Also, *Sumter National Forest* map. District Ranger, Andrew Pickens Ranger District, Walhalla, SC 29691.

South Dakota

Canoeing in South Dakota. Division of Parks & Recreation, 445 E. Capitol Ave., Pierre, SD 57501.

Tennessee

Tennessee Vacation Guide. Booklet listing and rating canoeable rivers throughout the state. Tennessee Tourist Development, P.O. Box 23170, Nashville, TN 37202.

Tennessee Recreational Waters. Department of Tourism, P.O. Box 23170, Nashville, TN 37202.

Texas

Big Bend National Park. Map. Superintendent, Big Bend National Park, TX 79834.

Suggested River Trips Through the Rio Grande River Canyons. Detailed notes, multilithed, with maps, prepared by Bob Burleson, president of the Texas Explorers Club. Bob Burleson, P.O. Box 844, Temple, TX 76503.

Utah

General information. Utah Travel Council, Council Hall/Capitol Hill, Salt Lake City, UT 84114.

Vermont

Canoe Vermont! Canoe Vermont, Box 610, Waitsfield, VT 05673.

Canoeing on the Connecticut River. Division of Recreation, 103 South Main St., Waterbury, VT 05676.

Canoe Trips in Vermont. Detailed resource sheet. Vermont Travel Division, 134 State St., Montpelier, VT 05602.

Vermont Canoeing. Vermont Development Commission, Montpelier, VT 05602.

Virginia

General information. State Travel Service, 6 North Richmond St., Richmond, VA 23219.

Canoeing White Water. Randy Carter. Paperback guide to wild rivers in Virginia, West Virginia, North Carolina's Great Smokies, Pennsylvania. Appalachian Outfitters, 2940 Chain Bridge Rd., Oakton, VA 22124.

Washington

General information. Travel Division, 101 General Administration Building, Olympia, WA 98504.

West Virginia

West Virginia Stream Map. Department of Natural Resources, 1800 Washington St. E., Charleston, WV 25305.

Wisconsin

Wisconsin Water Trails. Department of Natural Resources, P.O. Box 7921, Madison, WI 53707.

Canoe Trails of Southern Wisconsin. Wisconsin Trails, P.O. Box 5650, Madison, WI 53705.

Kickapoo Canoe Trail. Kickapoo Valley Association, Inc., Route 2, Box 211, La Farge, WI 54639.

Wyoming

General information. Wyoming Travel Commission, I-25 at College Drive, Cheyenne, WY 82002.

Bridger National Forest. Map (part of the Green River). Supervisor, Bridger National Forest, Forest Service Building, Kemmerer, WY 83101.

Floating the Snake River. Superintendent, Grand Teton National Park, Moose, WY 83012.

Medicine Bow National Forest. Map (part of the North Platte River). Supervisor, Medicine Bow National Forest, 605 Skyline Dr., Laramie, WY 82070.

CANADA

Detailed information and maps on Canadian rivers. Canadian Heritage Rivers Board, ⁒ Canadian Parks Service, Environment Canada, Ottawa, Ont. K1A 0H3.

Alberta

General information. Alberta Wilderness Association, Box 6398, Station D, Calgary, Alta. T2P 2E1.

British Columbia

General information.　Ministry of Tourism, Parliament Buildings, Victoria, B.C. V8V 1X4.

Booklets on provincial parks, with canoeing information, are available from Ministry of Environment and Parks, Conservation and Parks Division, 4000 Seymour Place, Victoria, B.C. V8V 1X5.

Maps of the provincial parks are available from Surveys and Mapping Branch, Department of Lands, Forests and Resources, Parliament Buildings, Victoria, B.C. V8V 1X4.

Manitoba

General information.　Department of Tourism, 7-155 Carlton St., Winnipeg, Man. R3C 3H8.

New Brunswick

Provincial maps.　Request a descriptive booklet, appropriate maps, and individual guidance from New Brunswick Dept. of Tourism Information Service, Box 12345, Fredericton, N.B. E3B 5C3

Newfoundland

General information.　Parks Division, Department of Culture, Recreation and Youth, P.O. Box 4750, St. John's, N.F. A1C 5T7.

Northwest Territories

Canoeing and Boating in the Northwest Territories; *Nahanni National Park*; and *The South Nahanni River* (multilithed descriptive notes) and general tourist information on the North, including lists of outfitters. TravelArctic, Government of the Northwest Territories, Yellowknife, N.W.T. X1A 2L9.

Ontario

Algonquin Provincial Park.　Canoe route booklets, maps, general information. Park Superintendent, Algonquin Provincial Park, Ontario Ministry of Natural Resources, Box 219, Whitney, Ont. K0J 2M0.

Canoe route pamphlets for Beaver River, Black Lake, Gull River system, Kishkebus Lake, Magnetawan River, Mississagi River, Upper Mississagi River, Lower Mississagi River, Mississippi River (Canada only), Rankin River, Saugeen River, Wolf and Pickerel rivers. Director, Park Management Branch, Ministry of Natural Resources, Public Information Centre, Room 1640, 99 Wellesley St. W., Toronto, Ont. M7A 1W3.

Mattawa Provincial Park.　Ministry of Natural Resources, Public Information Centre.

Quetico Provincial Park, booklet and maps.　District Manager, Ministry of Natural Resources, 108 Saturn Ave., Atikokan, Ont. P0T 1C0.

Quebec

General information.　Parks & Recreation, Place de la Capitale, 150 East St. Cyrille Blvd., Quebec City, Que. G1R 2B2.

Saskatchewan

Information on travel in Lac La Ronge Provincial Park.　Park Superintendent, DPRC, Box 5000, La Ronge, Sask. S0J 1L0.

Information on travel in Prince Albert National Park.　Park Superintendent, Prince Albert National Park, Box 100, Waskesin, Sask. S0J 2Y0.

Canoe Saskatchewan.　Listing of canoe routes within the province. Also, individual booklets under general title of *Saskatchewan Canoe Trips*, detailing, so far, 50 routes. Get both the general booklet and the specific guide or guides. Saskatchewan Economic Development and Tourism, 1919 Saskatchewan Dr., Regina, Sask. S4P 3V7.

Yukon Territory

General information.　Tourism Yukon, Box 2703, Whitehorse, Yukon Y1A 2C6.

APPENDIX 6

Canoe Manufacturers

ALUMACRAFT BOAT CO.
315 West St. Julien St.
St. Peter, MN 56082

BLUE HOLE CANOE CO.
P.O. Box 179
Sunbright, TN 37872

CHICAGOLAND CANOE BASE, INC.
4019 North Narragansett Ave.
Chicago, IL 60634

COLEMAN CO.
250 North St. Francis
Wichita, KS 67201

GREAT CANADIAN
65 Water St.
Worcester, MA 01604

GRUMMAN BOATS
P.O. Box 549
Marathon, NY 13803

MAD RIVER CANOE CO.
P.O. Box 610
Waitsfield, VT 05673

OLD TOWN CANOE CO.
58 Middle St.
Old Town, ME 04468

SAWYER CANOE CO.
P.O. Box 459
Oscoda, MI 48750

SPORTSPAL CANOES
Meyers Industries
P.O. Box E
Tecumseh, MI 49286

SUN RIVER CANOE CO.
P.O. Box 194
Wellston, MI 49689

WE-NO-NAH CANOE CO.
Box 247
Winona, MN 55987

WHITE CANOE CO.
P.O. Box 548
Old Town, ME 04468

APPENDIX 7

Paddles and Other Canoe Equipment

Most of the canoe builders listed in Appendix 6 also produce or market paddles, carrying yokes, cartop carriers, and other equipment. The following sources are specialists in the items indicated.

BARTON PADDLE CO.
6201 23-½ Mile Rd.
Homer, MI 49245 (paddles)

BENDING BRANCHES
1101 Stinson Blvd.
Minneapolis, MN 55413 (paddles)

GREY OWL PADDLE CO.
62 Cowansview Rd.
Cambridge, Ont.
Canada N1R 7N3 (paddles)

MITCHELL PADDLES, INC.
RD 2, Box 922
Canaan, NH 03741 (paddles)

NORSE PADDLE CO.
RD 1
Spring Mills, PA 16875 (paddles)

McCANN PADDLES
Rt. 2, Box 343
Cornell, WI 54732 (paddles)

GILLESPIE PADDLES
679 Furman Rd.
Fairport, NY 14450 (paddles)

CARLISLE PADDLES
P.O. Box 488
Grayling, MI 49738 (paddles)

ILIAD PADDLE CO.
208 Cherry St.
Sunbright, TN 37872 (paddles)

MOHAWK PADDLE CO.
963 N. Hwy. 427
Longwood, FL 32750 (paddles)

STEARNS MANUFACTURING CO.
P.O. Box 1498
St. Cloud, MN 56302 (PFDs)

VOYAGEUR'S
P.O. Box 409
Gardner, KS 66030 (PFDs, cartop carriers, canoe flotation bags)

YAKIMA PRODUCTS, INC.
P.O. Drawer 4899
Arcata, CA 95521

APPENDIX 8

Camping Equipment Manufacturers

Some manufacturers sell directly to the consumer and can supply you with a catalog or other purchase information. Others can recommend mail-order or local dealers who carry their products.

ALPINEAIRE FOODS
P.O. Box 1600
Nevada City, CA 95959 (freeze-dried foods)

BACKPACK PANTRY/DRI-LITE FOODS
1540 Charles Dr.
Redding, CA 96003 (freeze-dried foods)

CAMEL OUTDOOR PRODUCTS
P.O. Box 7225
Norcross, GA 30071 (tents)

CAMP TRAILS
625 Conklin Road
Binghamton, NY 13848 (packs)

CASCADE DESIGNS, INC.
4000 First Ave.
Seattle, WA 98134 (Therm-A-Rest mattresses)

COLEMAN CO.
250 N. St. Francis
Wichita, KS 67201 (tents, stoves, lanterns, cook kits)

DIAMOND BRAND
Hwy. 25
Naples, NC 28760 (packs, tents)

DULUTH TENT & AWNING
1610 West Superior St.
Duluth, MN 55816 (canvas packs)

EUREKA! TENT
625 Conklin Road
Binghamton, NY 13902 (tents)

GRADE VI EXPEDITION OUTFITTERS
P.O. Box 8
Urbana, IL 61801 (packs)

KATADYN USA
3020 N. Scottsdale Rd.
Scottsdale, AZ 85251 (water purification system)

MIRRO/METAL WARE CORPORATION
P.O. Box 237
Two Rivers, WI 54241 (cook kits, grills)

NALGE TRAIL PRODUCTS
Box 20365
Rochester, NY 14602 (food and fuel bottles)

THE NORTH FACE
999 Harrison St.
Berkeley, CA 94710 (packs, tents)

OLICAMP
P.O. Box 306
Montrose, CA 91020 (cook kits, stoves)

MOUNTAIN HOUSE/OREGON FREEZE DRY
P.O. Box 1048
Albany, OR 97321 (freeze-dried foods)

PELICAN PRODUCTS
2255 Jefferson St.
Torrance, CA 90501 (waterproof camera cases)

PRIMUS/CENTURY TOOL & MANUFACTURING CO.
P.O. Box 188
Cherry Valley, IL 61016 (cook kits, stoves, lanterns)

QUETICO SUPERIOR PACKS
P.O. Box 6687-M
Minneapolis, MN 55406 (packs)

SIGG/PRECISE INTERNATIONAL
3 Chestnut St.
Suffern, NY 10901 (fuel and beverage bottles)

SMOKY CANYON/VAN RICH
16850 Chicago Ave.
Lansing, IL 60438 (camp foods)

SPECIALTY FOOD & BEVERAGE SALES
198 Lincoln Ave.
West Milford, NJ 07480 (camp foods)

WHITE STAG/HENDERSON CAMP PRODUCTS
414 North Orleans St.
Chicago, IL 60610 (sleeping bags, tents)

APPENDIX 9

Retail Sources for Canoe-Camping Equipment

Each of the companies listed below produces a mail-order catalog with a variety of outdoor products, including canoe-camping gear.

L.L. BEAN
Freeport, ME 04033

CABELA'S
812 13th Ave.
Sidney, NE 69160

EASTERN MOUNTAIN SPORTS, INC.
1041 Commonwealth Ave.
Boston, MA 02215

GANDER MOUNTAIN
P.O. Box 248
Wilmot, WI 53192

NORTHWEST RIVER SUPPLIES
2009 South Maine
Moscow, ID 83843

APPENDIX 10

Outfitter Information

Many reputable canoe outfitters belong to associations that publish annual listings of their memberships. For an up-to-date list of outfitters, write to the appropriate group below.

For outfitter information in specific areas that are not included below, refer to Appendix 5.

U.S. OUTFITTERS

NATIONAL ASSOCIATION OF CANOE LIVERIES AND
  OUTFITTERS
P.O. Box 88866
Atlanta, GA 30356

CANADIAN OUTFITTERS

TRAVELARCTIC
Yellowknife, N.W.T. X1A 2L9

MINISTRY OF TOURISM
Queen's Park
Toronto, Ont. M7A 2R9

THE QUEBEC OUTFITTERS ASSOCIATION
2900, boul. Saint-Martin Ouest
Laval, Que. H7L 2J2

YUKON OUTFITTERS ASSOCIATION
Bag Service 2762
Whitehorse, Yukon Y1A 5B9

About the Authors

ROBERT DOUGLAS MEAD was a scholar, editor, writer, and outdoorsman. He was introduced to canoeing as a child going on canoe trips in the Quetico-Superior with his family. During those years he explored the rivers of Maine, New Jersey, Pennsylvania, and the Chesapeake Bay area, as well. Later, researching books took him to Alaska, where he canoed the Kenai and Gulkhana rivers. He also canoed the Mackenzie River, beginning in Fort McMurray and ending at the Beaufort Sea, north of Inuvik. Mead was the author of several books, including *Ultimate North* and *Journeys Down the Line*.

J. WAYNE FEARS is an outdoor writer and photographer who has written a dozen books on subjects ranging from trout fishing to outdoor survival, including *The Complete Book of Canoe Camping*. His articles have appeared in *Outdoor Life, Sports Afield, Field & Stream, Canoe, Farm Journal,* and many other magazines. Fears has worked as a canoe outfitter throughout North America and as a canoe-trails planner for the state of Georgia. He is the recipient of numerous writing and photography awards.